MznLnx

Missing Links Exam Preps

Exam Prep for

Auditing & Assurance Services

Louwers et al..., 3rd Edition

The MznLnx Exam Prep is your link from the texbook and lecture to your exams.
The MznLnx Exam Preps are unauthorized and comprehensive reviews of your textbooks.

All material provided by MznLnx and Rico Publications (c) 2010
Textbook publishers and textbook authors do not particpate in or contribute to these reviews.

MznLnx

Rico Publications

Exam Prep for Auditing & Assurance Services
3rd Edition
Louwers et al...

Publisher: Raymond Houge
Assistant Editor: Michael Rouger
Text and Cover Designer: Lisa Buckner
Marketing Manager: Sara Swagger
Project Manager, Editorial Production: Jerry Emerson
Art Director: Vernon Lowerui

Product Manager: Dave Mason
Editorial Assitant: Rachel Guzmanji
Pedagogy: Debra Long
Cover Image: Jim Reed/Getty Images
Text and Cover Printer: City Printing, Inc.
Compositor: Media Mix, Inc.

(c) 2010 Rico Publications
ALL RIGHTS RESERVED. No part of this work covered by the copyright may be reproduced or used in any form or by an means--graphic, electronic, or mechanical, including photocopying, recording, taping, Web distribution, information storage, and retrieval systems, or in any other manner--without the written permission of the publisher.

Printed in the United States
ISBN:

For more information about our products, contact us at:
Dave.Mason@RicoPublications.com

For permission to use material from this text or product, submit a request online to:
Dave.Mason@RicoPublications.com

Contents

CHAPTER 1
Auditing and Assurance Services — 1

CHAPTER 2
Professional Standards — 17

CHAPTER 3
Management Fraud and Audit Risk — 26

CHAPTER 4
Engagement Planning — 36

CHAPTER 5
Risk Assessment: Internal Control Evaluation — 47

CHAPTER 6
Employee Fraud and the Audit of Cash — 58

CHAPTER 7
Revenue and Collection Cycle — 64

CHAPTER 8
Acquisition and Expenditure Cycle — 72

CHAPTER 9
Production Cycle — 83

CHAPTER 10
Finance and Investment Cycle — 93

CHAPTER 11
Completing the Audit — 103

CHAPTER 12
Reports on Audited Financial Statements — 110

CHAPTER 13
Other Public Accounting Services — 118

CHAPTER 14
Professional Ethics — 127

CHAPTER 15
Legal Liability — 137

CHAPTER 16
Internal, Governmental, and Fraud Audits — 146

CHAPTER 17
Overview of Sampling — 151

CHAPTER 18
Attribute Sampling — 155

CHAPTER 19
Variables Sampling — 158

CHAPTER 20
Information Systems Auditing — 164

ANSWER KEY — 171

TO THE STUDENT

COMPREHENSIVE

The *MznLnx* Exam Prep series is designed to help you pass your exams. Editors at MznLnx review your textbooks and then prepare these practice exams to help you master the textbook material. Unlike study guides, workbooks, and practice tests provided by the texbook publisher and textbook authors, *MznLnx* gives you **all** of the material in each chapter in exam form, not just samples, so you can be sure to nail your exam.

MECHANICAL

The MznLnx Exam Prep series creates exams that will help you learn the subject matter as well as test you on your understanding. Each question is designed to help you master the concept. Just working through the exams, you gain an understanding of the subject--its a simple mechanical process that produces success.

INTEGRATED STUDY GUIDE AND REVIEW

MznLnx is not just a set of exams designed to test you, its also a comprehensive review of the subject content. Each exam question is also a review of the concept, making sure that you will get the answer correct without having to go to other sources of material. You learn as you go! Its the easiest way to pass an exam.

HUMOR

Studying can be tedious and dry. MznLnx's instructional design includes moderate humor within the exam questions on occassion, to break the tedium and revitalize the brain

Chapter 1. Auditing and Assurance Services

1. _____s have been defined by the American Institute of Certified Public Accountants (AICPA) as 'Independent Professional Services that improve information quality or its context'. _____s reduce the information risk; risk that the information provided is incorrect, on more than just financial data. The major purpose of _____s is to provide independent and professional opinions that improve the quality of information to management as well as other decision makers within a given firm.
   - a. Auditor independence
   - b. ITGCs
   - c. Institute of Chartered Accountants of India
   - d. Assurance service

2. The general definition of an _____ is an evaluation of a person, organization, system, process, project or product. _____s are performed to ascertain the validity and reliability of information; also to provide an assessment of a system's internal control. The goal of an _____ is to express an opinion on the person/organization/system (etc) in question, under evaluation based on work done on a test basis.
   - a. Audit regime
   - b. Assurance service
   - c. Institute of Chartered Accountants of India
   - d. Audit

3. _____ is a term that is commonly used in relation to the audit of the financial statements of an entity. (.
   - a. Audit working paper
   - b. Audit risk
   - c. Auditor independence
   - d. Engagement Letter

4. _____, in auditing, is the risk that a company's internal controls are insufficient to mitigate or detect errors or fraud.
   - a. Control risk
   - b. BMC Software, Inc.
   - c. BNSF Railway
   - d. 3M Company

5. The Federal National Mortgage Association (FNMA) (NYSE: FNM), commonly known as _____, is a stockholder-owned corporation chartered by Congress in 1968 as a government sponsored enterprise (GSE), but founded in 1938 during the Great Depression. The corporation's purpose is to purchase and securitize mortgages in order to ensure that funds are consistently available to the institutions that lend money to home buyers.

   On September 7, 2008, James Lockhart, director of the Federal Housing Finance Agency (FHFA), announced that _____ and Freddie Mac were being placed into conservatorship of the FHFA.
   - a. Freddie Mac
   - b. National Conference of Commissioners on Uniform State Laws
   - c. Public company
   - d. Fannie Mae

6. _____ are ten auditing standards, developed by the AICPA, consisting of general standards, standards of field work, and standards of reporting, along with interpretations. They were developed by the AICPA in 1947 and have undergone minor changes since then.

The _____ are as follows:

1. The auditor must have adequate technical training and proficiency to perform the audit
2. The auditor must maintain independence in mental attitude in all matters related to the audit.
3. The auditor must use due professional care during the performance of the audit and the preparation of the report.

1. The auditor must adequately plan the work and must properly supervise any assistants.
2. The auditor must obtain a sufficient understanding of the entity and its environment, including its internal control, to assess the risk of material misstatement of the financial statements whether due to error or fraud, and to design the nature, timing, and extent of further audit procedures.
3. The auditor must obtain sufficient appropriate audit evidence by performing audit procedures to afford a reasonable basis for an opinion regarding the financial statements under audit.

The new standards are in effect for audits of financial statements for periods beginning on or after December 15, 2006.

1. The auditor must state in the auditor's report whether the financial statements are in accordance with generally accepted accounting principles (GAAP.)
2. The auditor must identify in the auditor's report those circumstances in which such principles have not been consistently observed in the current period in relation to the preceding period.
3. When the auditor determines that informative disclosures are not reasonably adequate, the auditor must so state in the auditor's report.
4. The auditor must either express an opinion regarding the financial statements, taken as a whole the auditor should state the reasons therefore in the auditor's report. In all cases where the auditor's name is associated with the financial statements, the auditor should clearly indicate the character of the auditor's work, if any, and the degree of responsibility the auditor is taking, in the auditor's report.

a. Negative assurance
b. Continuous auditing
c. Joint audit
d. Generally accepted auditing standards

7. _____, in auditing, is the risk that the account or section being audited is materially misstated without considering internal controls due to error; _____ does not include an assessment of the risk of material misstatement due to fraud. The assessment of _____ depends on the professional judgement of the auditor, and it is done after assessing the business environment of the entity being audited.

_____ is typically assessed using a scale, with assessments being either low, medium, or high.

a. ABC Television Network
b. AIG
c. AMEX
d. Inherent risk

Chapter 1. Auditing and Assurance Services

8. An _____ is a term used in behavioral economics to describe those types of behaviors that impose costs on a person in the long-run that are not taken into account when making decisions in the present. Classical Economics discourages government from creating legislation that targets internalities, because it is assumed that the consumer takes these personal costs into account when paying for the good that causes the _____. For example, cigarettes should be taxed because of the negative consumption externalities that they impose, such as second-hand smoke, not because the smoker harms him or herself by smoking.
   - a. Authorised capital
   - b. Operating budget
   - c. Inventory turnover ratio
   - d. Internality

9. In accounting and organizational theory, _____ is defined as a process effected by an organization's structure, work and authority flows, people and management information systems, designed to help the organization accomplish specific goals or objectives. It is a means by which an organization's resources are directed, monitored, and measured. It plays an important role in preventing and detecting fraud and protecting the organization's resources, both physical (e.g., machinery and property) and intangible (e.g., reputation or intellectual property such as trademarks.)
   - a. Audit committee
   - b. Audit risk
   - c. Internal control
   - d. Auditor independence

10. A _____ is the transfer of an interest in property (or the equivalent in law - a charge) to a lender as a security for a debt - usually a loan of money. While a _____ in itself is not a debt, it is the lender's security for a debt. It is a transfer of an interest in land (or the equivalent) from the owner to the _____ lender, on the condition that this interest will be returned to the owner when the terms of the _____ have been satisfied or performed.
    - a. 3M Company
    - b. BMC Software, Inc.
    - c. BNSF Railway
    - d. Mortgage

11. _____ is a concept that denotes the precise probability of specific eventualities. Technically, the notion of _____ is independent from the notion of value and, as such, eventualities may have both beneficial and adverse consequences. However, in general usage the convention is to focus only on potential negative impact to some characteristic of value that may arise from a future event.
    - a. Discount factor
    - b. Risk
    - c. Discounting
    - d. Risk adjusted return on capital

12. _____ is that part of statistical practice concerned with the selection of individual observations intended to yield some knowledge about a population of concern, especially for the purposes of statistical inference. Each observation measures one or more properties (weight, location, etc.) of an observable entity enumerated to distinguish objects or individuals.
    - a. Arthur Betz Laffer
    - b. Abby Joseph Cohen
    - c. Alan Greenspan
    - d. Sampling

13. _____ is a specific term used in companies' financial reporting from the company-whole point of view. Because that use excludes the effects of changing ownership interest, an economic measure of _____ is necessary for financial analysis from the shareholders' point of view

_____ is defined by the Financial Accounting Standards Board, or FASB, as 'the change in equity [net assets] of a business enterprise during a period from transactions and other events and circumstances from nonowner sources. It includes all changes in equity during a period except those resulting from investments by owners and distributions to owners.'

_____ is the sum of net income and other items that must bypass the income statement because they have not been realized, including items like an unrealized holding gain or loss from available for sale securities and foreign currency translation gains or losses.

a. BMC Software, Inc.
b. 3M Company
c. BNSF Railway
d. Comprehensive income

14. _____ are the earnings returned on the initial investment amount.

In the US, the Financial Accounting Standards Board (FASB) requires companies' income statements to report _____ for each of the major categories of the income statement: continuing operations, discontinued operations, extraordinary items, and net income.

The _____ formula does not include preferred dividends for categories outside of continued operations and net income.

a. Average accounting return
b. Earnings yield
c. Invested capital
d. Earnings per share

15. _____ is a fee paid on borrowed assets. It is the price paid for the use of borrowed money, or, money earned by deposited funds. Assets that are sometimes lent with _____ include money, shares, consumer goods through hire purchase, major assets such as aircraft, and even entire factories in finance lease arrangements. The _____ is calculated upon the value of the assets in the same manner as upon money.

a. AIG
b. ABC Television Network
c. Insolvency
d. Interest

16. The _____ is a 'voluntary organization of persons interested in accounting education and research'. It was formed in 1916. Its main publication, the The Accounting Review, was first published in 1926.

a. International Accounting Standards Board
b. Institute of Management Accountants
c. Australian Accounting Standards Board
d. American Accounting Association

17. _____ is the term used to refer to the standard framework of guidelines for financial accounting used in any given jurisdiction. _____ includes the standards, conventions, and rules accountants follow in recording and summarizing transactions, and in the preparation of financial statements.

Financial accounting information must be assembled and reported objectively.

a. Long-term liabilities
b. General ledger
c. Current asset
d. Generally accepted accounting principles

18. The _____ is the main body of domestic statutory tax law of the United States organized topically, including laws covering the income tax, payroll taxes, gift taxes, estate taxes and statutory excise taxes. The _____ is published as Title 26 of the United States Code (USC), and is also known as the internal revenue title.

a. Income tax
b. Internal Revenue Code
c. Ordinary income
d. Equity of condition

19. _____ is a profession and activity involved in helping organisations achieve their stated objectives. It does this by using a systematic methodology for analyzing business processes, procedures and activities with the goal of highlighting organizational problems and recommending solutions. Professionals called internal auditors are employed by organizations to perform the _____ activity.

a. ITGCs
b. Assurance service
c. Information audit
d. Internal auditing

20. The _____ is the national, professional association of CPAs in the United States, with more than 330,000 members, including CPAs in business and industry, public practice, government, and education; student affiliates; and international associates. It sets ethical standards for the profession and U.S. auditing standards for audits of private companies; federal, state and local governments; and non-profit organizations.

Approximately 40% of its members are engaged in the practice of public accounting, in areas such as auditing, accounting, taxation, general business consulting, business valuation, personal financial planning and business technology.

a. AIG
b. Other postemployment benefits
c. ABC Television Network
d. American Institute of Certified Public Accountants

21. _____ is the statutory title of qualified accountants in the United States who have passed the Uniform _____ Examination and have met additional state education and experience requirements for certification as a _____. Individuals who have passed the Exam but have not either accomplished the required on-the-job experience or have previously met it but in the meantime have lapsed their continuing professional education are, in many states, permitted the designation '_____ Inactive' or an equivalent phrase. In most U.S. states, only _____s who are licensed are able to provide to the public attestation (including auditing) opinions on financial statements.

a. Certified public accountant
b. Chartered Accountant
c. Chartered Certified Accountant
d. Certified General Accountant

22. _____ are formal records of a business' financial activities.

In British English, including United Kingdom company law, _____ are often referred to as accounts, although the term _____ is also used, particularly by accountants.

_____ provide an overview of a business' financial condition in both short and long term.

a. Statement of retained earnings
b. 3M Company
c. Notes to the financial statements
d. Financial statements

23. The term _____ is a term applied to practices that are perfunctory, or seek to satisfy the minimum requirements or to conform to a convention or doctrine. It has different meanings in different fields.

In accounting, _____ earnings are those earnings of companies in addition to actual earnings calculated under the Generally Accepted Accounting Principles (GAAP) in their quarterly and yearly financial reports.

a. Bottom line
b. Payroll
c. Treasury stock
d. Pro Forma

24. An _____ is a practitioner of accountancy, which is the measurement, disclosure or provision of assurance about financial information that helps managers, investors, tax authorities and other decision makers make resource allocation decisions.

The word '_____' is derived from the French 'Compter' which took its origin from the Latin 'Computare'. The word was formerly written in English as 'Accomptant', but in process of time the word, which was always pronounced by dropping the 'p', became gradually changed both in pronunciation and in orthography to its present form.

a. Accountant
b. AMEX
c. ABC Television Network
d. AIG

25. _____ refers to a business or organization attempting to acquire goods or services to accomplish the goals of the enterprise. Though there are several organizations that attempt to set standards in the _____ process, processes can vary greatly between organizations. Typically the word e;_____e; is not used interchangeably with the word e;procuremente;, since procurement typically includes Expediting, Supplier Quality, and Traffic and Logistics (T'L) in addition to _____.

a. Free port
b. Consignor
c. Supply chain
d. Purchasing

26. _____ is one of a series of accounting transactions dealing with the billing of customers who owe money to a person, company or organization for goods and services that have been provided to the customer. In most business entities this is typically done by generating an invoice and mailing or electronically delivering it to the customer, who in turn must pay it within an established timeframe called credit or payment terms.

An example of a common payment term is Net 30, meaning payment is due in the amount of the invoice 30 days from the date of invoice.

a. Accrued revenue
b. Adjusting entries
c. Accrual
d. Accounts receivable

27. Established in 1988 the _____ is the professional organization that governs professional fraud examiners. Its activities include producing fraud information, tools and training. It also governs the professional designation of Certified Fraud Examiner.

a. Association of Certified Fraud Examiners
b. AMEX
c. ABC Television Network
d. AIG

28. _____ is the process of comparing the cost, cycle time, productivity, or quality of a specific process or method to another that is widely considered to be an industry standard or best practice. Essentially, _____ provides a snapshot of the performance of your business and helps you understand where you are in relation to a particular standard. The result is often a business case for making changes in order to make improvements.

a. Benchmarking
b. Strategic business unit
c. BMC Software, Inc.
d. 3M Company

29. _____ asserts that there is a technique, method, process, activity, incentive or reward that is more effective at delivering a particular outcome than any other technique, method, process, etc. The idea is that with proper processes, checks, and testing, a desired outcome can be delivered with fewer problems and unforeseen complications. _____s can also be defined as the most efficient (least amount of effort) and effective (best results) way of accomplishing a task, based on repeatable procedures that have proven themselves over time for large numbers of people.

a. Cash cow
b. Performance measurement
c. Management by objectives
d. Best practice

30. _____ is a designation awarded by the Association of _____s (ACertified Fraud Examiner.) The ACertified Fraud Examiner is a 41,000 member-based global association dedicated to providing anti-fraud education and training.

In order to become a _____ one must meet the following requirements:

- Be an Associate Member of the ACertified Fraud Examiner in good standing
- Meet minimum academic and professional requirements
- Be of high moral character
- Agree to abide by the Bylaws and Code of Professional Ethics of the Association of _____s

Generally, applicants for _____ certification have a minimum of a bachelor's degree or equivalent from an institution of higher education. Two years of professional experience related to fraud can be substituted for each year of college.

a. Certified public accountant
b. Certified Fraud Examiner
c. Chartered Certified Accountant
d. Chartered Accountant

31. A _____, also client, buyer or purchaser is the buyer or user of the paid products of an individual or organization, mostly called the supplier or seller. This is typically through purchasing or renting goods or services.

a. BNSF Railway
b. BMC Software, Inc.
c. 3M Company
d. Customer

32. _____, a business term, is a measure of how products and services supplied by a company meet or surpass customer expectation. It is seen as a key performance indicator within business and is part of the four perspectives of a Balanced Scorecard.

In a competitive marketplace where businesses compete for customers, _____ is seen as a key differentiator and increasingly has become a key element of business strategy.

a. Pre-determined overhead rate
b. Time to market
c. Procurement
d. Customer satisfaction

Chapter 1. Auditing and Assurance Services

33. A _____ has several related meanings:

- a daily record of events or business; a private _____ is usually referred to as a diary.
- a newspaper or other periodical, in the literal sense of one published each day;
- many publications issued at stated intervals, such as magazines, or scholarly academic _____s, or the record of the transactions of a society, are often called _____s. Although _____ is sometimes used, erroneously, as a synonym for 'magazine,' in academic use, a _____ refers to a serious, scholarly publication, most often peer-reviewed. A non-scholarly magazine written for an educated audience about an industry or an area of professional activity is usually called a professional magazine.

The word 'journalist' for one whose business is writing for the public press has been in use since the end of the 17th century.

Open access _____s are scholarly _____s that are available to the reader without financial or other barrier other than access to the internet itself. Some are subsidized, and some require payment on behalf of the author. Subsidized _____s are financed by an academic institution or a government information center.

a. BNSF Railway
b. 3M Company
c. Journal
d. BMC Software, Inc.

34. _____ is subcontracting a process, such as product design or manufacturing, to a third-party company. The decision to outsource is often made in the interest of lowering cost or making better use of time and energy costs, redirecting or conserving energy directed at the competencies of a particular business, or to make more efficient use of land, labor, capital, (information) technology and resources. _____ became part of the business lexicon during the 1980s.

a. USA Today
b. US Airways, Inc.
c. Economic Growth and Tax Relief Reconciliation Act of 2001
d. Outsourcing

35. A _____ is a fungible, negotiable instrument representing financial value. they are broadly categorized into debt securities (such as banknotes, bonds and debentures), and equity securities; e.g., common stocks. The company or other entity issuing the _____ is called the issuer.

a. Security
b. 3M Company
c. BMC Software, Inc.
d. Tracking stock

36. _____ is any physical or virtual entity that is owned by an individual or jointly by a group of individuals. An owner of _____ has the right to consume, sell, rent, mortgage, transfer and exchange his or her _____. Important widely-recognized types of _____ include real _____, personal _____ (other physical possessions), and intellectual _____ (rights over artistic creations, inventions, etc.), although the latter is not always as widely recognized or enforced.

a. Fiduciary
b. Primary authority
c. Disclosure requirement
d. Property

37. The U.S. _____ is an independent agency of the United States government which holds primary responsibility for enforcing the federal securities laws and regulating the securities industry, the nation's stock and options exchanges, and other electronic securities markets. The SEC was created by section 4 of the Securities Exchange Act of 1934 (now codified as 15 U.S.C. §§ 78d and commonly referred to as the 1934 Act.)

Chapter 1. Auditing and Assurance Services

a. BMC Software, Inc.
b. 3M Company
c. BNSF Railway
d. Securities and Exchange Commission

38. In a financial audit, _____ or financial statement assertions is the set of information that the preparer of financial statements (management) is providing to another party. Financial statements represent a very complex and interrelated set of assertions. At the most aggregate level, the financial statements include broad assertions such as 'total liabilities as at 31 December are $50 million', 'total revenue for the year is $9 million' and 'net income for the year is $3 million'.
   a. Mainframe audit
   b. Management assertions
   c. Lead Auditor
   d. Sales Tax Audit

39. A _____ or chief executive is one of the highest-ranking corporate officer (executive) or administrator in charge of total management. An individual selected as President and _____ of a corporation, company, organization, or agency, reports to the board of directors. In internal communication and press releases, many companies capitalize the term and those of other high positions, even when they are not proper nouns.
   a. Chief executive officer
   b. Return on equity
   c. Return on assets
   d. Kohlberg Kravis Roberts ' Co

40. The term _____ usually refers to a company that is permitted to offer its registered securities (stock, bonds, etc.) for sale to the general public, typically through a stock exchange, or occasionally a company whose stock is traded over the counter (OTC) via market makers who use non-exchange quotation services.

The term '_____' may also refer to a company owned by the government.

   a. Professional association
   b. Governmental Accounting Standards Board
   c. MicroStrategy
   d. Public Company

41. The _____ (sometimes called 'Peekaboo') is a private-sector, non-profit corporation created by the Sarbanes-Oxley Act, a 2002 United States federal law, to oversee the auditors of public companies. Its stated purpose is to 'protect the interests of investors and further the public interest in the preparation of informative, fair, and independent audit reports'. Although a private entity, the _____ has many government-like regulatory functions, making it in some ways similar to the private Self Regulatory Organizations (SROs) that regulate stock markets and other aspects of the financial markets in the United States.
   a. Public Company Accounting Oversight Board
   b. Pension Benefit Guaranty Corporation
   c. Financial Crimes Enforcement Network
   d. 3M Company

42. An _____ is the buying of one company by another. An _____ may be friendly or hostile. In the former case, the companies cooperate in negotiations; in the latter case, the takeover target is unwilling to be bought or the target's board has no prior knowledge of the offer. _____ usually refers to a purchase of a smaller firm by a larger one. Sometimes, however, a smaller firm will acquire management control of a larger or longer established company and keep its name for the combined entity. This is known as a reverse takeover.
   a. AIG
   b. ABC Television Network
   c. AMEX
   d. Acquisition

43. _____ refers to the confirmation of certain characteristics of an object, person, or organization. This confirmation is often, but not always, provided by some form of external review, education, or assessment. One of the most common types of _____ in modern society is professional _____, where a person is certified as being able to competently complete a job or task, usually by the passing of an examination.

    a. BMC Software, Inc.
    b. BNSF Railway
    c. 3M Company
    d. Certification

44. In financial accounting, a _____ is defined as an obligation of an entity arising from past transactions or events, the settlement of which may result in the transfer or use of assets, provision of services or other yielding of economic benefits in the future.

    a. Vested
    b. Liability
    c. False Claims Act
    d. Corporate governance

45. _____ is the state or fact of exclusive rights and control over property, which may be an object, land/real estate or intellectual property. An _____ right is also referred to as title.

_____ is the key building block in the development of the capitalist socio-economic system.

    a. Encumbrance
    b. Administrative proceeding
    c. ABC Television Network
    d. Ownership

46. _____ means the giving out of information, either voluntarily or to be in compliance with legal regulations or workplace rules.

- In Computer security, full _____ means disclosing full information about vulnerabilities.
- In computing, _____ widget
- Journalism, full _____ refers to disclosing the interests of the writer which may bear on the subject being written about, for example, if the writer has worked with an interview subject in the past.

- In law:
    - The law of England and Wales, _____ refers to a process that may form part of legal proceedings, whereby parties inform to other parties the existence of any relevant documents that are, or have been, in their control. This compares with the process known as discovery in the course of legal proceedings in the United States.
    - In U.S. civil procedure (litigation rules for civil cases), _____ is a stage prior to trial. In civil cases, each party must disclose to the opposing party the following: names of witnesses which it may use to support its side, copies of documents (or mere description of these documents) in its control which it may use to support its side, computation of damages claimed, and certain insurance information. _____ is related to, but technically prior to, the discovery stage.
    - In Company law (known as 'corporate law' in the United States), _____ refers to giving out information about public or limited companies or their officers, which might be kept secret if the company was a private company or a partnership.

- In real property transactions, _____ refers to providing to a buyer information known to the seller or broker/agent concerning the condition or other aspects of real property that would affect the property's value or desirability. These rules regarding what information must be disclosed, and whether the information must be disclosed even if a buyer does not ask, vary from one jurisdiction to the next.

a. Controlled Foreign Corporations
c. Trailing
b. Tax harmonisation
d. Disclosure

47. In finance, _____ is the process of estimating the potential market value of a financial asset or liability. They can be done on assets (for example, investments in marketable securities such as stocks, options, business enterprises, or intangible assets such as patents and trademarks) or on liabilities (e.g., Bonds issued by a company.) A _____ is required in many contexts including investment analysis, capital budgeting, merger and acquisition transactions, financial reporting, taxable events to determine the proper tax liability, and in litigation.

a. Vyborg Appeal
c. Daybook
b. Valuation
d. Disclosure

48. _____ LLP, based in Chicago, was once one of the 'Big Five' accounting firms among PricewaterhouseCoopers, Deloitte Touche Tohmatsu, Ernst ' Young and KPMG, providing auditing, tax, and consulting services to large corporations. In 2002, the firm voluntarily surrendered its licenses to practice as Certified Public Accountants in the United States after being found guilty of criminal charges relating to the firm's handling of the auditing of Enron, the energy corporation, resulting in the loss of 85,000 jobs. Although the verdict was subsequently overturned by the Supreme Court of the United States, it has not returned as a viable business.

a. AIG
b. AMEX
c. ABC Television Network
d. Arthur Andersen

49. _____ in economics and business is the result of an exchange and from that trade we assign a numerical monetary value to a good, service or asset. If Alice trades Bob 4 apples for an orange, the _____ of an orange is 4 apples. Inversely, the _____ of an apple is 1/4 oranges.
   a. Price
   b. Transactional Net Margin Method
   c. Price discrimination
   d. Discounts and allowances

50. Tax avoidance is the legal utilization of the tax regime to one's own advantage, in order to reduce the amount of tax that is payable by means that are within the law. By contrast _____ is the general term for efforts to not pay taxes by illegal means. According to the former British Chancellor of the Exchequer Denis Healey, the difference between tax avoidance and _____ is the thickness of a prison wall.
   a. Tax compliance solution
   b. Tax evasion
   c. Progressive tax
   d. Rational economic exchange

51. _____ is the world's largest professional services firm. It was formed in 1998 from a merger between Price Waterhouse and Coopers ' Lybrand, both formed in London.

_____ earned aggregated worldwide revenues of $28 billion for fiscal 2008, and employed over 146,000 people in 150 countries.

   a. PricewaterhouseCoopers
   b. Daybook
   c. Total-factor productivity
   d. Serial bonds

52. The _____ of 2002 (Pub.L. 107-204, 116 Stat. 745, enacted July 30, 2002), also known as the Public Company Accounting Reform and Investor Protection Act of 2002, is a United States federal law enacted on July 30, 2002 in response to a number of major corporate and accounting scandals including those affecting Enron, Tyco International, Adelphia, Peregrine Systems and WorldCom. The legislation establishes new or enhanced standards for all U.S. public company boards, management, and public accounting firms. It does not apply to privately held companies.
   a. Lease
   b. FCPA
   c. Fair Labor Standards Act
   d. Sarbanes-Oxley Act

53. _____ is the recording of the value of assets, liabilities, income, and expenses in the daybooks, journals, and ledgers, in which debit and credit entries are chronologically posted to record changes in value. _____ is often mistaken for accounting, which is the system of recording, verifying, and reporting such information. Practitioners of accounting are called accountants.
   a. Double-entry bookkeeping
   b. Controlling account
   c. Bookkeeping
   d. Debit and credit

54. _____ is an increasingly broadening term with which an organization knowledge and experience, Employee Relations and resource planning at various levels. The field draws upon concepts developed in Industrial/Organizational Psychology and System Theory. _____ has at least two related interpretations depending on context.
   a. 3M Company
   b. Separation of duties
   c. BMC Software, Inc.
   d. Human resources

55. _____, Quarterly Report Pursuant to Section 13 or 15(d) of the Securities Exchange Act of 1934, is an SEC filing that must be filed quarterly with the US Securities and Exchange Commission. It contains similar information to the annual form 10-K, however the information is generally less detailed, and the financial statements are generally unaudited. Information for the final quarter of a firm's fiscal year is included in the 10-K, so only three 10-Q filings are made each year.
   a. 3M Company
   b. Form 8-K
   c. Form 10-Q
   d. Form 20-F

56. _____ is a demonstration of a process -- such as a variable, term, or object -- relative in terms of the specific process or set of validation tests used to determine its presence and quantity. Properties described in this manner must be sufficiently accessible, so that persons other than the definer may independently measure or test for them at will. An _____ is generally designed to model a conceptual definition.
   a. AIG
   b. Operational definition
   c. ABC Television Network
   d. AMEX

57. _____ refers to the independence of the auditor from parties, that have an interest in the financial statements of an entity. It is essentially an attitude of mind characterized by integrity and an objective approach to the audit process. The concept requires the auditor to carry out his work freely and in an objective manner.
   a. Internal Auditing
   b. Auditor independence
   c. Information audit
   d. Audit

58. The _____ is the United States federal government agency that collects taxes and enforces the internal revenue laws. It is an agency within the U.S. Dept of the treasury responsible for interpretation and application of Federal tax law. The official U.S. Treasury regulations provide (in part):

The _____ is a bureau of the Department of the Treasury under the immediate direction of the Commissioner of Internal Revenue.

   a. Income tax
   b. Use tax
   c. Indirect tax
   d. Internal Revenue Service

59. _____ refers to an examination of a program, function, operation or the management systems and procedures of a governmental or non-profit entity to assess whether the entity is achieving economy, efficiency and effectiveness in the employment of available resources. The examination is objective and systematic, generally using structured and professionally adopted methodologies.

In most countries, _____s of governmental activities are carried out by the external audit bodies at federal or state level.

   a. Trustworthy Repositories Audit ' Certification
   b. Mainframe audit
   c. Performance audit
   d. Statements on Auditing Standards

60. _____ is a professional certification for IT audit professionals sponsored by the Information Systems Audit and Control Association (ISACA.) Candidates for the certification must meet requirements set by ISACA.

The _____ certification was established in 1978 for several reasons:

1. Develop and maintain a tool that could be used to evaluate an individuals' competency in conducting information system audits.
2. Provide a motivational tool for information systems auditors to maintain their skills, and monitor the success of the maintenance programs.
3. Provide criteria to help aid management in the selection of personnel and development.

The first _____ examination was administered in 1981, and registration numbers have grown each year. Over 60,000 candidates have earned the _____ designation.

a. BMC Software, Inc.
b. BNSF Railway
c. 3M Company
d. Certified information systems auditor

61. The title _____ is a professional designation awarded by various professional bodies around the world.

The _____ designation is a post-nominal award issued to individuals who have achieved a peer-based criteria of professional competency in the field of Management Accounting. Management accounting qualifications differ from those such as the ACA or CPA 'Chartered' or 'Public' accounting qualifications in a number of ways.

a. BMC Software, Inc.
b. 3M Company
c. Certified management accountant
d. Convey Compliance Systems

62. Internal auditing is a profession and activity involved in helping organisations achieve their stated objectives. It does this by utilizing a systematic methodology for analyzing business processes, procedures and activities with the goal of highlighting organizational problems and recommending solutions. Professionals called _____ are employed by organizations to perform the internal auditing activity.

a. Auditor independence
b. Internal auditors
c. Auditing Standards Board
d. Internal Auditing

63. _____ is concerned with the provisions and use of accounting information to managers within organizations, to provide them with the basis to make informed business decisions that will allow them to be better equipped in their management and control functions.

In contrast to financial accountancy information, _____ information is:

- usually confidential and used by management, instead of publicly reported;
- forward-looking, instead of historical;
- pragmatically computed using extensive management information systems and internal controls, instead of complying with accounting standards.

This is because of the different emphasis: _____ information is used within an organization, typically for decision-making.

a. Grenzplankostenrechnung
b. Management accounting
c. Governmental accounting
d. Nonassurance services

64. _____ is the title used by members of certain professional accountancy associations in the British Commonwealth countries and Ireland. The term chartered comes from the Royal Charter granted to the world's first professional body of accountants upon their establishment in 1854. The Edinburgh Society of Accountants (formed 1854), the Glasgow Institute of Accountants and Actuaries (1854) and the Aberdeen Society of Accountants (1867) were each granted a royal charter almost from their inception.
a. Chartered Certified Accountant
b. Chartered accountant
c. Certified General Accountant
d. Certified public accountant

65. An _____ is an examination of the controls within an Information technology (IT) infrastructure. An IT audit is the process of collecting and evaluating evidence of an organization's information systems, practices, and operations. The evaluation of obtained evidence determines if the information systems are safeguarding assets, maintaining data integrity, and operating effectively and efficiently to achieve the organization's goals or objectives.
a. Information technology audit
b. Information technology audit process
c. AIG
d. ABC Television Network

66. ISACA is an international professional association that deals with IT Governance. It is an affiliate member of IFAC. Previously known as the _____, ISACA now goes by its acronym only, to reflect the broad range of IT governance professionals it serves.
a. Information Systems Audit and Control Association
b. East Asia Economic Caucus
c. Amoco
d. American Accounting Association

67. Established in 1941, The _____ is internationally recognized as a trustworthy guidance-setting body. Serving members in 165 countries, The IIA is the internal audit profession's global voice, chief advocate, recognized authority, acknowledged leader, and principal educator, with global headquarters in Altamonte Springs, Fla., United States.

The stated mission of The _____ is to provide dynamic leadership for the global profession of internal auditing.

a. Institute of Internal Auditors
b. Audit regime
c. Event data
d. Auditor independence

68. The _____ is a professional organization headquartered in Montvale, New Jersey consisting of over 70,000 members worldwide. The IMA is dedicated to advancing the role of the management accountant and financial manager within the business organization, and provides relevant professional certification.

The IMA awards the Certified Management Accountant (CMA) designation in the United States.

a. Institute of Management Accountants
b. International Accounting Standards Committee
c. Emerging technologies
d. American Accounting Association

69. Core competency is something that a firm can do well and that meets the following three conditions:

   1. It provides consumer benefits
   2. It is not easy for competitors to imitate
   3. It can be leveraged widely to many products and markets.

A core competency can take various forms, including technical/subject matter know how, a reliable process, and/or close relationships with customers and suppliers (Mascarenhas et al. 1998.) It may also include product development or culture, such as employee dedication.

_____ are particular strengths relative to other organizations in the industry which provide the fundamental basis for the provision of added value.

   a. BMC Software, Inc.
   c. BNSF Railway
   b. Core competencies
   d. 3M Company

Chapter 2. Professional Standards 17

1. An _____ is a practitioner of accountancy, which is the measurement, disclosure or provision of assurance about financial information that helps managers, investors, tax authorities and other decision makers make resource allocation decisions.

The word '_____' is derived from the French 'Compter' which took its origin from the Latin 'Computare'. The word was formerly written in English as 'Accomptant', but in process of time the word, which was always pronounced by dropping the 'p', became gradually changed both in pronunciation and in orthography to its present form.

   a. Accountant   b. ABC Television Network
   c. AMEX   d. AIG

2. The _____ is the national, professional association of CPAs in the United States, with more than 330,000 members, including CPAs in business and industry, public practice, government, and education; student affiliates; and international associates. It sets ethical standards for the profession and U.S. auditing standards for audits of private companies; federal, state and local governments; and non-profit organizations.

Approximately 40% of its members are engaged in the practice of public accounting, in areas such as auditing, accounting, taxation, general business consulting, business valuation, personal financial planning and business technology.

   a. Other postemployment benefits   b. ABC Television Network
   c. AIG   d. American Institute of Certified Public Accountants

3. _____ is the statutory title of qualified accountants in the United States who have passed the Uniform _____ Examination and have met additional state education and experience requirements for certification as a _____. Individuals who have passed the Exam but have not either accomplished the required on-the-job experience or have previously met it but in the meantime have lapsed their continuing professional education are, in many states, permitted the designation '_____ Inactive' or an equivalent phrase. In most U.S. states, only _____s who are licensed are able to provide to the public attestation (including auditing) opinions on financial statements.

   a. Certified General Accountant   b. Chartered Accountant
   c. Chartered Certified Accountant   d. Certified Public Accountant

4. The _____ is the global organization for the accountancy profession. IFAC has 157 member bodies and associates in 123 countries and jurisdictions, representing more than 2.5 million accountants employed in public practice, industry and commerce, government, and academe. The organization, through its independent standard-setting boards, establishes international standards on ethics, auditing and assurance, education, and public sector accounting.

   a. American Payroll Association   b. International Federation of Accountants
   c. Emerging technologies   d. International Accounting Standards Committee

5. The term _____ usually refers to a company that is permitted to offer its registered securities (stock, bonds, etc.) for sale to the general public, typically through a stock exchange, or occasionally a company whose stock is traded over the counter (OTC) via market makers who use non-exchange quotation services.

The term '_____' may also refer to a company owned by the government.

a. Public Company
b. MicroStrategy
c. Professional association
d. Governmental Accounting Standards Board

6. The _____ (sometimes called 'Peekaboo') is a private-sector, non-profit corporation created by the Sarbanes-Oxley Act, a 2002 United States federal law, to oversee the auditors of public companies. Its stated purpose is to 'protect the interests of investors and further the public interest in the preparation of informative, fair, and independent audit reports'. Although a private entity, the _____ has many government-like regulatory functions, making it in some ways similar to the private Self Regulatory Organizations (SROs) that regulate stock markets and other aspects of the financial markets in the United States.
   a. 3M Company
   b. Public Company Accounting Oversight Board
   c. Pension Benefit Guaranty Corporation
   d. Financial Crimes Enforcement Network

7. The _____ of 2002 (Pub.L. 107-204, 116 Stat. 745, enacted July 30, 2002), also known as the Public Company Accounting Reform and Investor Protection Act of 2002, is a United States federal law enacted on July 30, 2002 in response to a number of major corporate and accounting scandals including those affecting Enron, Tyco International, Adelphia, Peregrine Systems and WorldCom. The legislation establishes new or enhanced standards for all U.S. public company boards, management, and public accounting firms. It does not apply to privately held companies.
   a. Lease
   b. FCPA
   c. Fair Labor Standards Act
   d. Sarbanes-Oxley Act

8. _____ refers to the independence of the auditor from parties, that have an interest in the financial statements of an entity. It is essentially an attitude of mind characterized by integrity and an objective approach to the audit process. The concept requires the auditor to carry out his work freely and in an objective manner.
   a. Information audit
   b. Internal Auditing
   c. Audit
   d. Auditor independence

9. _____ are ten auditing standards, developed by the AICPA, consisting of general standards, standards of field work, and standards of reporting, along with interpretations. They were developed by the AICPA in 1947 and have undergone minor changes since then.

The _____ are as follows:

1. The auditor must have adequate technical training and proficiency to perform the audit
2. The auditor must maintain independence in mental attitude in all matters related to the audit.
3. The auditor must use due professional care during the performance of the audit and the preparation of the report.

1. The auditor must adequately plan the work and must properly supervise any assistants.
2. The auditor must obtain a sufficient understanding of the entity and its environment, including its internal control, to assess the risk of material misstatement of the financial statements whether due to error or fraud, and to design the nature, timing, and extent of further audit procedures.
3. The auditor must obtain sufficient appropriate audit evidence by performing audit procedures to afford a reasonable basis for an opinion regarding the financial statements under audit.

Chapter 2. Professional Standards

The new standards are in effect for audits of financial statements for periods beginning on or after December 15, 2006.

1. The auditor must state in the auditor's report whether the financial statements are in accordance with generally accepted accounting principles (GAAP.)
2. The auditor must identify in the auditor's report those circumstances in which such principles have not been consistently observed in the current period in relation to the preceding period.
3. When the auditor determines that informative disclosures are not reasonably adequate, the auditor must so state in the auditor's report.
4. The auditor must either express an opinion regarding the financial statements, taken as a whole the auditor should state the reasons therefore in the auditor's report. In all cases where the auditor's name is associated with the financial statements, the auditor should clearly indicate the character of the auditor's work, if any, and the degree of responsibility the auditor is taking, in the auditor's report.

a. Negative assurance
b. Joint audit
c. Generally accepted auditing standards
d. Continuous auditing

10. Established in 1988 the _____ is the professional organization that governs professional fraud examiners. Its activities include producing fraud information, tools and training. It also governs the professional designation of Certified Fraud Examiner.

a. ABC Television Network
b. AMEX
c. AIG
d. Association of Certified Fraud Examiners

11. _____ is a designation awarded by the Association of _____s (ACertified Fraud Examiner.) The ACertified Fraud Examiner is a 41,000 member-based global association dedicated to providing anti-fraud education and training.

In order to become a _____ one must meet the following requirements:

- Be an Associate Member of the ACertified Fraud Examiner in good standing
- Meet minimum academic and professional requirements
- Be of high moral character
- Agree to abide by the Bylaws and Code of Professional Ethics of the Association of _____s

Generally, applicants for _____ certification have a minimum of a bachelor's degree or equivalent from an institution of higher education. Two years of professional experience related to fraud can be substituted for each year of college.

a. Chartered Accountant
b. Chartered Certified Accountant
c. Certified public accountant
d. Certified Fraud Examiner

Chapter 2. Professional Standards

12. _____, Quarterly Report Pursuant to Section 13 or 15(d) of the Securities Exchange Act of 1934, is an SEC filing that must be filed quarterly with the US Securities and Exchange Commission. It contains similar information to the annual form 10-K, however the information is generally less detailed, and the financial statements are generally unaudited. Information for the final quarter of a firm's fiscal year is included in the 10-K, so only three 10-Q filings are made each year.
   a. 3M Company
   b. Form 20-F
   c. Form 8-K
   d. Form 10-Q

13. An _____ is a term used in behavioral economics to describe those types of behaviors that impose costs on a person in the long-run that are not taken into account when making decisions in the present. Classical Economics discourages government from creating legislation that targets internalities, because it is assumed that the consumer takes these personal costs into account when paying for the good that causes the _____. For example, cigarettes should be taxed because of the negative consumption externalities that they impose, such as second-hand smoke, not because the smoker harms him or herself by smoking.
   a. Internality
   b. Inventory turnover ratio
   c. Operating budget
   d. Authorised capital

14. _____ is a profession and activity involved in helping organisations achieve their stated objectives. It does this by using a systematic methodology for analyzing business processes, procedures and activities with the goal of highlighting organizational problems and recommending solutions. Professionals called internal auditors are employed by organizations to perform the _____ activity.
   a. Assurance service
   b. Information audit
   c. ITGCs
   d. Internal Auditing

15. _____, commonly abbreviated as SAS, provide guidance to external auditors on generally accepted auditing standards in regards to auditing an entity and issuing a report. They are usually issued by the certified public accountant authoritative body in the region where the standards apply, such as the American Institute of Certified Public Accountants in the United States.

   - _____
   - _____ (Taiwan)

   a. Financial Instruments and Exchange Law
   b. Statements on Auditing Standards
   c. GASB 45
   d. RSM International

16. The general definition of an _____ is an evaluation of a person, organization, system, process, project or product. _____s are performed to ascertain the validity and reliability of information; also to provide an assessment of a system's internal control. The goal of an _____ is to express an opinion on the person/organization/system (etc) in question, under evaluation based on work done on a test basis.
   a. Audit regime
   b. Institute of Chartered Accountants of India
   c. Assurance service
   d. Audit

Chapter 2. Professional Standards

17. _____ is evidence obtained during a financial audit and recorded in the audit working papers.

- In the audit engagement acceptance or reappointment stage, _____ is the information that the auditor is to consider for the appointment. For examples, change in the entity control environment, inherent risk and nature of the entity business, and scope of audit work.

- In the audit planning stage, _____ is the information that the auditor is to consider for the most effective and efficient audit approach. For examples, reliability of internal control procedures, and analytical review systems.

- In the control testing stage, _____ is the information that the auditor is to consider for the mix of audit test of control and audit substantive tests.

- In the substantive testing stage, _____ is the information that the auditor is to make sure the appropriation of financial statement assertions. For examples, existence, rights and obligations, occurrence, completeness, valuation, measurement, presentation and disclosure of a particular transaction or account balance.

a. ITGCs
c. Institute of Chartered Accountants of India
b. Audit
d. Audit evidence

18. _____ is the world's largest professional services firm. It was formed in 1998 from a merger between Price Waterhouse and Coopers ' Lybrand, both formed in London.

_____ earned aggregated worldwide revenues of $28 billion for fiscal 2008, and employed over 146,000 people in 150 countries.

a. Serial bonds
c. Daybook
b. Total-factor productivity
d. PricewaterhouseCoopers

19. An _____ is a lease whose term is short compared to the useful life of the asset or piece of equipment (an airliner, a ship etc.) being leased. An _____ is commonly used to acquire equipment on a relatively short-term basis.
a. Operating lease
c. Express warranty
b. Employee Retirement Income Security Act
d. Issued shares

20. A _____ is a contract conferring a right on one person to possess property belonging to another person (called a landlord or lessor) to the exclusion of the owner landlord. It is a rental agreement between landlord and tenant. The relationship between the tenant and the landlord is called a tenancy, and the right to possession by the tenant is sometimes called a leasehold interest.
a. Lease
c. Model Code of Professional Responsibility
b. Federal Sentencing Guidelines
d. Robinson-Patman Act

21. _____, in auditing, is the risk that a company's internal controls are insufficient to mitigate or detect errors or fraud.
a. BMC Software, Inc.
c. 3M Company
b. BNSF Railway
d. Control risk

22. _____, in auditing, is the risk that the account or section being audited is materially misstated without considering internal controls due to error; _____ does not include an assessment of the risk of material misstatement due to fraud. The assessment of _____ depends on the professional judgement of the auditor, and it is done after assessing the business environment of the entity being audited.

_____ is typically assessed using a scale, with assessments being either low, medium, or high.

a. AIG
b. ABC Television Network
c. Inherent risk
d. AMEX

23. In accounting and organizational theory, _____ is defined as a process effected by an organization's structure, work and authority flows, people and management information systems, designed to help the organization accomplish specific goals or objectives. It is a means by which an organization's resources are directed, monitored, and measured. It plays an important role in preventing and detecting fraud and protecting the organization's resources, both physical (e.g., machinery and property) and intangible (e.g., reputation or intellectual property such as trademarks.)

a. Audit committee
b. Audit risk
c. Auditor independence
d. Internal control

24. An _____ is the buying of one company by another. An _____ may be friendly or hostile. In the former case, the companies cooperate in negotiations; in the latter case, the takeover target is unwilling to be bought or the target's board has no prior knowledge of the offer. _____ usually refers to a purchase of a smaller firm by a larger one. Sometimes, however, a smaller firm will acquire management control of a larger or longer established company and keep its name for the combined entity. This is known as a reverse takeover.

a. AMEX
b. Acquisition
c. ABC Television Network
d. AIG

25. _____ is a concept that denotes the precise probability of specific eventualities. Technically, the notion of _____ is independent from the notion of value and, as such, eventualities may have both beneficial and adverse consequences. However, in general usage the convention is to focus only on potential negative impact to some characteristic of value that may arise from a future event.

a. Discount factor
b. Risk adjusted return on capital
c. Risk
d. Discounting

26. _____ is that part of statistical practice concerned with the selection of individual observations intended to yield some knowledge about a population of concern, especially for the purposes of statistical inference. Each observation measures one or more properties (weight, location, etc.) of an observable entity enumerated to distinguish objects or individuals.

a. Alan Greenspan
b. Arthur Betz Laffer
c. Abby Joseph Cohen
d. Sampling

Chapter 2. Professional Standards

27. A _____ has several related meanings:

- a daily record of events or business; a private _____ is usually referred to as a diary.
- a newspaper or other periodical, in the literal sense of one published each day;
- many publications issued at stated intervals, such as magazines, or scholarly academic _____ s, or the record of the transactions of a society, are often called _____ s. Although _____ is sometimes used, erroneously, as a synonym for 'magazine,' in academic use, a _____ refers to a serious, scholarly publication, most often peer-reviewed. A non-scholarly magazine written for an educated audience about an industry or an area of professional activity is usually called a professional magazine.

The word 'journalist' for one whose business is writing for the public press has been in use since the end of the 17th century.

Open access _____ s are scholarly _____ s that are available to the reader without financial or other barrier other than access to the internet itself. Some are subsidized, and some require payment on behalf of the author. Subsidized _____ s are financed by an academic institution or a government information center.

a. Journal
b. BNSF Railway
c. 3M Company
d. BMC Software, Inc.

28. _____ is a letter issued by an auditor's client to the auditor in writing as one of audit evidences. The date of the document must not be later than the date of audit work completion. It is used to let the client's management declare in writing that the financial statements and other presentations to the auditor are sufficient and appropriate and without omission of material facts to the financial statements, to the best of the management's knowledge.

a. Joint audit
b. Management representation
c. Management assertions
d. Statements on Auditing Standards

29. A _____ proof is a mathematical proof that a particular theory is consistent. The early development of mathematical proof theory was driven by the desire to provide finitary _____ proofs for all of mathematics as part of Hilbert's program. Hilbert's program was strongly impacted by incompleteness theorems, which showed that sufficiently strong proof theories cannot prove their own _____

a. Daybook
b. Consumption
c. Monte Carlo methods
d. Consistency

30. The _____ is a private, not-for-profit organization whose primary purpose is to develop generally accepted accounting principles (GAAP) within the United States in the public's interest. The Securities and Exchange Commission (SEC) designated the _____ as the organization responsible for setting accounting standards for public companies in the U.S. It was created in 1973, replacing the Accounting Principles Board and the Committee on Accounting Procedure of the American Institute of Certified Public Accountants. The _____ 's mission is 'to establish and improve standards of financial accounting and reporting for the guidance and education of the public, including issuers, auditors, and users of financial information.'

The _____ is not a governmental body.

a. Public company
b. Governmental Accounting Standards Board
c. Fannie Mae
d. Financial Accounting Standards Board

31. _____ is the term used to refer to the standard framework of guidelines for financial accounting used in any given jurisdiction. _____ includes the standards, conventions, and rules accountants follow in recording and summarizing transactions, and in the preparation of financial statements.

Financial accounting information must be assembled and reported objectively.

a. General ledger
b. Generally accepted accounting principles
c. Current asset
d. Long-term liabilities

32. In a company, _____ is the sum of all financial records of salaries, wages, bonuses and deductions.

A paycheck, is traditionally a paper document issued by an employer to pay an employee for services rendered. While most commonly used in the United States, recently the physical paycheck has been increasingly replaced by electronic direct deposit to bank accounts.

a. Total Expense Ratio
b. Tax expense
c. 3M Company
d. Payroll

33. _____ are formal records of a business' financial activities.

In British English, including United Kingdom company law, _____ are often referred to as accounts, although the term _____ is also used, particularly by accountants.

_____ provide an overview of a business' financial condition in both short and long term.

a. Notes to the financial statements
b. Statement of retained earnings
c. 3M Company
d. Financial statements

34. _____s have been defined by the American Institute of Certified Public Accountants (AICPA) as 'Independent Professional Services that improve information quality or its context'. _____s reduce the information risk; risk that the information provided is incorrect, on more than just financial data. The major purpose of _____s is to provide independent and professional opinions that improve the quality of information to management as well as other decision makers within a given firm.

a. Assurance service
b. Institute of Chartered Accountants of India
c. ITGCs
d. Auditor independence

35. Accounting _____ define the basic standards for representing attestation engagements. Attestation is defined as an engagement in which a practitioner is hired to issue written communication that expresses a conclusion about the reliability of written assertions prepared by a separate party. The American Institute of Certified Public Accountants identified a number of different engagements that fall under the scope of _____, including: examining financial forecasts and projections, examining pro forma financial statements, evaluating internal control, assessing compliance with rules, regulations, and contractual obligations, as well as evaluating management discussions and analysis of financial results.

a. Institute of Chartered Accountants of India
b. Audit management
c. Audit working paper
d. Attestation standards

36. In engineering and manufacturing, _____ and quality engineering are used in developing systems to ensure products or services are designed and produced to meet or exceed customer requirements. Refer to the definition by Merriam-Webster for further information . These systems are often developed in conjunction with other business and engineering disciplines using a cross-functional approach.
   a. BNSF Railway
   b. BMC Software, Inc.
   c. 3M Company
   d. Quality Control

37. _____ principle is a cornerstone of accrual accounting together with matching principle. They both determine the accounting period, in which revenues and expenses are recognized. According to the principle, revenues are recognized when they are (1) realized or realizable, and are (2) earned (usually when goods are transferred or services rendered), no matter when cash is received.
   a. Net realizable value
   b. 3M Company
   c. BMC Software, Inc.
   d. Revenue recognition

Chapter 3. Management Fraud and Audit Risk

1. _____ LLP, based in Chicago, was once one of the 'Big Five' accounting firms among PricewaterhouseCoopers, Deloitte Touche Tohmatsu, Ernst ' Young and KPMG, providing auditing, tax, and consulting services to large corporations. In 2002, the firm voluntarily surrendered its licenses to practice as Certified Public Accountants in the United States after being found guilty of criminal charges relating to the firm's handling of the auditing of Enron, the energy corporation, resulting in the loss of 85,000 jobs. Although the verdict was subsequently overturned by the Supreme Court of the United States, it has not returned as a viable business.
    a. AMEX
    b. Arthur Andersen
    c. ABC Television Network
    d. AIG

2. Established in 1988 the _____ is the professional organization that governs professional fraud examiners. Its activities include producing fraud information, tools and training. It also governs the professional designation of Certified Fraud Examiner.
    a. AMEX
    b. ABC Television Network
    c. AIG
    d. Association of Certified Fraud Examiners

3. _____ is a designation awarded by the Association of _____s (ACertified Fraud Examiner.) The ACertified Fraud Examiner is a 41,000 member-based global association dedicated to providing anti-fraud education and training.

    In order to become a _____ one must meet the following requirements:

    - Be an Associate Member of the ACertified Fraud Examiner in good standing
    - Meet minimum academic and professional requirements
    - Be of high moral character
    - Agree to abide by the Bylaws and Code of Professional Ethics of the Association of _____s

    Generally, applicants for _____ certification have a minimum of a bachelor's degree or equivalent from an institution of higher education. Two years of professional experience related to fraud can be substituted for each year of college.

    a. Certified public accountant
    b. Chartered Certified Accountant
    c. Chartered Accountant
    d. Certified Fraud Examiner

4. The general definition of an _____ is an evaluation of a person, organization, system, process, project or product. _____s are performed to ascertain the validity and reliability of information; also to provide an assessment of a system's internal control. The goal of an _____ is to express an opinion on the person/organization/system (etc) in question, under evaluation based on work done on a test basis.
    a. Assurance service
    b. Audit regime
    c. Institute of Chartered Accountants of India
    d. Audit

5. Employment is a contract between two parties, one being the employer and the other being the _____. An _____ may be defined as: 'A person in the service of another under any contract of hire, express or implied, oral or written, where the employer has the power or right to control and direct the _____ in the material details of how the work is to be performed.' Black's Law Dictionary page 471 (5th ed. 1979).
    a. AMEX
    b. AIG
    c. ABC Television Network
    d. Employee

Chapter 3. Management Fraud and Audit Risk

6. _____ is a concept that denotes the precise probability of specific eventualities. Technically, the notion of _____ is independent from the notion of value and, as such, eventualities may have both beneficial and adverse consequences. However, in general usage the convention is to focus only on potential negative impact to some characteristic of value that may arise from a future event.

   a. Discount factor
   b. Risk adjusted return on capital
   c. Discounting
   d. Risk

7. _____ is the recording of the value of assets, liabilities, income, and expenses in the daybooks, journals, and ledgers, in which debit and credit entries are chronologically posted to record changes in value. _____ is often mistaken for accounting, which is the system of recording, verifying, and reporting such information. Practitioners of accounting are called accountants.

   a. Double-entry bookkeeping
   b. Bookkeeping
   c. Controlling account
   d. Debit and credit

8. _____ is a system of financial accounting where each transaction is recorded in at least two accounts: at least one account is debited and at least one account is credited, so that the total debits of the transaction equal to the total credits. For example, if Company A sells an item to Company B, and Company B pays by cheque, then the bookkeeper of Company A credits the account 'Sales' and debits the account 'Bank'. Conversely, the bookkeeper of Company B debits the account 'Purchases' and credits the account 'Bank'.

   a. Double-entry bookkeeping
   b. Cookie jar accounting
   c. Bookkeeping
   d. Debit and credit

9. A _____ has several related meanings:

   - a daily record of events or business; a private _____ is usually referred to as a diary.
   - a newspaper or other periodical, in the literal sense of one published each day;
   - many publications issued at stated intervals, such as magazines, or scholarly academic _____s, or the record of the transactions of a society, are often called _____s. Although _____ is sometimes used, erroneously, as a synonym for 'magazine,' in academic use, a _____ refers to a serious, scholarly publication, most often peer-reviewed. A non-scholarly magazine written for an educated audience about an industry or an area of professional activity is usually called a professional magazine.

The word 'journalist' for one whose business is writing for the public press has been in use since the end of the 17th century.

Open access _____s are scholarly _____s that are available to the reader without financial or other barrier other than access to the internet itself. Some are subsidized, and some require payment on behalf of the author. Subsidized _____s are financed by an academic institution or a government information center.

   a. Journal
   b. 3M Company
   c. BNSF Railway
   d. BMC Software, Inc.

10. In financial accounting, a _____ is defined as an obligation of an entity arising from past transactions or events, the settlement of which may result in the transfer or use of assets, provision of services or other yielding of economic benefits in the future.

a. Vested
b. False Claims Act
c. Liability
d. Corporate governance

11. _____ is that which is owed; usually referencing assets owed, but the term can also cover moral obligations and other interactions not requiring money. In the case of assets, _____ is a means of using future purchasing power in the present before a summation has been earned. Some companies and corporations use _____ as a part of their overall corporate finance strategy.
   a. Debenture
   b. Lender
   c. Debt
   d. Loan

12. _____ is a term that is commonly used in relation to the audit of the financial statements of an entity. (.
   a. Audit working paper
   b. Auditor independence
   c. Engagement Letter
   d. Audit risk

13. _____, in auditing, is the risk that a company's internal controls are insufficient to mitigate or detect errors or fraud.
   a. 3M Company
   b. BNSF Railway
   c. BMC Software, Inc.
   d. Control risk

14. _____ is a specific term used in companies' financial reporting from the company-whole point of view. Because that use excludes the effects of changing ownership interest, an economic measure of _____ is necessary for financial analysis from the shareholders' point of view

_____ is defined by the Financial Accounting Standards Board, or FASB, as 'the change in equity [net assets] of a business enterprise during a period from transactions and other events and circumstances from nonowner sources. It includes all changes in equity during a period except those resulting from investments by owners and distributions to owners.'

_____ is the sum of net income and other items that must bypass the income statement because they have not been realized, including items like an unrealized holding gain or loss from available for sale securities and foreign currency translation gains or losses.

   a. BMC Software, Inc.
   b. BNSF Railway
   c. 3M Company
   d. Comprehensive income

15. _____, in auditing, is the risk that the account or section being audited is materially misstated without considering internal controls due to error; _____ does not include an assessment of the risk of material misstatement due to fraud. The assessment of _____ depends on the professional judgement of the auditor, and it is done after assessing the business environment of the entity being audited.

_____ is typically assessed using a scale, with assessments being either low, medium, or high.

   a. AIG
   b. Inherent risk
   c. AMEX
   d. ABC Television Network

Chapter 3. Management Fraud and Audit Risk

16. An _____ is a term used in behavioral economics to describe those types of behaviors that impose costs on a person in the long-run that are not taken into account when making decisions in the present. Classical Economics discourages government from creating legislation that targets internalities, because it is assumed that the consumer takes these personal costs into account when paying for the good that causes the _____. For example, cigarettes should be taxed because of the negative consumption externalities that they impose, such as second-hand smoke, not because the smoker harms him or herself by smoking.

    a. Authorised capital   b. Operating budget
    c. Inventory turnover ratio   d. Internality

17. In accounting and organizational theory, _____ is defined as a process effected by an organization's structure, work and authority flows, people and management information systems, designed to help the organization accomplish specific goals or objectives. It is a means by which an organization's resources are directed, monitored, and measured. It plays an important role in preventing and detecting fraud and protecting the organization's resources, both physical (e.g., machinery and property) and intangible (e.g., reputation or intellectual property such as trademarks.)

    a. Audit committee   b. Auditor independence
    c. Audit risk   d. Internal control

18. _____ is that part of statistical practice concerned with the selection of individual observations intended to yield some knowledge about a population of concern, especially for the purposes of statistical inference. Each observation measures one or more properties (weight, location, etc.) of an observable entity enumerated to distinguish objects or individuals.

    a. Alan Greenspan   b. Abby Joseph Cohen
    c. Arthur Betz Laffer   d. Sampling

19. _____ is a term used in accounting, economics and finance to spread the cost of an asset over the span of several years.

In simple words we can say that _____ is the reduction in the value of an asset due to usage, passage of time, wear and tear, technological outdating or obsolescence, depletion, inadequacy, rot, rust, decay or other such factors.

In accounting, _____ is a term used to describe any method of attributing the historical or purchase cost of an asset across its useful life, roughly corresponding to normal wear and tear.

    a. Current asset   b. Depreciation
    c. Net profit   d. General ledger

20. _____ is the calculated approximation of a result which is usable even if input data may be incomplete or uncertain.

In statistics, see _____ theory, estimator.

In mathematics, approximation or _____ typically means finding upper or lower bounds of a quantity that cannot readily be computed precisely and is also an educated guess .

a. AIG
b. Estimation
c. AMEX
d. ABC Television Network

21. _____ is the corporate management term for the act of partially dismantling or otherwise reorganizing a company for the purpose of making it more profitable. Also known as corporate _____, debt _____ and financial _____.

_____ is often done as part of a bankruptcy or of a strategic takeover by another firm, such as a leveraged buyout by a private equity firm.

a. Net worth
b. Restructuring
c. Fair market value
d. Payback period

22. _____ is the collection, transport, processing, recycling or disposal, and monitoring of waste materials. The term usually relates to materials produced by human activity, and is generally undertaken to reduce their effect on health, the environment or aesthetics. _____ is also carried out to recover resources from it.

a. Waste Management
b. BNSF Railway
c. 3M Company
d. BMC Software, Inc.

23. In a publicly-held company, an _____ is an operating committee of the Board of Directors, typically charged with oversight of financial reporting and disclosure. Committee members are drawn from members of the Company's board of directors, with a Chairperson selected from among the members. An _____ of a publicly-traded company in the United States is composed of independent and outside directors referred to as non-executive directors, at least one of which is typically a financial expert.

a. Event data
b. External auditor
c. Audit working paper
d. Audit committee

24. An _____ is the buying of one company by another. An _____ may be friendly or hostile. In the former case, the companies cooperate in negotiations; in the latter case, the takeover target is unwilling to be bought or the target's board has no prior knowledge of the offer. _____ usually refers to a purchase of a smaller firm by a larger one. Sometimes, however, a smaller firm will acquire management control of a larger or longer established company and keep its name for the combined entity. This is known as a reverse takeover.

a. Acquisition
b. AIG
c. ABC Television Network
d. AMEX

25. The _____ is the national, professional association of CPAs in the United States, with more than 330,000 members, including CPAs in business and industry, public practice, government, and education; student affiliates; and international associates. It sets ethical standards for the profession and U.S. auditing standards for audits of private companies; federal, state and local governments; and non-profit organizations.

Approximately 40% of its members are engaged in the practice of public accounting, in areas such as auditing, accounting, taxation, general business consulting, business valuation, personal financial planning and business technology.

a. American Institute of Certified Public Accountants
b. Other postemployment benefits
c. AIG
d. ABC Television Network

26. _____ means the giving out of information, either voluntarily or to be in compliance with legal regulations or workplace rules.

- In Computer security, full _____ means disclosing full information about vulnerabilities.
- In computing, _____ widget
- Journalism, full _____ refers to disclosing the interests of the writer which may bear on the subject being written about, for example, if the writer has worked with an interview subject in the past.

- In law:
    - The law of England and Wales, _____ refers to a process that may form part of legal proceedings, whereby parties inform to other parties the existence of any relevant documents that are, or have been, in their control. This compares with the process known as discovery in the course of legal proceedings in the United States.
    - In U.S. civil procedure (litigation rules for civil cases), _____ is a stage prior to trial. In civil cases, each party must disclose to the opposing party the following: names of witnesses which it may use to support its side, copies of documents (or mere description of these documents) in its control which it may use to support its side, computation of damages claimed, and certain insurance information. _____ is related to, but technically prior to, the discovery stage.
    - In Company law (known as 'corporate law' in the United States), _____ refers to giving out information about public or limited companies or their officers, which might be kept secret if the company was a private company or a partnership.

- In real property transactions, _____ refers to providing to a buyer information known to the seller or broker/agent concerning the condition or other aspects of real property that would affect the property's value or desirability. These rules regarding what information must be disclosed, and whether the information must be disclosed even if a buyer does not ask, vary from one jurisdiction to the next.

a. Tax harmonisation
b. Controlled Foreign Corporations
c. Trailing
d. Disclosure

27. _____ is a report required to be filed by public companies with the United States Securities and Exchange Commission pursuant to the Securities Exchange Act of 1934, as amended. After a significant event like bankruptcy or departure of a CEO, a public company generally must file a Current Report on _____ within four business days to provide an update to previously filed quarterly reports on Form 10-Q and/or Annual Reports on Form 10-K. _____ is a very broad form used to notify investors of any unscheduled material event that is important to shareholders or the SEC.
a. Form 10-Q
b. Form 8-K
c. 3M Company
d. Form 20-F

28. _____ refers to the independence of the auditor from parties, that have an interest in the financial statements of an entity. It is essentially an attitude of mind characterized by integrity and an objective approach to the audit process. The concept requires the auditor to carry out his work freely and in an objective manner.
a. Information audit
b. Internal Auditing
c. Audit
d. Auditor independence

Chapter 3. Management Fraud and Audit Risk

29. A _____ is a fungible, negotiable instrument representing financial value. they are broadly categorized into debt securities (such as banknotes, bonds and debentures), and equity securities; e.g., common stocks. The company or other entity issuing the _____ is called the issuer.

a. 3M Company
b. BMC Software, Inc.
c. Tracking stock
d. Security

30. _____ are ten auditing standards, developed by the AICPA, consisting of general standards, standards of field work, and standards of reporting, along with interpretations. They were developed by the AICPA in 1947 and have undergone minor changes since then.

The _____ are as follows:

1. The auditor must have adequate technical training and proficiency to perform the audit
2. The auditor must maintain independence in mental attitude in all matters related to the audit.
3. The auditor must use due professional care during the performance of the audit and the preparation of the report.

1. The auditor must adequately plan the work and must properly supervise any assistants.
2. The auditor must obtain a sufficient understanding of the entity and its environment, including its internal control, to assess the risk of material misstatement of the financial statements whether due to error or fraud, and to design the nature, timing, and extent of further audit procedures.
3. The auditor must obtain sufficient appropriate audit evidence by performing audit procedures to afford a reasonable basis for an opinion regarding the financial statements under audit.

The new standards are in effect for audits of financial statements for periods beginning on or after December 15, 2006.

1. The auditor must state in the auditor's report whether the financial statements are in accordance with generally accepted accounting principles (GAAP.)
2. The auditor must identify in the auditor's report those circumstances in which such principles have not been consistently observed in the current period in relation to the preceding period.
3. When the auditor determines that informative disclosures are not reasonably adequate, the auditor must so state in the auditor's report.
4. The auditor must either express an opinion regarding the financial statements, taken as a whole the auditor should state the reasons therefore in the auditor's report. In all cases where the auditor's name is associated with the financial statements, the auditor should clearly indicate the character of the auditor's work, if any, and the degree of responsibility the auditor is taking, in the auditor's report.

a. Continuous auditing
b. Generally accepted auditing standards
c. Negative assurance
d. Joint audit

31. _____ is a business, economics or investment term that refers to an asset's ability to be easily converted through an act of buying or selling without causing a significant movement in the price and with minimum loss of value. Money, or cash on hand, is the most liquid asset. An act of exchange of a less liquid asset with a more liquid asset is called liquidation.

Chapter 3. Management Fraud and Audit Risk

a. Financial instruments
b. Spot rate
c. Market liquidity
d. Transfer agent

32. _____, in auditing, is the risk that the auditing procedures used will not find a material misstatement in the financial statements of the company being audited. .

a. Detection risk
b. BNSF Railway
c. 3M Company
d. BMC Software, Inc.

33. _____, Quarterly Report Pursuant to Section 13 or 15(d) of the Securities Exchange Act of 1934, is an SEC filing that must be filed quarterly with the US Securities and Exchange Commission. It contains similar information to the annual form 10-K, however the information is generally less detailed, and the financial statements are generally unaudited. Information for the final quarter of a firm's fiscal year is included in the 10-K, so only three 10-Q filings are made each year.

a. Form 20-F
b. 3M Company
c. Form 8-K
d. Form 10-Q

34. _____ is equal to the income that a firm has after subtracting costs and expenses from the total revenue. _____ can be distributed among holders of common stock as a dividend or held by the firm as retained earnings.

The items deducted will typically include tax expense, financing expense (interest expense), and minority interest. Likewise, preferred stock dividends will be subtracted too, though they are not an expense.

a. Matching principle
b. Generally accepted accounting principles
c. Net income
d. Long-term liabilities

35. _____ is evidence obtained during a financial audit and recorded in the audit working papers.

- In the audit engagement acceptance or reappointment stage, _____ is the information that the auditor is to consider for the appointment. For examples, change in the entity control environment, inherent risk and nature of the entity business, and scope of audit work.

- In the audit planning stage, _____ is the information that the auditor is to consider for the most effective and efficient audit approach. For examples, reliability of internal control procedures, and analytical review systems.

- In the control testing stage, _____ is the information that the auditor is to consider for the mix of audit test of control and audit substantive tests.

- In the substantive testing stage, _____ is the information that the auditor is to make sure the appropriation of financial statement assertions. For examples, existence, rights and obligations, occurrence, completeness, valuation, measurement, presentation and disclosure of a particular transaction or account balance.

a. Audit
b. Institute of Chartered Accountants of India
c. ITGCs
d. Audit evidence

36. In law, tangibility is the attribute of being detectable with the senses.

In criminal law, one of the elements of an offense of larceny is that the stolen property must be _____.

In the context of intellectual property, expression in _____ form is one of the requirements for copyright protection.

a. Tangible
c. Contingent liabilities
b. Headnote
d. Nonacquiescence

37. In finance, _____ is the process of estimating the potential market value of a financial asset or liability. They can be done on assets (for example, investments in marketable securities such as stocks, options, business enterprises, or intangible assets such as patents and trademarks) or on liabilities (e.g., Bonds issued by a company.) A _____ is required in many contexts including investment analysis, capital budgeting, merger and acquisition transactions, financial reporting, taxable events to determine the proper tax liability, and in litigation.

a. Daybook
c. Disclosure
b. Vyborg Appeal
d. Valuation

38. _____ is a file or account that contains money that a person or company owes to suppliers, but has not paid yet (a form of debt.) When you receive an invoice you add it to the file, and then you remove it when you pay. Thus, the A/P is a form of credit that suppliers offer to their purchasers by allowing them to pay for a product or service after it has already been received.

a. Earnings before interest, taxes, depreciation and amortization
b. Accrual
c. Accounts receivable
d. Accounts payable

39. In business and accounting, _____ are everything of value that is owned by a person or company. It is a claim on the property your income of a borrower. The balance sheet of a firm records the monetary value of the _____ owned by the firm.

a. Assets
c. Accounts receivable
b. Accrual basis accounting
d. Earnings before interest, taxes, depreciation and amortization

40. _____ is one of financial audit skill which help an auditor understand the client's business and changes in the business, to identify potential risk areas and to plan other audit procedures.

_____ include comparison of financial information (data in financial statement) with

1. prior periods
2. budgets
3. forecasts
4. similar industries and so on.

It also includes consideration of predictable relationships, such as:

1. gross profit to sales,
2. payroll costs to employees,
3. financial information and non-financial information, for examples the CEO's reports and the industry news.

possible sources of information about the client include:

1. interim financial information
2. Budgets
3. Management accounts
4. Non-Financial information
5. Bank and cash records
6. VAT returns
7. Board minutes
8. Discussion or correspondance with the client at they year-end

a. Analytical procedures
b. External auditor
c. Assurance service
d. International Federation of Audit Bureaux of Circulations

41. An _____ invented by esteemed professor Karen Osterheld is the system of records a business keeps to maintain its accounting system. This includes the purchase, sales, and other financial processes of the business. The purpose of an _____ is to accumulate data and provide decision makers (investors, creditors, and managers) with information to make decision While this was previously a paper-based process, most modern businesses now use accounting software such as UBS, MYOB etc.

a. Accounting information system
b. ABC Television Network
c. AMEX
d. AIG

42. _____ is one of a series of accounting transactions dealing with the billing of customers who owe money to a person, company or organization for goods and services that have been provided to the customer. In most business entities this is typically done by generating an invoice and mailing or electronically delivering it to the customer, who in turn must pay it within an established timeframe called credit or payment terms.

An example of a common payment term is Net 30, meaning payment is due in the amount of the invoice 30 days from the date of invoice.

a. Accrued revenue
b. Accounts receivable
c. Adjusting entries
d. Accrual

Chapter 4. Engagement Planning

1. _____ LLP, based in Chicago, was once one of the 'Big Five' accounting firms among PricewaterhouseCoopers, Deloitte Touche Tohmatsu, Ernst ' Young and KPMG, providing auditing, tax, and consulting services to large corporations. In 2002, the firm voluntarily surrendered its licenses to practice as Certified Public Accountants in the United States after being found guilty of criminal charges relating to the firm's handling of the auditing of Enron, the energy corporation, resulting in the loss of 85,000 jobs. Although the verdict was subsequently overturned by the Supreme Court of the United States, it has not returned as a viable business.
   a. AMEX
   b. AIG
   c. ABC Television Network
   d. Arthur Andersen

2. The general definition of an _____ is an evaluation of a person, organization, system, process, project or product. _____s are performed to ascertain the validity and reliability of information; also to provide an assessment of a system's internal control. The goal of an _____ is to express an opinion on the person/organization/system (etc) in question, under evaluation based on work done on a test basis.
   a. Audit regime
   b. Assurance service
   c. Institute of Chartered Accountants of India
   d. Audit

3. _____ is a term that is commonly used in relation to the audit of the financial statements of an entity. (.
   a. Audit working paper
   b. Audit risk
   c. Auditor independence
   d. Engagement Letter

4. _____, in auditing, is the risk that a company's internal controls are insufficient to mitigate or detect errors or fraud.
   a. BNSF Railway
   b. BMC Software, Inc.
   c. 3M Company
   d. Control risk

5. _____, in auditing, is the risk that the account or section being audited is materially misstated without considering internal controls due to error; _____ does not include an assessment of the risk of material misstatement due to fraud. The assessment of _____ depends on the professional judgement of the auditor, and it is done after assessing the business environment of the entity being audited.

   _____ is typically assessed using a scale, with assessments being either low, medium, or high.

   a. Inherent risk
   b. AMEX
   c. ABC Television Network
   d. AIG

6. An _____ is a term used in behavioral economics to describe those types of behaviors that impose costs on a person in the long-run that are not taken into account when making decisions in the present. Classical Economics discourages government from creating legislation that targets internalities, because it is assumed that the consumer takes these personal costs into account when paying for the good that causes the _____. For example, cigarettes should be taxed because of the negative consumption externalities that they impose, such as second-hand smoke, not because the smoker harms him or herself by smoking.
   a. Authorised capital
   b. Inventory turnover ratio
   c. Operating budget
   d. Internality

Chapter 4. Engagement Planning

7. In accounting and organizational theory, _____ is defined as a process effected by an organization's structure, work and authority flows, people and management information systems, designed to help the organization accomplish specific goals or objectives. It is a means by which an organization's resources are directed, monitored, and measured. It plays an important role in preventing and detecting fraud and protecting the organization's resources, both physical (e.g., machinery and property) and intangible (e.g., reputation or intellectual property such as trademarks.)
   a. Audit committee
   b. Audit risk
   c. Auditor independence
   d. Internal control

8. _____ is a concept that denotes the precise probability of specific eventualities. Technically, the notion of _____ is independent from the notion of value and, as such, eventualities may have both beneficial and adverse consequences. However, in general usage the convention is to focus only on potential negative impact to some characteristic of value that may arise from a future event.
   a. Risk adjusted return on capital
   b. Risk
   c. Discounting
   d. Discount factor

9. _____ is that part of statistical practice concerned with the selection of individual observations intended to yield some knowledge about a population of concern, especially for the purposes of statistical inference. Each observation measures one or more properties (weight, location, etc.) of an observable entity enumerated to distinguish objects or individuals.
   a. Arthur Betz Laffer
   b. Alan Greenspan
   c. Abby Joseph Cohen
   d. Sampling

10. A _____ is an annual report required by the U.S. Securities and Exchange Commission (SEC), that gives a comprehensive summary of a public company's performance. Although similarly named, the annual report on _____ is distinct from the often glossy 'annual report to shareholders', which a company must send to its shareholders when it holds an annual meeting to elect directors (though some companies combine the annual report and the 10-K into one document.) The 10-K includes information such as company history, organizational structure, executive compensation, equity, subsidiaries, and audited financial statements, among other information.
   a. Form 10-Q
   b. Form 8-K
   c. Form 10-K
   d. 3M Company

11. _____ is the world's largest professional services firm. It was formed in 1998 from a merger between Price Waterhouse and Coopers ' Lybrand, both formed in London.

   _____ earned aggregated worldwide revenues of $28 billion for fiscal 2008, and employed over 146,000 people in 150 countries.

   a. Daybook
   b. PricewaterhouseCoopers
   c. Serial bonds
   d. Total-factor productivity

12. An _____ is the buying of one company by another. An _____ may be friendly or hostile. In the former case, the companies cooperate in negotiations; in the latter case, the takeover target is unwilling to be bought or the target's board has no prior knowledge of the offer. _____ usually refers to a purchase of a smaller firm by a larger one. Sometimes, however, a smaller firm will acquire management control of a larger or longer established company and keep its name for the combined entity. This is known as a reverse takeover.

a. AIG
b. ABC Television Network
c. AMEX
d. Acquisition

13. _____ is a report required to be filed by public companies with the United States Securities and Exchange Commission pursuant to the Securities Exchange Act of 1934, as amended. After a significant event like bankruptcy or departure of a CEO, a public company generally must file a Current Report on _____ within four business days to provide an update to previously filed quartely reports on Form 10-Q and/or Annual Reports on Form 10-K. _____ is a very broad form used to notify investors of any unscheduled material event that is important to shareholders or the SEC.
   a. Form 10-Q
   b. Form 20-F
   c. 3M Company
   d. Form 8-K

14. The U.S. _____ is an independent agency of the United States government which holds primary responsibility for enforcing the federal securities laws and regulating the securities industry, the nation's stock and options exchanges, and other electronic securities markets. The SEC was created by section 4 of the Securities Exchange Act of 1934 (now codified as 15 U.S.C. §§ 78d and commonly referred to as the 1934 Act.)
   a. Securities and Exchange Commission
   b. 3M Company
   c. BNSF Railway
   d. BMC Software, Inc.

15. The _____ is the national, professional association of CPAs in the United States, with more than 330,000 members, including CPAs in business and industry, public practice, government, and education; student affiliates; and international associates. It sets ethical standards for the profession and U.S. auditing standards for audits of private companies; federal, state and local governments; and non-profit organizations.

Approximately 40% of its members are engaged in the practice of public accounting, in areas such as auditing, accounting, taxation, general business consulting, business valuation, personal financial planning and business technology.

   a. AIG
   b. ABC Television Network
   c. Other postemployment benefits
   d. American Institute of Certified Public Accountants

16. An _____ defines the legal relationship (or engagement) between a professional firm (e.g., law, investment banking, consulting, advisory or accountancy firm) and its client(s.) This letter states the terms and conditions of the engagement, principally addressing the scope of the engagement and the terms of compensation for the firm.

Most _____s follow a standard format.

   a. Audit risk
   b. Audit evidence
   c. Internal control
   d. Engagement letter

17. Project _____: The project _____ is a prediction of the costs associated with a particular company project. These costs include labor, materials, and other related expenses. The project _____ is often broken down into specific tasks, with task _____s assigned to each.
   a. BNSF Railway
   b. Budget
   c. 3M Company
   d. BMC Software, Inc.

Chapter 4. Engagement Planning

18. _____ in business includes the methods and processes used by organizations to manage risks and seize opportunities related to the achievement of their objectives. _____ provides a framework for risk management, which typically involves identifying particular events or circumstances relevant to the organization's objectives (risks and opportunities), assessing them in terms of likelihood and magnitude of impact, determining a response strategy, and monitoring progress. By identifying and proactively addressing risks and opportunities, business enterprises protect and create value for their stakeholders, including owners, employees, customers, regulators, and society overall.

   a. Enterprise risk management
   b. AMEX
   c. ABC Television Network
   d. AIG

19. _____ refers to a business or organization attempting to acquire goods or services to accomplish the goals of the enterprise. Though there are several organizations that attempt to set standards in the _____ process, processes can vary greatly between organizations. Typically the word e;_____e; is not used interchangeably with the word e;procuremente;, since procurement typically includes Expediting, Supplier Quality, and Traffic and Logistics (T'L) in addition to _____.

   a. Supply chain
   b. Purchasing
   c. Consignor
   d. Free port

20. _____ is activity directed towards the assessing, mitigating (to an acceptable level) and monitoring of risks. In some cases the acceptable risk may be near zero. Risks can come from accidents, natural causes and disasters as well as deliberate attacks from an adversary.

   a. Risk management
   b. Trademark
   c. FIFO
   d. Kanban

21. A _____ is a fungible, negotiable instrument representing financial value. they are broadly categorized into debt securities (such as banknotes, bonds and debentures), and equity securities; e.g., common stocks. The company or other entity issuing the _____ is called the issuer.

   a. BMC Software, Inc.
   b. Security
   c. 3M Company
   d. Tracking stock

22. _____ are payments made by a corporation to its shareholder members. It is the portion of corporate profits paid out to stockholders. When a corporation earns a profit or surplus, that money can be put to two uses: it can either be re-invested in the business (called retained earnings), or it can be paid to the shareholders as a dividend.

   a. Dividend payout ratio
   b. Dividend stripping
   c. Dividend yield
   d. Dividends

23. A _____ has several related meanings:

   - a daily record of events or business; a private _____ is usually referred to as a diary.
   - a newspaper or other periodical, in the literal sense of one published each day;
   - many publications issued at stated intervals, such as magazines, or scholarly academic _____s, or the record of the transactions of a society, are often called _____s. Although _____ is sometimes used, erroneously, as a synonym for 'magazine,' in academic use, a _____ refers to a serious, scholarly publication, most often peer-reviewed. A non-scholarly magazine written for an educated audience about an industry or an area of professional activity is usually called a professional magazine.

Chapter 4. Engagement Planning

The word 'journalist' for one whose business is writing for the public press has been in use since the end of the 17th century.

Open access _____s are scholarly _____s that are available to the reader without financial or other barrier other than access to the internet itself. Some are subsidized, and some require payment on behalf of the author. Subsidized _____s are financed by an academic institution or a government information center.

    a. BNSF Railway
    b. Journal
    c. 3M Company
    d. BMC Software, Inc.

24.   In finance, an _____ is a contract between a buyer and a seller that gives the buyer the right--but not the obligation-- to buy or to sell a particular asset (the underlying asset) at a later time at an agreed price. In return for granting the _____, the seller collects a payment (the premium) from the buyer. A call _____ gives the buyer the right to buy the underlying asset; a put _____ gives the buyer of the _____ the right to sell the underlying asset.

    a. AIG
    b. Option
    c. AMEX
    d. ABC Television Network

25.   A _____ is a type of business entity in which partners (owners) share with each other the profits or losses of the business undertaking in which all have invested. _____s are often favored over corporations for taxation purposes, as the _____ structure does not generally incur a tax on profits before it is distributed to the partners (i.e. there is no dividend tax levied.) However, depending on the _____ structure and the jurisdiction in which it operates, owners of a _____ may be exposed to greater personal liability than they would as shareholders of a corporation.

    a. Partnership
    b. National Information Infrastructure Protection Act
    c. Corporate governance
    d. Resource Conservation and Recovery Act

26.   The _____ is one of a number of uniform acts that have been promulgated in conjunction with efforts to harmonize the law of sales and other commercial transactions in all 50 states within the United States of America. This objective is deemed important because of the prevalence today of commercial transactions that extend beyond one state (for example, where the goods are manufactured in state A, warehoused in state B, sold from state C and delivered in state D.) The _____ deals primarily with transactions involving personal property (movable property), not real property (immovable property).

    a. Employee Retirement Income Security Act
    b. Uniform Commercial Code
    c. Issued shares
    d. Escheat

27.   In business and accounting, _____ are everything of value that is owned by a person or company. It is a claim on the property your income of a borrower. The balance sheet of a firm records the monetary value of the _____ owned by the firm.

    a. Accounts receivable
    b. Assets
    c. Accrual basis accounting
    d. Earnings before interest, taxes, depreciation and amortization

28.   _____ is a profession and activity involved in helping organisations achieve their stated objectives. It does this by using a systematic methodology for analyzing business processes, procedures and activities with the goal of highlighting organizational problems and recommending solutions. Professionals called internal auditors are employed by organizations to perform the _____ activity.

Chapter 4. Engagement Planning

a. ITGCs
b. Information audit
c. Internal auditing
d. Assurance service

29. _____ is one of financial audit skill which help an auditor understand the client's business and changes in the business, to identify potential risk areas and to plan other audit procedures.

_____ include comparison of financial information (data in financial statement) with

1. prior periods
2. budgets
3. forecasts
4. similar industries and so on.

It also includes consideration of predictable relationships, such as:

1. gross profit to sales,
2. payroll costs to employees,
3. financial information and non-financial information, for examples the CEO's reports and the industry news.

possible sources of information about the client include:

1. interim financial information
2. Budgets
3. Management accounts
4. Non-Financial information
5. Bank and cash records
6. VAT returns
7. Board minutes
8. Discussion or correspondance with the client at they year-end

a. International Federation of Audit Bureaux of Circulations
b. Assurance service
c. External auditor
d. Analytical procedures

30. _____ are formal records of a business' financial activities.

In British English, including United Kingdom company law, _____ are often referred to as accounts, although the term _____ is also used, particularly by accountants.

_____ provide an overview of a business' financial condition in both short and long term.

a. 3M Company
b. Statement of retained earnings
c. Notes to the financial statements
d. Financial statements

Chapter 4. Engagement Planning

31. An _____ is a practitioner of accountancy, which is the measurement, disclosure or provision of assurance about financial information that helps managers, investors, tax authorities and other decision makers make resource allocation decisions.

The word '_____' is derived from the French 'Compter' which took its origin from the Latin 'Computare'. The word was formerly written in English as 'Accomptant', but in process of time the word, which was always pronounced by dropping the 'p', became gradually changed both in pronunciation and in orthography to its present form.

   a. ABC Television Network
   b. AIG
   c. Accountant
   d. AMEX

32. _____ is the process of understanding the stock/product mix combined with the knowledge of the demand for stock/product.
   a. AIG
   b. ABC Television Network
   c. AMEX
   d. Inventory analysis

33. _____ is the balance of the amounts of cash being received and paid by a business during a defined period of time, sometimes tied to a specific project. Measurement of _____ can be used

   - to evaluate the state or performance of a business or project.
   - to determine problems with liquidity. Being profitable does not necessarily mean being liquid. A company can fail because of a shortage of cash, even while profitable.
   - to project rate of returns. The time of _____s into and out of projects are used as inputs to financial models such as internal rate of return, and net present value.
   - to examine income or growth of a business when it is believed that accrual accounting concepts do not represent economic realities. Alternately, _____ can be used to 'validate' the net income generated by accrual accounting.

_____ as a generic term may be used differently depending on context, and certain _____ definitions may be adapted by analysts and users for their own uses. Common terms include operating _____ and free _____.

   a. Cash flow
   b. Flow-through entity
   c. Controlling interest
   d. Commercial paper

34. _____ is the calculated approximation of a result which is usable even if input data may be incomplete or uncertain.

In statistics, see _____ theory, estimator.

In mathematics, approximation or _____ typically means finding upper or lower bounds of a quantity that cannot readily be computed precisely and is also an educated guess.

   a. Estimation
   b. AMEX
   c. AIG
   d. ABC Television Network

Chapter 4. Engagement Planning

35. Established in 1988 the _____ is the professional organization that governs professional fraud examiners. Its activities include producing fraud information, tools and training. It also governs the professional designation of Certified Fraud Examiner.
    a. AMEX
    b. Association of Certified Fraud Examiners
    c. ABC Television Network
    d. AIG

36. _____ or audit log is a chronological sequence of audit records, each of which contains evidence directly pertaining to and resulting from the execution of a business process or system function.

    Audit records typically result from activities such as transactions or communications by individual people, systems, accounts or other entities.

    Webopedia defines an _____ as 'a record showing who has accessed a computer system and what operations he or she has performed during a given period of time.' ()

    In telecommunication, the term means a record of both completed and attempted accesses and service, or data forming a logical path linking a sequence of events, used to trace the transactions that have affected the contents of a record.

    a. AIG
    b. AMEX
    c. ABC Television Network
    d. Audit trail

37. _____ is a designation awarded by the Association of _____s (ACertified Fraud Examiner.) The ACertified Fraud Examiner is a 41,000 member-based global association dedicated to providing anti-fraud education and training.

    In order to become a _____ one must meet the following requirements:

    - Be an Associate Member of the ACertified Fraud Examiner in good standing
    - Meet minimum academic and professional requirements
    - Be of high moral character
    - Agree to abide by the Bylaws and Code of Professional Ethics of the Association of _____s

    Generally, applicants for _____ certification have a minimum of a bachelor's degree or equivalent from an institution of higher education. Two years of professional experience related to fraud can be substituted for each year of college.

    a. Certified public accountant
    b. Chartered Certified Accountant
    c. Certified Fraud Examiner
    d. Chartered Accountant

38. _____ is a file or account that contains money that a person or company owes to suppliers, but has not paid yet (a form of debt.) When you receive an invoice you add it to the file, and then you remove it when you pay. Thus, the A/P is a form of credit that suppliers offer to their purchasers by allowing them to pay for a product or service after it has already been received.

a. Accounts receivable
b. Accrual
c. Earnings before interest, taxes, depreciation and amortization
d. Accounts payable

39. In economics, business, retail, and accounting, a _____ is the value of money that has been used up to produce something, and hence is not available for use anymore. In economics, a _____ is an alternative that is given up as a result of a decision. In business, the _____ may be one of acquisition, in which case the amount of money expended to acquire it is counted as _____.
a. Cost allocation
b. Prime cost
c. Cost
d. Cost of quality

40. In financial accounting, _____ or cost of sales includes the direct costs attributable to the production of the goods sold by a company. This amount includes the materials cost used in creating the goods along with the direct labor costs used to produce the good. It excludes indirect expenses such as distribution costs and sales force costs.
a. Cost of goods sold
b. Reorder point
c. FIFO and LIFO accounting
d. 3M Company

41. The _____ is a financial ratio that measures whether or not a firm has enough resources to pay its debts over the next 12 months. It compares a firm's current assets to its current liabilities. It is expressed as follows:

$$\text{Current ratio} = \frac{\text{Current Assets}}{\text{Current Liabilities}}$$

For example, if WXY Company's current assets are $50,000,000 and its current liabilities are $40,000,000, then its _____ would be $50,000,000 divided by $40,000,000, which equals 1.25.

a. Return on capital
b. Current ratio
c. Times interest earned
d. Net Interest Income

42. In finance, a _____ or accounting ratio is a ratio of two selected numerical values taken from an enterprise's financial statements. There are many standard ratios used to try to evaluate the overall financial condition of a corporation or other organization. _____s may be used by managers within a firm, by current and potential shareholders (owners) of a firm, and by a firm's creditors.
a. Financial ratio
b. Current ratio
c. Return of capital
d. Price/cash flow ratio

43. _____, Gross profit margin or Gross Profit Rate can be defined as the amount of contribution to the business enterprise, after paying for direct-fixed and direct-variable unit costs, required to cover overheads (fixed commitments) and provide a buffer for unknown items. It expresses the relationship between gross profit and sales revenue.

It can be expressed in absolute terms:

Gross Profit = Revenue − Cost of Goods Sold

or as the ratio of gross profit to sales revenue, usually in the form of a percentage:

_____ Percentage = (Revenue-Cost of Goods Sold)/Revenue

Cost of goods sold includes variable costs and fixed costs directly linked to the product, such as material and labor.

a. 3M Company
c. BMC Software, Inc.
b. BNSF Railway
d. Gross margin

44. The _____ is an equation that equals the cost of goods sold divided by the average inventory. Average inventory equals beginning inventory plus ending inventory divided by 2.

The formula for _____:

$$\text{Inventory Turnover} = \frac{\text{Cost of Goods Sold}}{\text{Average Inventory}}$$

The formula for average inventory:

$$\text{Average Inventory} = \frac{\text{Beginning inventory} + \text{Ending inventory}}{2}$$

A low turnover rate may point to overstocking, obsolescence, or deficiencies in the product line or marketing effort.

a. Inventory turnover
c. Earnings per share
b. Upside potential ratio
d. Enterprise Value/Sales

45. _____ is one of the Accounting Liquidity ratios, a financial ratio. This ratio measures the number of times, on average, the inventory is sold during the period. Its purpose is to measure the liquidity of the inventory.

a. Inventory turnover ratio
c. ABC Television Network
b. AIG
d. Ending inventory

46. _____ is one of the accounting liquidity ratios, a financial ratio. This ratio measures the number of times, on average, receivables (e.g. Accounts Receivable) are collected during the period. A popular variant of the _____ is to convert it into an Average Collection Period in terms of days.

a. Price-to-sales ratio
c. Receivable turnover ratio
b. Shrinkage
d. Capital

47. The _____ is a financial ratio indicating the relative proportion of equity to all used to finance a company's assets. The two components are often taken from the firm's balance sheet or statement of financial position (so-called book value), but the ratio may also be calculated using market values for both, if the company's equities are publicly traded.

The _____ is especially in Central Europe a very common financial ratio while in the US the debt to _____ is more often used in financial (research) reports.

a. Efficiency ratio
b. Average accounting return
c. Earnings yield
d. Equity ratio

48. A _____ is the pinnacle activity involved in selling products or services in return for money or other compensation. It is an act of completion of a commercial activity.

A _____ is completed by the seller, the owner of the goods.

a. Maturity
b. Tertiary sector of economy
c. High yield stock
d. Sale

Chapter 5. Risk Assessment: Internal Control Evaluation

1. An _____ is a term used in behavioral economics to describe those types of behaviors that impose costs on a person in the long-run that are not taken into account when making decisions in the present. Classical Economics discourages government from creating legislation that targets internalities, because it is assumed that the consumer takes these personal costs into account when paying for the good that causes the _____. For example, cigarettes should be taxed because of the negative consumption externalities that they impose, such as second-hand smoke, not because the smoker harms him or herself by smoking.
   - a. Authorised capital
   - b. Inventory turnover ratio
   - c. Operating budget
   - d. Internality

2. In accounting and organizational theory, _____ is defined as a process effected by an organization's structure, work and authority flows, people and management information systems, designed to help the organization accomplish specific goals or objectives. It is a means by which an organization's resources are directed, monitored, and measured. It plays an important role in preventing and detecting fraud and protecting the organization's resources, both physical (e.g., machinery and property) and intangible (e.g., reputation or intellectual property such as trademarks.)
   - a. Auditor independence
   - b. Internal control
   - c. Audit risk
   - d. Audit committee

3. A _____ is an annual report required by the U.S. Securities and Exchange Commission (SEC), that gives a comprehensive summary of a public company's performance. Although similarly named, the annual report on _____ is distinct from the often glossy 'annual report to shareholders', which a company must send to its shareholders when it holds an annual meeting to elect directors (though some companies combine the annual report and the 10-K into one document.) The 10-K includes information such as company history, organizational structure, executive compensation, equity, subsidiaries, and audited financial statements, among other information.
   - a. 3M Company
   - b. Form 10-Q
   - c. Form 10-K
   - d. Form 8-K

4. The _____ (acronym of National Association of Securities Dealers Automated Quotations) is an American stock exchange. It is the largest electronic screen-based equity securities trading market in the United States. With approximately 3,800 companies, it has more trading volume per hour than any other stock exchange in the world.
   - a. Sale of goods
   - b. Variance
   - c. Sustainability measurement
   - d. NASDAQ

5. The _____ is the national, professional association of CPAs in the United States, with more than 330,000 members, including CPAs in business and industry, public practice, government, and education; student affiliates; and international associates. It sets ethical standards for the profession and U.S. auditing standards for audits of private companies; federal, state and local governments; and non-profit organizations.

   Approximately 40% of its members are engaged in the practice of public accounting, in areas such as auditing, accounting, taxation, general business consulting, business valuation, personal financial planning and business technology.
   - a. AIG
   - b. American Institute of Certified Public Accountants
   - c. Other postemployment benefits
   - d. ABC Television Network

Chapter 5. Risk Assessment: Internal Control Evaluation

6. A _____ or chief executive is one of the highest-ranking corporate officer (executive) or administrator in charge of total management. An individual selected as President and _____ of a corporation, company, organization, or agency, reports to the board of directors. In internal communication and press releases, many companies capitalize the term and those of other high positions, even when they are not proper nouns.
   a. Chief executive officer
   b. Kohlberg Kravis Roberts ' Co
   c. Return on assets
   d. Return on equity

7. _____, in auditing, is the risk that a company's internal controls are insufficient to mitigate or detect errors or fraud.
   a. BMC Software, Inc.
   b. Control risk
   c. BNSF Railway
   d. 3M Company

8. The _____ of 2002 (Pub.L. 107-204, 116 Stat. 745, enacted July 30, 2002), also known as the Public Company Accounting Reform and Investor Protection Act of 2002, is a United States federal law enacted on July 30, 2002 in response to a number of major corporate and accounting scandals including those affecting Enron, Tyco International, Adelphia, Peregrine Systems and WorldCom. The legislation establishes new or enhanced standards for all U.S. public company boards, management, and public accounting firms. It does not apply to privately held companies.
   a. Lease
   b. FCPA
   c. Fair Labor Standards Act
   d. Sarbanes-Oxley Act

9. _____, commonly abbreviated as SAS, provide guidance to external auditors on generally accepted auditing standards in regards to auditing an entity and issuing a report. They are usually issued by the certified public accountant authoritative body in the region where the standards apply, such as the American Institute of Certified Public Accountants in the United States.

   - _____
   - _____ (Taiwan)

   a. Statements on Auditing Standards
   b. Financial Instruments and Exchange Law
   c. RSM International
   d. GASB 45

10. An _____ is the buying of one company by another. An _____ may be friendly or hostile. In the former case, the companies cooperate in negotiations; in the latter case, the takeover target is unwilling to be bought or the target's board has no prior knowledge of the offer. _____ usually refers to a purchase of a smaller firm by a larger one. Sometimes, however, a smaller firm will acquire management control of a larger or longer established company and keep its name for the combined entity. This is known as a reverse takeover.
    a. AMEX
    b. ABC Television Network
    c. AIG
    d. Acquisition

11. _____ refers to the confirmation of certain characteristics of an object, person, or organization. This confirmation is often, but not always, provided by some form of external review, education, or assessment. One of the most common types of _____ in modern society is professional _____, where a person is certified as being able to competently complete a job or task, usually by the passing of an examination.
    a. BMC Software, Inc.
    b. BNSF Railway
    c. 3M Company
    d. Certification

Chapter 5. Risk Assessment: Internal Control Evaluation

12. _____ are ten auditing standards, developed by the AICPA, consisting of general standards, standards of field work, and standards of reporting, along with interpretations. They were developed by the AICPA in 1947 and have undergone minor changes since then.

The _____ are as follows:

1. The auditor must have adequate technical training and proficiency to perform the audit
2. The auditor must maintain independence in mental attitude in all matters related to the audit.
3. The auditor must use due professional care during the performance of the audit and the preparation of the report.

1. The auditor must adequately plan the work and must properly supervise any assistants.
2. The auditor must obtain a sufficient understanding of the entity and its environment, including its internal control, to assess the risk of material misstatement of the financial statements whether due to error or fraud, and to design the nature, timing, and extent of further audit procedures.
3. The auditor must obtain sufficient appropriate audit evidence by performing audit procedures to afford a reasonable basis for an opinion regarding the financial statements under audit.

The new standards are in effect for audits of financial statements for periods beginning on or after December 15, 2006.

1. The auditor must state in the auditor's report whether the financial statements are in accordance with generally accepted accounting principles (GAAP.)
2. The auditor must identify in the auditor's report those circumstances in which such principles have not been consistently observed in the current period in relation to the preceding period.
3. When the auditor determines that informative disclosures are not reasonably adequate, the auditor must so state in the auditor's report.
4. The auditor must either express an opinion regarding the financial statements, taken as a whole the auditor should state the reasons therefore in the auditor's report. In all cases where the auditor's name is associated with the financial statements, the auditor should clearly indicate the character of the auditor's work, if any, and the degree of responsibility the auditor is taking, in the auditor's report.

a. Generally accepted auditing standards
c. Continuous auditing
b. Joint audit
d. Negative assurance

13. _____ is a concept that denotes the precise probability of specific eventualities. Technically, the notion of _____ is independent from the notion of value and, as such, eventualities may have both beneficial and adverse consequences. However, in general usage the convention is to focus only on potential negative impact to some characteristic of value that may arise from a future event.

a. Discounting
c. Discount factor
b. Risk adjusted return on capital
d. Risk

14. _____ is that part of statistical practice concerned with the selection of individual observations intended to yield some knowledge about a population of concern, especially for the purposes of statistical inference. Each observation measures one or more properties (weight, location, etc.) of an observable entity enumerated to distinguish objects or individuals.
   a. Abby Joseph Cohen
   b. Alan Greenspan
   c. Sampling
   d. Arthur Betz Laffer

15. An _____ is a practitioner of accountancy, which is the measurement, disclosure or provision of assurance about financial information that helps managers, investors, tax authorities and other decision makers make resource allocation decisions.

The word '_____' is derived from the French 'Compter' which took its origin from the Latin 'Computare'. The word was formerly written in English as 'Accomptant', but in process of time the word, which was always pronounced by dropping the 'p', became gradually changed both in pronunciation and in orthography to its present form.

   a. AIG
   b. AMEX
   c. ABC Television Network
   d. Accountant

16. The _____ is a 'voluntary organization of persons interested in accounting education and research'. It was formed in 1916. Its main publication, the The Accounting Review, was first published in 1926.
   a. International Accounting Standards Board
   b. Australian Accounting Standards Board
   c. Institute of Management Accountants
   d. American Accounting Association

17. The general definition of an _____ is an evaluation of a person, organization, system, process, project or product. _____s are performed to ascertain the validity and reliability of information; also to provide an assessment of a system's internal control. The goal of an _____ is to express an opinion on the person/organization/system (etc) in question, under evaluation based on work done on a test basis.
   a. Institute of Chartered Accountants of India
   b. Audit regime
   c. Audit
   d. Assurance service

18. _____ are formal records of a business' financial activities.

In British English, including United Kingdom company law, _____ are often referred to as accounts, although the term _____ is also used, particularly by accountants.

_____ provide an overview of a business' financial condition in both short and long term.

   a. Notes to the financial statements
   b. Statement of retained earnings
   c. 3M Company
   d. Financial statements

19. _____ is the term used to refer to the standard framework of guidelines for financial accounting used in any given jurisdiction. _____ includes the standards, conventions, and rules accountants follow in recording and summarizing transactions, and in the preparation of financial statements.

Financial accounting information must be assembled and reported objectively.

a. Current asset
c. General ledger
b. Generally accepted accounting principles
d. Long-term liabilities

20. Established in 1941, The _____ is internationally recognized as a trustworthy guidance-setting body. Serving members in 165 countries, The IIA is the internal audit profession's global voice, chief advocate, recognized authority, acknowledged leader, and principal educator, with global headquarters in Altamonte Springs, Fla., United States.

The stated mission of The _____ is to provide dynamic leadership for the global profession of internal auditing.

a. Audit regime
c. Auditor independence
b. Institute of Internal Auditors
d. Event data

21. The _____ is a professional organization headquartered in Montvale, New Jersey consisting of over 70,000 members worldwide. The IMA is dedicated to advancing the role of the management accountant and financial manager within the business organization, and provides relevant professional certification.

The IMA awards the Certified Management Accountant (CMA) designation in the United States.

a. Institute of Management Accountants
c. American Accounting Association
b. Emerging technologies
d. International Accounting Standards Committee

22. Internal auditing is a profession and activity involved in helping organisations achieve their stated objectives. It does this by utilizing a systematic methodology for analyzing business processes, procedures and activities with the goal of highlighting organizational problems and recommending solutions. Professionals called _____ are employed by organizations to perform the internal auditing activity.

a. Internal Auditing
c. Auditing Standards Board
b. Auditor independence
d. Internal auditors

23. _____ is concerned with the provisions and use of accounting information to managers within organizations, to provide them with the basis to make informed business decisions that will allow them to be better equipped in their management and control functions.

In contrast to financial accountancy information, _____ information is:

- usually confidential and used by management, instead of publicly reported;
- forward-looking, instead of historical;
- pragmatically computed using extensive management information systems and internal controls, instead of complying with accounting standards.

This is because of the different emphasis: _____ information is used within an organization, typically for decision-making.

a. Management accounting
c. Governmental accounting
b. Nonassurance services
d. Grenzplankostenrechnung

Chapter 5. Risk Assessment: Internal Control Evaluation

24. The term _____ usually refers to a company that is permitted to offer its registered securities (stock, bonds, etc.) for sale to the general public, typically through a stock exchange, or occasionally a company whose stock is traded over the counter (OTC) via market makers who use non-exchange quotation services.

The term '_____' may also refer to a company owned by the government.

   a. Governmental Accounting Standards Board
   b. Professional association
   c. MicroStrategy
   d. Public Company

25. _____ also called 'Internal _____'. It is a term of financial audit, internal audit and Enterprise Risk Management. It means the overall attitude, awareness and actions of directors and management (i.e. 'those charged with governance') regarding the internal control system and its importance to the entity.

   a. Mainframe audit
   b. Negative assurance
   c. SOFT audit
   d. Control environment

26. _____ is systematic determination of merit, worth, and significance of something or someone using criteria against a set of standards. _____ often is used to characterize and appraise subjects of interest in a wide range of human enterprises, including the arts, criminal justice, foundations and non-profit organizations, government, health care, and other human services.

Depending on the topic of interest, there are professional groups which look to the quality and rigor of the _____ process.

   a. ABC Television Network
   b. AIG
   c. AMEX
   d. Evaluation

27. _____ LLP, based in Chicago, was once one of the 'Big Five' accounting firms among PricewaterhouseCoopers, Deloitte Touche Tohmatsu, Ernst ' Young and KPMG, providing auditing, tax, and consulting services to large corporations. In 2002, the firm voluntarily surrendered its licenses to practice as Certified Public Accountants in the United States after being found guilty of criminal charges relating to the firm's handling of the auditing of Enron, the energy corporation, resulting in the loss of 85,000 jobs. Although the verdict was subsequently overturned by the Supreme Court of the United States, it has not returned as a viable business.

   a. AMEX
   b. AIG
   c. ABC Television Network
   d. Arthur Andersen

28. The Federal Home Loan Mortgage Corporation (FHLMC) (NYSE: FRE) is an insolvent government sponsored enterprise (GSE) of the United States federal government.

The FHLMC was created in 1970 to expand the secondary market for mortgages in the US. Along with other GSEs, _____ buys mortgages on the secondary market, pools them, and sells them as mortgage-backed securities to investors on the open market.

   a. MicroStrategy
   b. Butterfield Bank
   c. Limited liability partnership
   d. Freddie Mac

29. _____ is a term that is commonly used in relation to the audit of the financial statements of an entity. (.

Chapter 5. Risk Assessment: Internal Control Evaluation

a. Audit risk
c. Engagement Letter
b. Auditor independence
d. Audit working paper

30. _____ in business includes the methods and processes used by organizations to manage risks and seize opportunities related to the achievement of their objectives. _____ provides a framework for risk management, which typically involves identifying particular events or circumstances relevant to the organization's objectives (risks and opportunities), assessing them in terms of likelihood and magnitude of impact, determining a response strategy, and monitoring progress. By identifying and proactively addressing risks and opportunities, business enterprises protect and create value for their stakeholders, including owners, employees, customers, regulators, and society overall.

a. AMEX
c. ABC Television Network
b. Enterprise risk management
d. AIG

31. _____, in auditing, is the risk that the account or section being audited is materially misstated without considering internal controls due to error; _____ does not include an assessment of the risk of material misstatement due to fraud. The assessment of _____ depends on the professional judgement of the auditor, and it is done after assessing the business environment of the entity being audited.

_____ is typically assessed using a scale, with assessments being either low, medium, or high.

a. ABC Television Network
c. AMEX
b. AIG
d. Inherent risk

32. _____ is a step in a risk management process. _____ is the determination of quantitative or qualitative value of risk related to a concrete situation and a recognized threat (also called hazard.) Quantitative _____ requires calculations of two components of risk: R, the magnitude of the potential loss L, and the probability p that the loss will occur.

a. 3M Company
c. Risk assessment
b. BNSF Railway
d. BMC Software, Inc.

33. _____ is activity directed towards the assessing, mitigating (to an acceptable level) and monitoring of risks. In some cases the acceptable risk may be near zero. Risks can come from accidents, natural causes and disasters as well as deliberate attacks from an adversary.

a. Trademark
c. Risk management
b. FIFO
d. Kanban

34. _____ is the concept of having more than one person required to complete a task. It is alternatively called segregation of duties or, in the political realm, separation of powers.

_____ is one of the key concepts of internal control and is the most difficult and sometimes the most costly one to achieve. The term _____ is already well-known in financial accounting systems. Companies in all sizes understand not to combine roles such as receiving checks (payment on account) and approving write-offs, depositing cash and reconciling bank statements, approving time cards and have custody of pay checks, etc.

a. Salary
c. BMC Software, Inc.
b. 3M Company
d. Separation of duties

35. In business and accounting, _____ are everything of value that is owned by a person or company. It is a claim on the property your income of a borrower. The balance sheet of a firm records the monetary value of the _____ owned by the firm.
    a. Accrual basis accounting
    b. Earnings before interest, taxes, depreciation and amortization
    c. Accounts receivable
    d. Assets

36. _____ is the specialty practice area of accountancy that describes engagements that result from actual or anticipated disputes or litigation. 'Forensic' means 'suitable for use in a court of law', and it is to that standard and potential outcome that forensic accountants generally have to work. Forensic accountants, also referred to as forensic auditors or investigative auditors, often have to give expert evidence at the eventual trial.
    a. Forensic Accounting
    b. Nonassurance services
    c. Governmental accounting
    d. Grenzplankostenrechnung

37. A _____ is a computer application that simulates a paper worksheet. It displays multiple cells that together make up a grid consisting of rows and columns, each cell containing either alphanumeric text or numeric values. A _____ cell may alternatively contain a formula that defines how the contents of that cell is to be calculated from the contents of any other cell (or combination of cells) each time any cell is updated.
    a. Merck ' Co., Inc.
    b. Linear regression
    c. Spreadsheet
    d. Mutual fund

38. The Federal National Mortgage Association (FNMA) (NYSE: FNM), commonly known as _____, is a stockholder-owned corporation chartered by Congress in 1968 as a government sponsored enterprise (GSE), but founded in 1938 during the Great Depression. The corporation's purpose is to purchase and securitize mortgages in order to ensure that funds are consistently available to the institutions that lend money to home buyers.

On September 7, 2008, James Lockhart, director of the Federal Housing Finance Agency (FHFA), announced that _____ and Freddie Mac were being placed into conservatorship of the FHFA.

    a. Freddie Mac
    b. Public company
    c. National Conference of Commissioners on Uniform State Laws
    d. Fannie Mae

39. A _____ is the transfer of an interest in property (or the equivalent in law - a charge) to a lender as a security for a debt - usually a loan of money. While a _____ in itself is not a debt, it is the lender's security for a debt. It is a transfer of an interest in land (or the equivalent) from the owner to the _____ lender, on the condition that this interest will be returned to the owner when the terms of the _____ have been satisfied or performed.
    a. BMC Software, Inc.
    b. 3M Company
    c. BNSF Railway
    d. Mortgage

40. A _____ is any one of a variety of different systems, institutions, procedures, social relations and infrastructures whereby persons trade, and goods and services are exchanged, forming part of the economy. It is an arrangement that allows buyers and sellers to exchange things. _____s vary in size, range, geographic scale, location, types and variety of human communities, as well as the types of goods and services traded.

a. Market
b. Market Failure
c. Perfect competition
d. Recession

41. _____ or audit log is a chronological sequence of audit records, each of which contains evidence directly pertaining to and resulting from the execution of a business process or system function.

Audit records typically result from activities such as transactions or communications by individual people, systems, accounts or other entities.

Webopedia defines an _____ as 'a record showing who has accessed a computer system and what operations he or she has performed during a given period of time.' ()

In telecommunication, the term means a record of both completed and attempted accesses and service, or data forming a logical path linking a sequence of events, used to trace the transactions that have affected the contents of a record.

a. Audit trail
b. AIG
c. ABC Television Network
d. AMEX

42. A _____ is a common type of chart, that represents an algorithm or process, showing the steps as boxes of various kinds, and their order by connecting these with arrows. _____s are used in analyzing, designing, documenting or managing a process or program in various fields.

The first structured method for documenting process flow, the 'flow process chart', was introduced by Frank Gilbreth to members of ASME in 1921 as the presentation e;Process Charts--First Steps in Finding the One Best Waye;.

a. BNSF Railway
b. 3M Company
c. BMC Software, Inc.
d. Flowchart

43. The _____ (sometimes called 'Peekaboo') is a private-sector, non-profit corporation created by the Sarbanes-Oxley Act, a 2002 United States federal law, to oversee the auditors of public companies. Its stated purpose is to 'protect the interests of investors and further the public interest in the preparation of informative, fair, and independent audit reports'. Although a private entity, the _____ has many government-like regulatory functions, making it in some ways similar to the private Self Regulatory Organizations (SROs) that regulate stock markets and other aspects of the financial markets in the United States.

a. Financial Crimes Enforcement Network
b. 3M Company
c. Pension Benefit Guaranty Corporation
d. Public Company Accounting Oversight Board

44. _____ and bottom-up are strategies of information processing and knowledge ordering, mostly involving software, but also other humanistic and scientific theories In practice, they can be seen as a style of thinking and teaching. In many cases _____ is used as a synonym of analysis or decomposition, and bottom-up of synthesis.

a. BNSF Railway
b. BMC Software, Inc.
c. 3M Company
d. Top-down

Chapter 5. Risk Assessment: Internal Control Evaluation

45. In finance, an _____ is a contract between a buyer and a seller that gives the buyer the right--but not the obligation-- to buy or to sell a particular asset (the underlying asset) at a later time at an agreed price. In return for granting the _____, the seller collects a payment (the premium) from the buyer. A call _____ gives the buyer the right to buy the underlying asset; a put _____ gives the buyer of the _____ the right to sell the underlying asset.
   a. Option
   b. ABC Television Network
   c. AMEX
   d. AIG

46. An _____ is a comprehensive report on a company's activities throughout the preceding year. _____s are intended to give shareholders and other interested persons information about the company's activities and financial performance. Most jurisdictions require companies to prepare and disclose _____s, and many require the _____ to be filed at the company's registry.
   a. ABC Television Network
   b. AMEX
   c. AIG
   d. Annual report

47. A _____ is a contract conferring a right on one person to possess property belonging to another person (called a landlord or lessor) to the exclusion of the owner landlord. It is a rental agreement between landlord and tenant. The relationship between the tenant and the landlord is called a tenancy, and the right to possession by the tenant is sometimes called a leasehold interest.
   a. Model Code of Professional Responsibility
   b. Robinson-Patman Act
   c. Federal Sentencing Guidelines
   d. Lease

48. _____ principle is a cornerstone of accrual accounting together with matching principle. They both determine the accounting period, in which revenues and expenses are recognized. According to the principle, revenues are recognized when they are (1) realized or realizable, and are (2) earned (usually when goods are transferred or services rendered), no matter when cash is received.
   a. BMC Software, Inc.
   b. Revenue recognition
   c. Net realizable value
   d. 3M Company

49. _____ is an agreement, usually secretive, which occurs between two or more persons to deceive, mislead, or defraud others of their legal rights, or to obtain an objective forbidden by law typically involving fraud or gaining an unfair advantage. It is an agreement among firms to divide the market, set prices kickbacks, or misrepresenting the independence of the relationship between the colluding parties.' All acts effected by _____ are considered void.
   a. Limited partnership
   b. Debt
   c. Collusion
   d. Bond market

50. The _____ is a private, not-for-profit organization whose primary purpose is to develop generally accepted accounting principles (GAAP) within the United States in the public's interest. The Securities and Exchange Commission (SEC) designated the _____ as the organization responsible for setting accounting standards for public companies in the U.S. It was created in 1973, replacing the Accounting Principles Board and the Committee on Accounting Procedure of the American Institute of Certified Public Accountants. The _____'s mission is 'to establish and improve standards of financial accounting and reporting for the guidance and education of the public, including issuers, auditors, and users of financial information.'

The _____ is not a governmental body.

a. Governmental Accounting Standards Board
b. Public company
c. Fannie Mae
d. Financial Accounting Standards Board

Chapter 6. Employee Fraud and the Audit of Cash

1. Established in 1988 the _____ is the professional organization that governs professional fraud examiners. Its activities include producing fraud information, tools and training. It also governs the professional designation of Certified Fraud Examiner.
   a. ABC Television Network
   b. Association of Certified Fraud Examiners
   c. AIG
   d. AMEX

2. _____ is a designation awarded by the Association of _____s (ACertified Fraud Examiner.) The ACertified Fraud Examiner is a 41,000 member-based global association dedicated to providing anti-fraud education and training.

   In order to become a _____ one must meet the following requirements:

   - Be an Associate Member of the ACertified Fraud Examiner in good standing
   - Meet minimum academic and professional requirements
   - Be of high moral character
   - Agree to abide by the Bylaws and Code of Professional Ethics of the Association of _____s

   Generally, applicants for _____ certification have a minimum of a bachelor's degree or equivalent from an institution of higher education. Two years of professional experience related to fraud can be substituted for each year of college.

   a. Chartered Accountant
   b. Certified public accountant
   c. Chartered Certified Accountant
   d. Certified Fraud Examiner

3. Employment is a contract between two parties, one being the employer and the other being the _____. An _____ may be defined as: 'A person in the service of another under any contract of hire, express or implied, oral or written, where the employer has the power or right to control and direct the _____ in the material details of how the work is to be performed.' Black's Law Dictionary page 471 (5th ed. 1979.)
   a. AIG
   b. ABC Television Network
   c. Employee
   d. AMEX

4. _____ is an agreement, usually secretive, which occurs between two or more persons to deceive, mislead, or defraud others of their legal rights, or to obtain an objective forbidden by law typically involving fraud or gaining an unfair advantage. It is an agreement among firms to divide the market, set prices kickbacks, or misrepresenting the independence of the relationship between the colluding parties.' All acts effected by _____ are considered void.
   a. Debt
   b. Bond market
   c. Limited partnership
   d. Collusion

5. An _____ is a term used in behavioral economics to describe those types of behaviors that impose costs on a person in the long-run that are not taken into account when making decisions in the present. Classical Economics discourages government from creating legislation that targets internalities, because it is assumed that the consumer takes these personal costs into account when paying for the good that causes the _____. For example, cigarettes should be taxed because of the negative consumption externalities that they impose, such as second-hand smoke, not because the smoker harms him or herself by smoking.
   a. Authorised capital
   b. Inventory turnover ratio
   c. Operating budget
   d. Internality

Chapter 6. Employee Fraud and the Audit of Cash

6. In accounting and organizational theory, _____ is defined as a process effected by an organization's structure, work and authority flows, people and management information systems, designed to help the organization accomplish specific goals or objectives. It is a means by which an organization's resources are directed, monitored, and measured. It plays an important role in preventing and detecting fraud and protecting the organization's resources, both physical (e.g., machinery and property) and intangible (e.g., reputation or intellectual property such as trademarks.)
   a. Internal control
   b. Auditor independence
   c. Audit committee
   d. Audit risk

7. The general definition of an _____ is an evaluation of a person, organization, system, process, project or product. _____s are performed to ascertain the validity and reliability of information; also to provide an assessment of a system's internal control. The goal of an _____ is to express an opinion on the person/organization/system (etc) in question, under evaluation based on work done on a test basis.
   a. Audit regime
   b. Audit
   c. Institute of Chartered Accountants of India
   d. Assurance service

8. A _____ has several related meanings:

   - a daily record of events or business; a private _____ is usually referred to as a diary.
   - a newspaper or other periodical, in the literal sense of one published each day;
   - many publications issued at stated intervals, such as magazines, or scholarly academic _____s, or the record of the transactions of a society, are often called _____s. Although _____ is sometimes used, erroneously, as a synonym for 'magazine,' in academic use, a _____ refers to a serious, scholarly publication, most often peer-reviewed. A non-scholarly magazine written for an educated audience about an industry or an area of professional activity is usually called a professional magazine.

The word 'journalist' for one whose business is writing for the public press has been in use since the end of the 17th century.

Open access _____s are scholarly _____s that are available to the reader without financial or other barrier other than access to the internet itself. Some are subsidized, and some require payment on behalf of the author. Subsidized _____s are financed by an academic institution or a government information center.

   a. 3M Company
   b. BMC Software, Inc.
   c. BNSF Railway
   d. Journal

9. In accounting, _____ has a very specific meaning. It is an outflow of cash or other valuable assets from a person or company to another person or company. This outflow of cash is generally one side of a trade for products or services that have equal or better current or future value to the buyer than to the seller.
   a. Expense
   b. AMEX
   c. ABC Television Network
   d. AIG

10. Internal auditing is a profession and activity involved in helping organisations achieve their stated objectives. It does this by utilizing a systematic methodology for analyzing business processes, procedures and activities with the goal of highlighting organizational problems and recommending solutions. Professionals called _____ are employed by organizations to perform the internal auditing activity.

Chapter 6. Employee Fraud and the Audit of Cash

a. Auditor independence	b. Auditing Standards Board
c. Internal Auditing	d. Internal auditors

11. In finance, a _____ is a debt security, in which the authorized issuer owes the holders a debt and, depending on the terms of the _____, is obliged to pay interest (the coupon) and/or to repay the principal at a later date, termed maturity. It is a formal contract to repay borrowed money with interest at fixed intervals.

Thus a _____ is like a loan: the issuer is the borrower, the _____ holder is the lender, and the coupon is the interest.

a. Coupon rate	b. Zero-coupon bond
c. Revenue bonds	d. Bond

12. An _____ is the buying of one company by another. An _____ may be friendly or hostile. In the former case, the companies cooperate in negotiations; in the latter case, the takeover target is unwilling to be bought or the target's board has no prior knowledge of the offer. _____ usually refers to a purchase of a smaller firm by a larger one. Sometimes, however, a smaller firm will acquire management control of a larger or longer established company and keep its name for the combined entity. This is known as a reverse takeover.

a. AIG	b. Acquisition
c. AMEX	d. ABC Television Network

13. _____ is one of a series of accounting transactions dealing with the billing of customers who owe money to a person, company or organization for goods and services that have been provided to the customer. In most business entities this is typically done by generating an invoice and mailing or electronically delivering it to the customer, who in turn must pay it within an established timeframe called credit or payment terms.

An example of a common payment term is Net 30, meaning payment is due in the amount of the invoice 30 days from the date of invoice.

a. Accrual	b. Accrued revenue
c. Accounts receivable	d. Adjusting entries

14. In business and accounting, _____ are everything of value that is owned by a person or company. It is a claim on the property your income of a borrower. The balance sheet of a firm records the monetary value of the _____ owned by the firm.

a. Accrual basis accounting	b. Assets
c. Accounts receivable	d. Earnings before interest, taxes, depreciation and amortization

15. _____s have been defined by the American Institute of Certified Public Accountants (AICPA) as 'Independent Professional Services that improve information quality or its context'. _____s reduce the information risk; risk that the information provided is incorrect, on more than just financial data. The major purpose of _____s is to provide independent and professional opinions that improve the quality of information to management as well as other decision makers within a given firm.

a. Institute of Chartered Accountants of India
b. ITGCs
c. Auditor independence
d. Assurance service

16. _____ is evidence obtained during a financial audit and recorded in the audit working papers.

- In the audit engagement acceptance or reappointment stage, _____ is the information that the auditor is to consider for the appointment. For examples, change in the entity control environment, inherent risk and nature of the entity business, and scope of audit work.

- In the audit planning stage, _____ is the information that the auditor is to consider for the most effective and efficient audit approach. For examples, reliability of internal control procedures, and analytical review systems.

- In the control testing stage, _____ is the information that the auditor is to consider for the mix of audit test of control and audit substantive tests.

- In the substantive testing stage, _____ is the information that the auditor is to make sure the appropriation of financial statement assertions. For examples, existence, rights and obligations, occurrence, completeness, valuation, measurement, presentation and disclosure of a particular transaction or account balance.

a. ITGCs
b. Institute of Chartered Accountants of India
c. Audit
d. Audit evidence

17. _____ is a concept that denotes the precise probability of specific eventualities. Technically, the notion of _____ is independent from the notion of value and, as such, eventualities may have both beneficial and adverse consequences. However, in general usage the convention is to focus only on potential negative impact to some characteristic of value that may arise from a future event.

a. Risk
b. Discount factor
c. Discounting
d. Risk adjusted return on capital

18. _____ is the process of matching and comparing figures from accounting records against those presented on a bank statement. Less any items which have no relation to the bank statement, the balance of the accounting ledger should reconcile (match) to the balance of the bank statement.

_____ allows companies or individuals to compare their account records to the bank's records of their account balance in order to uncover any possible discrepancies.

a. Bank reconciliation
b. Bankruptcy prediction
c. Credit memo
d. Lower of Cost or Market

19. An account statement or a _____ is a summary of all financial transactions occurring over a given period of time on a deposit account, a credit card, or any other type of account offered by a financial institution.

_____s are typically printed on one or several pieces of paper and either mailed directly to the account holder's address, or kept at the financial institution's local branch for pick-up. Certain ATMs offer the possibility to print, at any time, a condensed version of a _____.

a. BMC Software, Inc.
c. Bank statement
b. BNSF Railway
d. 3M Company

20. _____ is that part of statistical practice concerned with the selection of individual observations intended to yield some knowledge about a population of concern, especially for the purposes of statistical inference. Each observation measures one or more properties (weight, location, etc.) of an observable entity enumerated to distinguish objects or individuals.
   a. Alan Greenspan
   c. Arthur Betz Laffer
   b. Abby Joseph Cohen
   d. Sampling

21. _____ is a file or account that contains money that a person or company owes to suppliers, but has not paid yet (a form of debt.) When you receive an invoice you add it to the file, and then you remove it when you pay. Thus, the A/P is a form of credit that suppliers offer to their purchasers by allowing them to pay for a product or service after it has already been received.
   a. Earnings before interest, taxes, depreciation and amortization
   b. Accounts receivable
   c. Accrual
   d. Accounts payable

22. _____ refers to a category of criminal acts that involve making the unlawful use of checks in order to illegally acquire or borrow funds that do not exist within the account balance or account-holder's legal ownership. Most methods involve taking advantage of the float (the time between the negotiation of the cheque and its clearance at the cheque-writer's bank) to draw out these funds. Specific kinds of cheque fraud include cheque kiting, where funds are deposited before the end of the float period to cover the fraud, and paper hanging, where the float offers the opportunity to commit the crime but the account is never replenished.
   a. BNSF Railway
   c. BMC Software, Inc.
   b. 3M Company
   d. Check fraud

23. _____ is often a small amount of discretionary funds in the form of cash used for expenditures where it is not sensible to make the disbursement by check, because of the inconvenience and costs of writing, signing and then cashing the check.

The most common way of accounting expenditures is to use the imprest system. The initial fund would be created by issuing a check for the desired amount.

   a. Fixed asset
   c. Remittance advice
   b. Petty cash
   d. Minority interest

24. _____ or audit log is a chronological sequence of audit records, each of which contains evidence directly pertaining to and resulting from the execution of a business process or system function.

Audit records typically result from activities such as transactions or communications by individual people, systems, accounts or other entities.

Webopedia defines an _____ as 'a record showing who has accessed a computer system and what operations he or she has performed during a given period of time.' ()

In telecommunication, the term means a record of both completed and attempted accesses and service, or data forming a logical path linking a sequence of events, used to trace the transactions that have affected the contents of a record.

a. AMEX
b. Audit trail
c. ABC Television Network
d. AIG

25. In business, _____ is the total assets minus total outside liabilities of an individual or a company. For a company, this is called shareholders' equity and may be referred to as book value. _____ is stated as at a particular point in time.
a. Creditor
b. Debtor
c. Restructuring
d. Net worth

Chapter 7. Revenue and Collection Cycle

1. The general definition of an _____ is an evaluation of a person, organization, system, process, project or product. _____s are performed to ascertain the validity and reliability of information; also to provide an assessment of a system's internal control. The goal of an _____ is to express an opinion on the person/organization/system (etc) in question, under evaluation based on work done on a test basis.
   a. Assurance service
   b. Institute of Chartered Accountants of India
   c. Audit regime
   d. Audit

2. _____ is a term that is commonly used in relation to the audit of the financial statements of an entity. (.
   a. Auditor independence
   b. Audit working paper
   c. Engagement Letter
   d. Audit risk

3. Just in Time could refer to the following:

   - _____, an inventory strategy that reduces in-process inventory
   - _____ compilation, a technique for improving the performance of bytecode-compiled programming systems

   a. Comparable
   b. Help desk and incident reporting auditing
   c. Just-in-time
   d. Fiscal

4. An _____ is the buying of one company by another. An _____ may be friendly or hostile. In the former case, the companies cooperate in negotiations; in the latter case, the takeover target is unwilling to be bought or the target's board has no prior knowledge of the offer. _____ usually refers to a purchase of a smaller firm by a larger one. Sometimes, however, a smaller firm will acquire management control of a larger or longer established company and keep its name for the combined entity. This is known as a reverse takeover.
   a. AIG
   b. AMEX
   c. Acquisition
   d. ABC Television Network

5. _____ is a concept that denotes the precise probability of specific eventualities. Technically, the notion of _____ is independent from the notion of value and, as such, eventualities may have both beneficial and adverse consequences. However, in general usage the convention is to focus only on potential negative impact to some characteristic of value that may arise from a future event.
   a. Discount factor
   b. Discounting
   c. Risk adjusted return on capital
   d. Risk

6. _____, in auditing, is the risk that the account or section being audited is materially misstated without considering internal controls due to error; _____ does not include an assessment of the risk of material misstatement due to fraud. The assessment of _____ depends on the professional judgement of the auditor, and it is done after assessing the business environment of the entity being audited.

   _____ is typically assessed using a scale, with assessments being either low, medium, or high.

   a. AIG
   b. ABC Television Network
   c. Inherent risk
   d. AMEX

Chapter 7. Revenue and Collection Cycle

7. _____ principle is a cornerstone of accrual accounting together with matching principle. They both determine the accounting period, in which revenues and expenses are recognized. According to the principle, revenues are recognized when they are (1) realized or realizable, and are (2) earned (usually when goods are transferred or services rendered), no matter when cash is received.
- a. 3M Company
- b. Net realizable value
- c. Revenue recognition
- d. BMC Software, Inc.

8. A _____ or transnational corporation (TNC) is a corporation or enterprise that manages production or delivers services in more than one country. It can also be referred to as an international corporation. The first modern _____ is generally thought to be the British East India Company, established in 1600.
- a. Privately held
- b. MicroStrategy
- c. Butterfield Bank
- d. Multinational corporation

9. _____ refers to the independence of the auditor from parties, that have an interest in the financial statements of an entity. It is essentially an attitude of mind characterized by integrity and an objective approach to the audit process. The concept requires the auditor to carry out his work freely and in an objective manner.
- a. Internal Auditing
- b. Information audit
- c. Audit
- d. Auditor independence

10. _____ is one of a series of accounting transactions dealing with the billing of customers who owe money to a person, company or organization for goods and services that have been provided to the customer. In most business entities this is typically done by generating an invoice and mailing or electronically delivering it to the customer, who in turn must pay it within an established timeframe called credit or payment terms.

An example of a common payment term is Net 30, meaning payment is due in the amount of the invoice 30 days from the date of invoice.

- a. Accrued revenue
- b. Adjusting entries
- c. Accounts receivable
- d. Accrual

11. The _____ (sometimes called 'Peekaboo') is a private-sector, non-profit corporation created by the Sarbanes-Oxley Act, a 2002 United States federal law, to oversee the auditors of public companies. Its stated purpose is to 'protect the interests of investors and further the public interest in the preparation of informative, fair, and independent audit reports'. Although a private entity, the _____ has many government-like regulatory functions, making it in some ways similar to the private Self Regulatory Organizations (SROs) that regulate stock markets and other aspects of the financial markets in the United States.
- a. 3M Company
- b. Public Company Accounting Oversight Board
- c. Financial Crimes Enforcement Network
- d. Pension Benefit Guaranty Corporation

12. _____ in economics and business is the result of an exchange and from that trade we assign a numerical monetary value to a good, service or asset. If Alice trades Bob 4 apples for an orange, the _____ of an orange is 4 apples. Inversely, the _____ of an apple is 1/4 oranges.
- a. Discounts and allowances
- b. Transactional Net Margin Method
- c. Price discrimination
- d. Price

Chapter 7. Revenue and Collection Cycle

13. In business and accounting, _____ are everything of value that is owned by a person or company. It is a claim on the property your income of a borrower. The balance sheet of a firm records the monetary value of the _____ owned by the firm.

   a. Earnings before interest, taxes, depreciation and amortization
   b. Accounts receivable
   c. Accrual basis accounting
   d. Assets

14. A _____ is the pinnacle activity involved in selling products or services in return for money or other compensation. It is an act of completion of a commercial activity.

   A _____ is completed by the seller, the owner of the goods.

   a. Tertiary sector of economy
   b. Sale
   c. High yield stock
   d. Maturity

15. An _____ or bill is a commercial document issued by a seller to the buyer, indicating the products, quantities, and agreed prices for products or services the seller has provided the buyer. An _____ indicates the buyer must pay the seller, according to the payment terms.

   In the rental industry, an _____ must include a specific reference to the duration of the time being billed, so rather than quantity, price and discount the invoicing amount is based on quantity, price, discount and duration.

   a. AMEX
   b. ABC Television Network
   c. AIG
   d. Invoice

16. In accounting, the _____ is a worksheet listing the balance at a certain date, of each ledger account in two columns, namely debit and credit. Under the double-entry system, in any transaction the total of any debits must equal the total of any credits, so in a _____ the total of the debit side should always be equal to the total of the credit side. The _____ thus serves as a tool to detect errors, which can result in the totals not being equal.

   a. Depreciation
   b. Current asset
   c. Bottom line
   d. Trial balance

17. _____, in auditing, is the risk that a company's internal controls are insufficient to mitigate or detect errors or fraud.
   a. 3M Company
   b. BMC Software, Inc.
   c. Control risk
   d. BNSF Railway

18. A _____, also client, buyer or purchaser is the buyer or user of the paid products of an individual or organization, mostly called the supplier or seller. This is typically through purchasing or renting goods or services.
   a. BNSF Railway
   b. 3M Company
   c. BMC Software, Inc.
   d. Customer

19. An _____ is a term used in behavioral economics to describe those types of behaviors that impose costs on a person in the long-run that are not taken into account when making decisions in the present. Classical Economics discourages government from creating legislation that targets internalities, because it is assumed that the consumer takes these personal costs into account when paying for the good that causes the _____. For example, cigarettes should be taxed because of the negative consumption externalities that they impose, such as second-hand smoke, not because the smoker harms him or herself by smoking.
   a. Inventory turnover ratio
   b. Operating budget
   c. Internality
   d. Authorised capital

20. In accounting and organizational theory, _____ is defined as a process effected by an organization's structure, work and authority flows, people and management information systems, designed to help the organization accomplish specific goals or objectives. It is a means by which an organization's resources are directed, monitored, and measured. It plays an important role in preventing and detecting fraud and protecting the organization's resources, both physical (e.g., machinery and property) and intangible (e.g., reputation or intellectual property such as trademarks.)
   a. Audit committee
   b. Audit risk
   c. Auditor independence
   d. Internal control

21. _____ is a step in a risk management process. _____ is the determination of quantitative or qualitative value of risk related to a concrete situation and a recognized threat (also called hazard.) Quantitative _____ requires calculations of two components of risk: R, the magnitude of the potential loss L, and the probability p that the loss will occur.
   a. Risk assessment
   b. 3M Company
   c. BNSF Railway
   d. BMC Software, Inc.

22. _____ is an organization's process of defining its strategy and making decisions on allocating its resources to pursue this strategy, including its capital and people. Various business analysis techniques can be used in _____, including SWOT analysis (Strengths, Weaknesses, Opportunities, and Threats) and PEST analysis (Political, Economic, Social, and Technological analysis) or STEER analysis involving Socio-cultural, Technological, Economic, Ecological, and Regulatory factors and EPISTEL (Environment, Political, Informatic, Social, Technological, Economic and Legal)

_____ is the formal consideration of an organization's future course. All _____ deals with at least one of three key questions:

   1. 'What do we do?'
   2. 'For whom do we do it?'
   3. 'How do we excel?'

In business _____, the third question is better phrased 'How can we beat or avoid competition?'. (Bradford and Duncan, page 1.)

   a. BMC Software, Inc.
   b. 3M Company
   c. BNSF Railway
   d. Strategic planning

23. In economics, the _____, (or _____) measures the payments that flow between any individual country and all other countries. It is used to summarize all international economic transactions for that country during a specific time period, usually a year. The _____ is determined by the country's exports and imports of goods, services, and financial capital, as well as financial transfers.

a. Moving average	b. Stock split
c. Yield to maturity	d. Balance of payments

24. _____ is that part of statistical practice concerned with the selection of individual observations intended to yield some knowledge about a population of concern, especially for the purposes of statistical inference. Each observation measures one or more properties (weight, location, etc.) of an observable entity enumerated to distinguish objects or individuals.

a. Alan Greenspan	b. Abby Joseph Cohen
c. Arthur Betz Laffer	d. Sampling

25. The _____ is the national, professional association of CPAs in the United States, with more than 330,000 members, including CPAs in business and industry, public practice, government, and education; student affiliates; and international associates. It sets ethical standards for the profession and U.S. auditing standards for audits of private companies; federal, state and local governments; and non-profit organizations.

Approximately 40% of its members are engaged in the practice of public accounting, in areas such as auditing, accounting, taxation, general business consulting, business valuation, personal financial planning and business technology.

a. Other postemployment benefits	b. ABC Television Network
c. AIG	d. American Institute of Certified Public Accountants

26. _____ is one of financial audit skill which help an auditor understand the client's business and changes in the business, to identify potential risk areas and to plan other audit procedures.

_____ include comparison of financial information (data in financial statement) with

1. prior periods
2. budgets
3. forecasts
4. similar industries and so on.

It also includes consideration of predictable relationships, such as:

1. gross profit to sales,
2. payroll costs to employees,
3. financial information and non-financial information, for examples the CEO's reports and the industry news.

possible sources of information about the client include:

1. interim financial information
2. Budgets
3. Management accounts
4. Non-Financial information
5. Bank and cash records
6. VAT returns
7. Board minutes
8. Discussion or correspondance with the client at they year-end

a. Analytical procedures

b. International Federation of Audit Bureaux of Circulations

c. Assurance service

d. External auditor

27. _____ represents claims for which formal instruments of credit are issued as evidence of debt, such as a promissory note. The credit instrument normally requires the debtor to pay interest and extends for time periods of 60-90 days or longer.

a. Restricted stock

b. Moving average

c. Public offering

d. Notes receivable

28. _____, commonly abbreviated as SAS, provide guidance to external auditors on generally accepted auditing standards in regards to auditing an entity and issuing a report. They are usually issued by the certified public accountant authoritative body in the region where the standards apply, such as the American Institute of Certified Public Accountants in the United States.

- _____
- _____ (Taiwan)

a. Statements on Auditing Standards

b. GASB 45

c. Financial Instruments and Exchange Law

d. RSM International

29. _____ is a file or account that contains money that a person or company owes to suppliers, but has not paid yet (a form of debt.) When you receive an invoice you add it to the file, and then you remove it when you pay. Thus, the A/P is a form of credit that suppliers offer to their purchasers by allowing them to pay for a product or service after it has already been received.

a. Accrual

b. Accounts payable

c. Earnings before interest, taxes, depreciation and amortization

d. Accounts receivable

30. _____ is the state or fact of exclusive rights and control over property, which may be an object, land/real estate or intellectual property. An _____ right is also referred to as title.

_____ is the key building block in the development of the capitalist socio-economic system.

a. Encumbrance
c. Administrative proceeding
b. ABC Television Network
d. Ownership

31. In a company, _____ is the sum of all financial records of salaries, wages, bonuses and deductions.

A paycheck, is traditionally a paper document issued by an employer to pay an employee for services rendered. While most commonly used in the United States, recently the physical paycheck has been increasingly replaced by electronic direct deposit to bank accounts.

a. Total Expense Ratio
c. 3M Company
b. Tax expense
d. Payroll

32. _____ means the giving out of information, either voluntarily or to be in compliance with legal regulations or workplace rules.

- In Computer security, full _____ means disclosing full information about vulnerabilities.
- In computing, _____ widget
- Journalism, full _____ refers to disclosing the interests of the writer which may bear on the subject being written about, for example, if the writer has worked with an interview subject in the past.

- In law:
    - The law of England and Wales, _____ refers to a process that may form part of legal proceedings, whereby parties inform to other parties the existence of any relevant documents that are, or have been, in their control. This compares with the process known as discovery in the course of legal proceedings in the United States.
    - In U.S. civil procedure (litigation rules for civil cases), _____ is a stage prior to trial. In civil cases, each party must disclose to the opposing party the following: names of witnesses which it may use to support its side, copies of documents (or mere description of these documents) in its control which it may use to support its side, computation of damages claimed, and certain insurance information. _____ is related to, but technically prior to, the discovery stage.
    - In Company law (known as 'corporate law' in the United States), _____ refers to giving out information about public or limited companies or their officers, which might be kept secret if the company was a private company or a partnership.

- In real property transactions, _____ refers to providing to a buyer information known to the seller or broker/agent concerning the condition or other aspects of real property that would affect the property's value or desirability. These rules regarding what information must be disclosed, and whether the information must be disclosed even if a buyer does not ask, vary from one jurisdiction to the next.

a. Controlled Foreign Corporations
c. Disclosure
b. Tax harmonisation
d. Trailing

Chapter 7. Revenue and Collection Cycle

33. Established in 1988 the _____ is the professional organization that governs professional fraud examiners. Its activities include producing fraud information, tools and training. It also governs the professional designation of Certified Fraud Examiner.

   a. AIG
   b. ABC Television Network
   c. AMEX
   d. Association of Certified Fraud Examiners

34. _____ is a designation awarded by the Association of _____s (ACertified Fraud Examiner.) The ACertified Fraud Examiner is a 41,000 member-based global association dedicated to providing anti-fraud education and training.

   In order to become a _____ one must meet the following requirements:

   - Be an Associate Member of the ACertified Fraud Examiner in good standing
   - Meet minimum academic and professional requirements
   - Be of high moral character
   - Agree to abide by the Bylaws and Code of Professional Ethics of the Association of _____s

   Generally, applicants for _____ certification have a minimum of a bachelor's degree or equivalent from an institution of higher education. Two years of professional experience related to fraud can be substituted for each year of college.

   a. Certified Fraud Examiner
   b. Chartered Certified Accountant
   c. Certified public accountant
   d. Chartered Accountant

35. A _____ has several related meanings:

   - a daily record of events or business; a private _____ is usually referred to as a diary.
   - a newspaper or other periodical, in the literal sense of one published each day;
   - many publications issued at stated intervals, such as magazines, or scholarly academic _____s, or the record of the transactions of a society, are often called _____s. Although _____ is sometimes used, erroneously, as a synonym for 'magazine,' in academic use, a _____ refers to a serious, scholarly publication, most often peer-reviewed. A non-scholarly magazine written for an educated audience about an industry or an area of professional activity is usually called a professional magazine.

   The word 'journalist' for one whose business is writing for the public press has been in use since the end of the 17th century.

   Open access _____s are scholarly _____s that are available to the reader without financial or other barrier other than access to the internet itself. Some are subsidized, and some require payment on behalf of the author. Subsidized _____s are financed by an academic institution or a government information center.

   a. BMC Software, Inc.
   b. 3M Company
   c. BNSF Railway
   d. Journal

Chapter 8. Acquisition and Expenditure Cycle

1. An _____ is the buying of one company by another. An _____ may be friendly or hostile. In the former case, the companies cooperate in negotiations; in the latter case, the takeover target is unwilling to be bought or the target's board has no prior knowledge of the offer. _____ usually refers to a purchase of a smaller firm by a larger one. Sometimes, however, a smaller firm will acquire management control of a larger or longer established company and keep its name for the combined entity. This is known as a reverse takeover.

    a. AIG
    b. ABC Television Network
    c. Acquisition
    d. AMEX

2. A _____ has several related meanings:

    - a daily record of events or business; a private _____ is usually referred to as a diary.
    - a newspaper or other periodical, in the literal sense of one published each day;
    - many publications issued at stated intervals, such as magazines, or scholarly academic _____s, or the record of the transactions of a society, are often called _____s. Although _____ is sometimes used, erroneously, as a synonym for 'magazine,' in academic use, a _____ refers to a serious, scholarly publication, most often peer-reviewed. A non-scholarly magazine written for an educated audience about an industry or an area of professional activity is usually called a professional magazine.

    The word 'journalist' for one whose business is writing for the public press has been in use since the end of the 17th century.

    Open access _____s are scholarly _____s that are available to the reader without financial or other barrier other than access to the internet itself. Some are subsidized, and some require payment on behalf of the author. Subsidized _____s are financed by an academic institution or a government information center.

    a. BMC Software, Inc.
    b. 3M Company
    c. BNSF Railway
    d. Journal

3. In a company, _____ is the sum of all financial records of salaries, wages, bonuses and deductions.

    A paycheck, is traditionally a paper document issued by an employer to pay an employee for services rendered. While most commonly used in the United States, recently the physical paycheck has been increasingly replaced by electronic direct deposit to bank accounts.

    a. Tax expense
    b. Payroll
    c. 3M Company
    d. Total Expense Ratio

4. In accounting, _____ has a very specific meaning. It is an outflow of cash or other valuable assets from a person or company to another person or company. This outflow of cash is generally one side of a trade for products or services that have equal or better current or future value to the buyer than to the seller.

    a. AMEX
    b. ABC Television Network
    c. AIG
    d. Expense

5. _____, in auditing, is the risk that the account or section being audited is materially misstated without considering internal controls due to error; _____ does not include an assessment of the risk of material misstatement due to fraud. The assessment of _____ depends on the professional judgement of the auditor, and it is done after assessing the business environment of the entity being audited.

Chapter 8. Acquisition and Expenditure Cycle

_____ is typically assessed using a scale, with assessments being either low, medium, or high.

a. AIG
c. AMEX
b. Inherent risk
d. ABC Television Network

6. In financial accounting, a _____ is defined as an obligation of an entity arising from past transactions or events, the settlement of which may result in the transfer or use of assets, provision of services or other yielding of economic benefits in the future.
a. Vested
c. Corporate governance
b. Liability
d. False Claims Act

7. _____ is the collection, transport, processing, recycling or disposal, and monitoring of waste materials. The term usually relates to materials produced by human activity, and is generally undertaken to reduce their effect on health, the environment or aesthetics. _____ is also carried out to recover resources from it.
a. Waste Management
c. BMC Software, Inc.
b. 3M Company
d. BNSF Railway

8. _____ refers to the independence of the auditor from parties, that have an interest in the financial statements of an entity. It is essentially an attitude of mind characterized by integrity and an objective approach to the audit process. The concept requires the auditor to carry out his work freely and in an objective manner.
a. Information audit
c. Internal Auditing
b. Audit
d. Auditor independence

9. In economics, business, retail, and accounting, a _____ is the value of money that has been used up to produce something, and hence is not available for use anymore. In economics, a _____ is an alternative that is given up as a result of a decision. In business, the _____ may be one of acquisition, in which case the amount of money expended to acquire it is counted as _____.
a. Prime cost
c. Cost allocation
b. Cost
d. Cost of quality

10. _____ is a concept that denotes the precise probability of specific eventualities. Technically, the notion of _____ is independent from the notion of value and, as such, eventualities may have both beneficial and adverse consequences. However, in general usage the convention is to focus only on potential negative impact to some characteristic of value that may arise from a future event.
a. Risk
c. Discounting
b. Discount factor
d. Risk adjusted return on capital

11. The _____ is the national, professional association of CPAs in the United States, with more than 330,000 members, including CPAs in business and industry, public practice, government, and education; student affiliates; and international associates. It sets ethical standards for the profession and U.S. auditing standards for audits of private companies; federal, state and local governments; and non-profit organizations.

Approximately 40% of its members are engaged in the practice of public accounting, in areas such as auditing, accounting, taxation, general business consulting, business valuation, personal financial planning and business technology.

Chapter 8. Acquisition and Expenditure Cycle

a. Other postemployment benefits
b. American Institute of Certified Public Accountants
c. AIG
d. ABC Television Network

12. _____ refers to the structured transmission of data between organizations by electronic means. It is used to transfer electronic documents from one computer system to another (ie) from one trading partner to another trading partner. It is more than mere E-mail; for instance, organizations might replace bills of lading and even checks with appropriate _____ messages.

a. AIG
b. ABC Television Network
c. Electronic commerce
d. Electronic data interchange

13. A _____ is a commercial document issued by a buyer to a seller, indicating types, quantities, and agreed prices for products or services the seller will provide to the buyer. Sending a _____ to a supplier constitutes a legal offer to buy products or services. Acceptance of a _____ by a seller usually forms a once-off contract between the buyer and seller, so no contract exists until the _____ is accepted.

a. Voucher
b. 3M Company
c. BMC Software, Inc.
d. Purchase order

14. A _____ is a bond which is worth a certain monetary value and which may only be spent for specific reasons or on specific goods. Examples include -- but are not limited to -- housing, travel and food _____s. The term _____ is also a synonym for receipt, and is often used to refer to receipts used as evidence of, for example, the declaration that a service has been performed or that an expenditure has been made.

a. BMC Software, Inc.
b. Source document
c. 3M Company
d. Voucher

15. _____, in auditing, is the risk that a company's internal controls are insufficient to mitigate or detect errors or fraud.

a. 3M Company
b. Control risk
c. BNSF Railway
d. BMC Software, Inc.

16. _____ is a file or account that contains money that a person or company owes to suppliers, but has not paid yet (a form of debt.) When you receive an invoice you add it to the file, and then you remove it when you pay. Thus, the A/P is a form of credit that suppliers offer to their purchasers by allowing them to pay for a product or service after it has already been received.

a. Accounts payable
b. Earnings before interest, taxes, depreciation and amortization
c. Accrual
d. Accounts receivable

17. The general definition of an _____ is an evaluation of a person, organization, system, process, project or product. _____s are performed to ascertain the validity and reliability of information; also to provide an assessment of a system's internal control. The goal of an _____ is to express an opinion on the person/organization/system (etc) in question, under evaluation based on work done on a test basis.

a. Institute of Chartered Accountants of India
b. Audit
c. Assurance service
d. Audit regime

18. An _____ or bill is a commercial document issued by a seller to the buyer, indicating the products, quantities, and agreed prices for products or services the seller has provided the buyer. An _____ indicates the buyer must pay the seller, according to the payment terms.

In the rental industry, an _____ must include a specific reference to the duration of the time being billed, so rather than quantity, price and discount the invoicing amount is based on quantity, price, discount and duration.

    a. AIG   b. ABC Television Network
    c. AMEX   d. Invoice

19. _____ is evidence obtained during a financial audit and recorded in the audit working papers.

- In the audit engagement acceptance or reappointment stage, _____ is the information that the auditor is to consider for the appointment. For examples, change in the entity control environment, inherent risk and nature of the entity business, and scope of audit work.

- In the audit planning stage, _____ is the information that the auditor is to consider for the most effective and efficient audit approach. For examples, reliability of internal control procedures, and analytical review systems.

- In the control testing stage, _____ is the information that the auditor is to consider for the mix of audit test of control and audit substantive tests.

- In the substantive testing stage, _____ is the information that the auditor is to make sure the appropriation of financial statement assertions. For examples, existence, rights and obligations, occurrence, completeness, valuation, measurement, presentation and disclosure of a particular transaction or account balance.

    a. Audit   b. Institute of Chartered Accountants of India
    c. Audit evidence   d. ITGCs

20. _____, also known as property, plant, and equipment (PP&E), is a term used in accountancy for assets and property which cannot easily be converted into cash. This can be compared with current assets such as cash or bank accounts, which are described as liquid assets. In most cases, only tangible assets are referred to as fixed.
    a. Subledger   b. Minority interest
    c. Fixed asset   d. Bankruptcy prediction

21. An _____ is a term used in behavioral economics to describe those types of behaviors that impose costs on a person in the long-run that are not taken into account when making decisions in the present. Classical Economics discourages government from creating legislation that targets internalities, because it is assumed that the consumer takes these personal costs into account when paying for the good that causes the _____. For example, cigarettes should be taxed because of the negative consumption externalities that they impose, such as second-hand smoke, not because the smoker harms him or herself by smoking.
    a. Internality   b. Operating budget
    c. Inventory turnover ratio   d. Authorised capital

Chapter 8. Acquisition and Expenditure Cycle

22. In accounting and organizational theory, _____ is defined as a process effected by an organization's structure, work and authority flows, people and management information systems, designed to help the organization accomplish specific goals or objectives. It is a means by which an organization's resources are directed, monitored, and measured. It plays an important role in preventing and detecting fraud and protecting the organization's resources, both physical (e.g., machinery and property) and intangible (e.g., reputation or intellectual property such as trademarks.)
   a. Auditor independence
   b. Audit risk
   c. Audit committee
   d. Internal control

23. _____ refers to a business or organization attempting to acquire goods or services to accomplish the goals of the enterprise. Though there are several organizations that attempt to set standards in the _____ process, processes can vary greatly between organizations. Typically the word e;_____ e; is not used interchangeably with the word e;procuremente;, since procurement typically includes Expediting, Supplier Quality, and Traffic and Logistics (T'L) in addition to _____.
   a. Supply chain
   b. Consignor
   c. Free port
   d. Purchasing

24. In business and accounting, _____ are everything of value that is owned by a person or company. It is a claim on the property your income of a borrower. The balance sheet of a firm records the monetary value of the _____ owned by the firm.
   a. Earnings before interest, taxes, depreciation and amortization
   b. Accounts receivable
   c. Accrual basis accounting
   d. Assets

25. _____ is a step in a risk management process. _____ is the determination of quantitative or qualitative value of risk related to a concrete situation and a recognized threat (also called hazard.) Quantitative _____ requires calculations of two components of risk: R, the magnitude of the potential loss L, and the probability p that the loss will occur.
   a. BMC Software, Inc.
   b. BNSF Railway
   c. 3M Company
   d. Risk assessment

26. _____ is one of a series of accounting transactions dealing with the billing of customers who owe money to a person, company or organization for goods and services that have been provided to the customer. In most business entities this is typically done by generating an invoice and mailing or electronically delivering it to the customer, who in turn must pay it within an established timeframe called credit or payment terms.

An example of a common payment term is Net 30, meaning payment is due in the amount of the invoice 30 days from the date of invoice.

   a. Accrual
   b. Adjusting entries
   c. Accounts receivable
   d. Accrued revenue

27. _____ is any physical or virtual entity that is owned by an individual or jointly by a group of individuals. An owner of _____ has the right to consume, sell, rent, mortgage, transfer and exchange his or her _____. Important widely-recognized types of _____ include real _____, personal _____ (other physical possessions), and intellectual _____ (rights over artistic creations, inventions, etc.), although the latter is not always as widely recognized or enforced.

Chapter 8. Acquisition and Expenditure Cycle

a. Fiduciary
b. Disclosure requirement
c. Property
d. Primary authority

28. _____ is that part of statistical practice concerned with the selection of individual observations intended to yield some knowledge about a population of concern, especially for the purposes of statistical inference. Each observation measures one or more properties (weight, location, etc.) of an observable entity enumerated to distinguish objects or individuals.
   a. Abby Joseph Cohen
   b. Arthur Betz Laffer
   c. Alan Greenspan
   d. Sampling

29. _____ are liabilities which have occurred, but have not been paid or logged under accounts payable during an accounting period; in other words, obligations for goods and services provided to a company for which invoices have not yet been received. Examples would include accrued wages payable, accrued sales tax payable, and accrued rent payable.

There are two general types of _____:

- Routine and recurring
- Infrequent or non-routine

Most companies pay their employees on a predetermined schedule. Let's say that the 'Imaginary company Ltd.' pays its employees each Friday for the hours worked that week.

   a. ABC Television Network
   b. Accrued liabilities
   c. AMEX
   d. AIG

30. An _____ is a tax levied on the financial income of people, corporations, or other legal entities. Various _____ systems exist, with varying degrees of tax incidence. Income taxation can be progressive, proportional, or regressive.
   a. Individual Retirement Arrangement
   b. Ordinary income
   c. Implied level of government service
   d. Income tax

31. _____ refers to services paid for in advance. Examples include tolls, pay as you go cell phones, and stored-value cards such as gift cards and preloaded credit cards. _____ accounts are assets, and they are increased by debiting the account(s.)
   a. BMC Software, Inc.
   b. BNSF Railway
   c. 3M Company
   d. Prepaid

32. _____, in accrual accounting, is any account where the asset or liability is not realized until a future date (accounting period), e.g. annuities, charges, taxes, income, etc. The _____ item may be carried, dependent on type of deferral, as either an asset or liability.
   a. Pro forma
   b. Cash basis accounting
   c. Deferred
   d. Payroll

Chapter 8. Acquisition and Expenditure Cycle

33. The _____ of 2002 (Pub.L. 107-204, 116 Stat. 745, enacted July 30, 2002), also known as the Public Company Accounting Reform and Investor Protection Act of 2002, is a United States federal law enacted on July 30, 2002 in response to a number of major corporate and accounting scandals including those affecting Enron, Tyco International, Adelphia, Peregrine Systems and WorldCom. The legislation establishes new or enhanced standards for all U.S. public company boards, management, and public accounting firms. It does not apply to privately held companies.

    a. Lease
    b. FCPA
    c. Fair Labor Standards Act
    d. Sarbanes-Oxley Act

34. _____ of something is, in finance, the adding together of interest or different investments over a period of time such as atoms (1 - the act or process of accruing; 2 - the amount that accrues.) It holds specific meanings in accounting and payroll.

    _____, in accounting, describes the accounting method known as _____ basis, whereby revenues and expenses are recognized when they are accrued, i.e. accumulated (earned or incurred), regardless when the actual cash is received or paid out.

    a. Earnings before interest, taxes, depreciation and amortization
    b. Accrual
    c. Assets
    d. Accounts receivable

35. U.S. _____ refers to accounting for tax purposes in the United States. Unlike most countries, the United States has a comprehensive set of accounting principles for tax purposes, prescribed by tax law, which are separate and distinct from Generally Accepted Accounting Principles.

    The Internal Revenue Code governs the application of _____.

    a. BMC Software, Inc.
    b. Tax accounting
    c. BNSF Railway
    d. 3M Company

36. _____ is the process of increasing, or accounting for, an amount over a period of time. Particular instances of the term include:

    - _____, the allocation of a lump sum amount to different time periods, particularly for loans and other forms of finance, including related interest or other finance charges.
        - _____ schedule, a table detailing each periodic payment on a loan (typically a mortgage), as generated by an _____ calculator.
        - Negative _____, an _____ schedule where the loan amount actually increases through not paying the full interest
    - Amortized analysis, analyzing the execution cost of algorithms over a sequence of operations.
        - _____ of capital expenditures of certain assets under accounting rules, particularly intangible assets, in a manner analogous to depreciation.
    - _____

    a. EBIT
    b. Amortization
    c. Intangible
    d. Annuity

Chapter 8. Acquisition and Expenditure Cycle

37. _____ is a term used in accounting, economics and finance to spread the cost of an asset over the span of several years.

In simple words we can say that _____ is the reduction in the value of an asset due to usage, passage of time, wear and tear, technological outdating or obsolescence, depletion, inadequacy, rot, rust, decay or other such factors.

In accounting, _____ is a term used to describe any method of attributing the historical or purchase cost of an asset across its useful life, roughly corresponding to normal wear and tear.

- a. Current asset
- b. Net profit
- c. General ledger
- d. Depreciation

38. _____ are defined as identifiable non-monetary assets that cannot be seen, touched or physically measured, which are created through time and/or effort and that are identifiable as a separate asset. There are two primary forms of intangibles - legal intangibles (such as trade secrets (e.g., customer lists), copyrights, patents, trademarks, and goodwill) and competitive intangibles (such as knowledge activities (know-how, knowledge), collaboration activities, leverage activities, and structural activities.) Legal intangibles are known under the generic term intellectual property and generate legal property rights defensible in a court of law.

- a. AIG
- b. ABC Television Network
- c. Overhead
- d. Intangible assets

39. In finance, _____ is the process of estimating the potential market value of a financial asset or liability. They can be done on assets (for example, investments in marketable securities such as stocks, options, business enterprises, or intangible assets such as patents and trademarks) or on liabilities (e.g., Bonds issued by a company.) A _____ is required in many contexts including investment analysis, capital budgeting, merger and acquisition transactions, financial reporting, taxable events to determine the proper tax liability, and in litigation.

- a. Daybook
- b. Vyborg Appeal
- c. Valuation
- d. Disclosure

40. In business or economics a _____ is a combination of two companies into one larger company. Such actions are commonly voluntary and involve stock swap or cash payment to the target. Stock swap is often used as it allows the shareholders of the two companies to share the risk involved in the deal. A _____ can resemble a takeover but result in a new company name (often combining the names of the original companies) and in new branding; in some cases, terming the combination a '_____' rather than an acquisition is done purely for political or marketing reasons.

- a. BMC Software, Inc.
- b. Merger
- c. 3M Company
- d. BNSF Railway

41. The phrase _____ refers to the aspect of corporate strategy, corporate finance and management dealing with the buying, selling and combining of different companies that can aid, finance, or help a growing company in a given industry grow rapidly without having to create another business entity.

- a. BMC Software, Inc.
- b. BNSF Railway
- c. 3M Company
- d. Mergers and acquisitions

42. _____ is a term that is commonly used in relation to the audit of the financial statements of an entity. (.

a. Auditor independence
c. Engagement Letter
b. Audit risk
d. Audit working paper

43. _____ means the giving out of information, either voluntarily or to be in compliance with legal regulations or workplace rules.

- In Computer security, full _____ means disclosing full information about vulnerabilities.
- In computing, _____ widget
- Journalism, full _____ refers to disclosing the interests of the writer which may bear on the subject being written about, for example, if the writer has worked with an interview subject in the past.

- In law:
  - The law of England and Wales, _____ refers to a process that may form part of legal proceedings, whereby parties inform to other parties the existence of any relevant documents that are, or have been, in their control. This compares with the process known as discovery in the course of legal proceedings in the United States.
  - In U.S. civil procedure (litigation rules for civil cases), _____ is a stage prior to trial. In civil cases, each party must disclose to the opposing party the following: names of witnesses which it may use to support its side, copies of documents (or mere description of these documents) in its control which it may use to support its side, computation of damages claimed, and certain insurance information. _____ is related to, but technically prior to, the discovery stage.
  - In Company law (known as 'corporate law' in the United States), _____ refers to giving out information about public or limited companies or their officers, which might be kept secret if the company was a private company or a partnership.

- In real property transactions, _____ refers to providing to a buyer information known to the seller or broker/agent concerning the condition or other aspects of real property that would affect the property's value or desirability. These rules regarding what information must be disclosed, and whether the information must be disclosed even if a buyer does not ask, vary from one jurisdiction to the next.

a. Controlled Foreign Corporations
c. Trailing
b. Tax harmonisation
d. Disclosure

44. The term _____ usually refers to a company that is permitted to offer its registered securities (stock, bonds, etc.) for sale to the general public, typically through a stock exchange, or occasionally a company whose stock is traded over the counter (OTC) via market makers who use non-exchange quotation services.

The term '_____' may also refer to a company owned by the government.

a. MicroStrategy
c. Governmental Accounting Standards Board
b. Professional association
d. Public Company

Chapter 8. Acquisition and Expenditure Cycle

45. The _____ (sometimes called 'Peekaboo') is a private-sector, non-profit corporation created by the Sarbanes-Oxley Act, a 2002 United States federal law, to oversee the auditors of public companies. Its stated purpose is to 'protect the interests of investors and further the public interest in the preparation of informative, fair, and independent audit reports'. Although a private entity, the _____ has many government-like regulatory functions, making it in some ways similar to the private Self Regulatory Organizations (SROs) that regulate stock markets and other aspects of the financial markets in the United States.
   a. 3M Company
   b. Public Company Accounting Oversight Board
   c. Pension Benefit Guaranty Corporation
   d. Financial Crimes Enforcement Network

46. Employment is a contract between two parties, one being the employer and the other being the _____. An _____ may be defined as: 'A person in the service of another under any contract of hire, express or implied, oral or written, where the employer has the power or right to control and direct the _____ in the material details of how the work is to be performed.' Black's Law Dictionary page 471 (5th ed. 1979.)
   a. AMEX
   b. ABC Television Network
   c. AIG
   d. Employee

47. In management accounting, _____ establishes budget and actual cost of operations, processes, departments or product and the analysis of variances, profitability or social use of funds. Managers use _____ to support decision-making to cut a company's costs and improve profitability. As a form of management accounting, _____ need not follow standards such as GAAP, because its primary use is for internal managers, rather than outside users, and what to compute is instead decided pragmatically.
   a. Cost-volume-profit analysis
   b. Cost accounting
   c. Prime cost
   d. Marginal cost

48. A _____ is usually a temporary account containing costs or amounts that are to be transferred to another account. An example is the income summary account containing revenue and expense amounts to be transferred to retained earnings at the close of a fiscal period.
   a. Special assessment
   b. Tax Analysts
   c. Fixed tax
   d. Clearing account

49. _____ is a specific term used in companies' financial reporting from the company-whole point of view. Because that use excludes the effects of changing ownership interest, an economic measure of _____ is necessary for financial analysis from the shareholders' point of view

   _____ is defined by the Financial Accounting Standards Board, or FASB, as 'the change in equity [net assets] of a business enterprise during a period from transactions and other events and circumstances from nonowner sources. It includes all changes in equity during a period except those resulting from investments by owners and distributions to owners.'

   _____ is the sum of net income and other items that must bypass the income statement because they have not been realized, including items like an unrealized holding gain or loss from available for sale securities and foreign currency translation gains or losses.

   a. 3M Company
   b. BNSF Railway
   c. BMC Software, Inc.
   d. Comprehensive income

Chapter 8. Acquisition and Expenditure Cycle

50. A _____ is a fungible, negotiable instrument representing financial value. they are broadly categorized into debt securities (such as banknotes, bonds and debentures), and equity securities; e.g., common stocks. The company or other entity issuing the _____ is called the issuer.

a. 3M Company
b. Tracking stock
c. BMC Software, Inc.
d. Security

51. _____ in the United States currently refers to the federal Old-Age, Survivors, and Disability Insurance (OASDI) program.

The original _____ Act and the current version of the Act, as amended encompass several social welfare and social insurance programs. The larger and better known programs are:

- Federal Old-Age, Survivors, and Disability Insurance
- Unemployment benefits
- Temporary Assistance for Needy Families
- Health Insurance for Aged and Disabled (Medicare)
- Grants to States for Medical Assistance Programs (Medicaid)
- State Children's Health Insurance Program (SCHIP)
- Supplemental Security Income (Social Securityl)

U.S. _____ is a social insurance program funded through dedicated payroll taxes called Federal Insurance Contributions Act (FICA.) Tax deposits are formally entrusted to Federal Old-Age and Survivors Insurance Trust Fund, or Federal Disability Insurance Trust Fund, Federal Hospital Insurance Trust Fund or the Federal Supplementary Medical Insurance Trust Fund.

a. Sale
b. Price-to-sales ratio
c. Comparable
d. Social Security

52. The United States _____ is an independent agency of the United States federal government that administers Social Security, a social insurance program consisting of retirement, disability, and survivors' benefits. To qualify for these benefits, most American workers pay Social Security taxes on their earnings; future benefits are based on the employees' contributions.

The _____ was established by a law currently codified at 42 U.S.C.

a. Return on assets
b. Minority interest
c. Time value of money
d. Social Security Administration

Chapter 9. Production Cycle

1. _____ is that part of statistical practice concerned with the selection of individual observations intended to yield some knowledge about a population of concern, especially for the purposes of statistical inference. Each observation measures one or more properties (weight, location, etc.) of an observable entity enumerated to distinguish objects or individuals.

   a. Alan Greenspan
   b. Sampling
   c. Abby Joseph Cohen
   d. Arthur Betz Laffer

2. The Exxon Mobil Corporation is an American oil and gas corporation. It is a direct descendant of John D. Rockefeller's Standard Oil company, formed on November 30, 1999, by the merger of Exxon and Mobil.

   _____ is the world's largest publicly traded company when measured by either revenue or market capitalization.

   a. Alan Greenspan
   b. Abby Joseph Cohen
   c. Arthur Betz Laffer
   d. ExxonMobil

3. _____ is an acronym for First In, First Out, an abstraction in ways of organizing and manipulation of data relative to time and prioritization. This expression describes the principle of a queue processing technique or servicing conflicting demands by ordering process by first-come, first-served (FCFS) behaviour: what comes in first is handled first, what comes in next waits until the first is finished, etc.

   Thus it is analogous to the behaviour of persons queueing (or 'standing in line', in common American parlance), where the persons leave the queue in the order they arrive, or waiting one's turn at a traffic control signal.

   a. Risk management
   b. Kanban
   c. Trademark
   d. FIFO

4. _____ are ten auditing standards, developed by the AICPA, consisting of general standards, standards of field work, and standards of reporting, along with interpretations. They were developed by the AICPA in 1947 and have undergone minor changes since then.

   The _____ are as follows:

   1. The auditor must have adequate technical training and proficiency to perform the audit
   2. The auditor must maintain independence in mental attitude in all matters related to the audit.
   3. The auditor must use due professional care during the performance of the audit and the preparation of the report.

   1. The auditor must adequately plan the work and must properly supervise any assistants.
   2. The auditor must obtain a sufficient understanding of the entity and its environment, including its internal control, to assess the risk of material misstatement of the financial statements whether due to error or fraud, and to design the nature, timing, and extent of further audit procedures.
   3. The auditor must obtain sufficient appropriate audit evidence by performing audit procedures to afford a reasonable basis for an opinion regarding the financial statements under audit.

The new standards are in effect for audits of financial statements for periods beginning on or after December 15, 2006.

1. The auditor must state in the auditor's report whether the financial statements are in accordance with generally accepted accounting principles (GAAP.)
2. The auditor must identify in the auditor's report those circumstances in which such principles have not been consistently observed in the current period in relation to the preceding period.
3. When the auditor determines that informative disclosures are not reasonably adequate, the auditor must so state in the auditor's report.
4. The auditor must either express an opinion regarding the financial statements, taken as a whole the auditor should state the reasons therefore in the auditor's report. In all cases where the auditor's name is associated with the financial statements, the auditor should clearly indicate the character of the auditor's work, if any, and the degree of responsibility the auditor is taking, in the auditor's report.

a. Continuous auditing
b. Joint audit
c. Negative assurance
d. Generally accepted auditing standards

5. _____, in auditing, is the risk that the account or section being audited is materially misstated without considering internal controls due to error; _____ does not include an assessment of the risk of material misstatement due to fraud. The assessment of _____ depends on the professional judgement of the auditor, and it is done after assessing the business environment of the entity being audited.

_____ is typically assessed using a scale, with assessments being either low, medium, or high.

a. AMEX
b. Inherent risk
c. ABC Television Network
d. AIG

6. A _____ has several related meanings:

- a daily record of events or business; a private _____ is usually referred to as a diary.
- a newspaper or other periodical, in the literal sense of one published each day;
- many publications issued at stated intervals, such as magazines, or scholarly academic _____s, or the record of the transactions of a society, are often called _____s. Although _____ is sometimes used, erroneously, as a synonym for 'magazine,' in academic use, a _____ refers to a serious, scholarly publication, most often peer-reviewed. A non-scholarly magazine written for an educated audience about an industry or an area of professional activity is usually called a professional magazine.

The word 'journalist' for one whose business is writing for the public press has been in use since the end of the 17th century.

Open access _____s are scholarly _____s that are available to the reader without financial or other barrier other than access to the internet itself. Some are subsidized, and some require payment on behalf of the author. Subsidized _____s are financed by an academic institution or a government information center.

a. BNSF Railway
c. 3M Company
b. BMC Software, Inc.
d. Journal

7. _____ methods are means of managing inventory and financial matters involving the money a company ties up within inventory of produced goods, raw materials, parts, components, or feed stocks. FIFO stands for first-in, first-out, meaning that the oldest inventory items are recorded as sold first. LIFO stands for last-in, first-out, meaning that the most recently purchased items are recorded as sold first.
a. 3M Company
c. Finished good
b. Reorder point
d. FIFO and LIFO accounting

8. _____ is a method of evaluating an asset's worth when held in inventory, in the field of accounting. _____ is part of the Generally Accepted Accounting Principles that apply to valuing inventory, so as to not overstate or understate the value of inventory goods. Net realisable value is generally equal to the selling price of the inventory goods less the selling costs (completion and disposal).
a. Revenue recognition
c. BMC Software, Inc.
b. 3M Company
d. Net realizable value

9. An _____ is the buying of one company by another. An _____ may be friendly or hostile. In the former case, the companies cooperate in negotiations; in the latter case, the takeover target is unwilling to be bought or the target's board has no prior knowledge of the offer. _____ usually refers to a purchase of a smaller firm by a larger one. Sometimes, however, a smaller firm will acquire management control of a larger or longer established company and keep its name for the combined entity. This is known as a reverse takeover.
a. AIG
c. ABC Television Network
b. Acquisition
d. AMEX

10. _____ is a concept that denotes the precise probability of specific eventualities. Technically, the notion of _____ is independent from the notion of value and, as such, eventualities may have both beneficial and adverse consequences. However, in general usage the convention is to focus only on potential negative impact to some characteristic of value that may arise from a future event.
a. Discount factor
c. Risk
b. Discounting
d. Risk adjusted return on capital

11. In finance, _____ is the process of estimating the potential market value of a financial asset or liability. They can be done on assets (for example, investments in marketable securities such as stocks, options, business enterprises, or intangible assets such as patents and trademarks) or on liabilities (e.g., Bonds issued by a company.) A _____ is required in many contexts including investment analysis, capital budgeting, merger and acquisition transactions, financial reporting, taxable events to determine the proper tax liability, and in litigation.
a. Vyborg Appeal
c. Valuation
b. Disclosure
d. Daybook

12. A _____ is something that is acted upon or used by or by human labour or industry, for use as a building material to create some product or structure. Often the term is used to denote material that came from nature and is in an unprocessed or minimally processed state. Iron ore, logs, and crude oil, would be examples.
a. BMC Software, Inc.
c. 3M Company
b. BNSF Railway
d. Raw material

13. A _____ is the pinnacle activity involved in selling products or services in return for money or other compensation. It is an act of completion of a commercial activity.

A _____ is completed by the seller, the owner of the goods.

   a. Tertiary sector of economy
   b. Sale
   c. High yield stock
   d. Maturity

14. An _____ is a term used in behavioral economics to describe those types of behaviors that impose costs on a person in the long-run that are not taken into account when making decisions in the present. Classical Economics discourages government from creating legislation that targets internalities, because it is assumed that the consumer takes these personal costs into account when paying for the good that causes the _____. For example, cigarettes should be taxed because of the negative consumption externalities that they impose, such as second-hand smoke, not because the smoker harms him or herself by smoking.
   a. Internality
   b. Inventory turnover ratio
   c. Operating budget
   d. Authorised capital

15. The general definition of an _____ is an evaluation of a person, organization, system, process, project or product. _____s are performed to ascertain the validity and reliability of information; also to provide an assessment of a system's internal control. The goal of an _____ is to express an opinion on the person/organization/system (etc) in question, under evaluation based on work done on a test basis.
   a. Audit regime
   b. Assurance service
   c. Institute of Chartered Accountants of India
   d. Audit

16. _____ is evidence obtained during a financial audit and recorded in the audit working papers.

   - In the audit engagement acceptance or reappointment stage, _____ is the information that the auditor is to consider for the appointment. For examples, change in the entity control environment, inherent risk and nature of the entity business, and scope of audit work.

   - In the audit planning stage, _____ is the information that the auditor is to consider for the most effective and efficient audit approach. For examples, reliability of internal control procedures, and analytical review systems.

   - In the control testing stage, _____ is the information that the auditor is to consider for the mix of audit test of control and audit substantive tests.

   - In the substantive testing stage, _____ is the information that the auditor is to make sure the appropriation of financial statement assertions. For examples, existence, rights and obligations, occurrence, completeness, valuation, measurement, presentation and disclosure of a particular transaction or account balance.

   a. Audit evidence
   b. Audit
   c. ITGCs
   d. Institute of Chartered Accountants of India

Chapter 9. Production Cycle

17. In economics, business, retail, and accounting, a _____ is the value of money that has been used up to produce something, and hence is not available for use anymore. In economics, a _____ is an alternative that is given up as a result of a decision. In business, the _____ may be one of acquisition, in which case the amount of money expended to acquire it is counted as _____.
    a. Cost allocation
    b. Cost
    c. Prime cost
    d. Cost of quality

18. In management accounting, _____ establishes budget and actual cost of operations, processes, departments or product and the analysis of variances, profitability or social use of funds. Managers use _____ to support decision-making to cut a company's costs and improve profitability. As a form of management accounting, _____ need not follow standards such as GAAP, because its primary use is for internal managers, rather than outside users, and what to compute is instead decided pragmatically.
    a. Cost accounting
    b. Marginal cost
    c. Prime cost
    d. Cost-volume-profit analysis

19. In financial accounting, _____ or cost of sales includes the direct costs attributable to the production of the goods sold by a company. This amount includes the materials cost used in creating the goods along with the direct labor costs used to produce the good. It excludes indirect expenses such as distribution costs and sales force costs.
    a. FIFO and LIFO accounting
    b. 3M Company
    c. Reorder point
    d. Cost of goods sold

20. In business, _____, Overhead cost or _____ expense refers to an ongoing expense of operating a business. The term _____ is usually used to group expenses that are necessary to the continued functioning of the business, but do not directly generate profits.

    _____ expenses are all costs on the income statement except for direct labor and direct materials.

    a. Overhead
    b. ABC Television Network
    c. Intangible assets
    d. AIG

21. _____, in auditing, is the risk that a company's internal controls are insufficient to mitigate or detect errors or fraud.
    a. 3M Company
    b. BNSF Railway
    c. Control risk
    d. BMC Software, Inc.

22. In accounting and organizational theory, _____ is defined as a process effected by an organization's structure, work and authority flows, people and management information systems, designed to help the organization accomplish specific goals or objectives. It is a means by which an organization's resources are directed, monitored, and measured. It plays an important role in preventing and detecting fraud and protecting the organization's resources, both physical (e.g., machinery and property) and intangible (e.g., reputation or intellectual property such as trademarks.)
    a. Audit risk
    b. Auditor independence
    c. Internal control
    d. Audit committee

23. _____ is a step in a risk management process. _____ is the determination of quantitative or qualitative value of risk related to a concrete situation and a recognized threat (also called hazard.) Quantitative _____ requires calculations of two components of risk: R, the magnitude of the potential loss L, and the probability p that the loss will occur.

a. BNSF Railway
b. Risk assessment
c. 3M Company
d. BMC Software, Inc.

24. In business and accounting, _____ are everything of value that is owned by a person or company. It is a claim on the property your income of a borrower. The balance sheet of a firm records the monetary value of the _____ owned by the firm.

a. Accrual basis accounting
b. Accounts receivable
c. Earnings before interest, taxes, depreciation and amortization
d. Assets

25. _____ is a specific term used in companies' financial reporting from the company-whole point of view. Because that use excludes the effects of changing ownership interest, an economic measure of _____ is necessary for financial analysis from the shareholders' point of view

_____ is defined by the Financial Accounting Standards Board, or FASB, as 'the change in equity [net assets] of a business enterprise during a period from transactions and other events and circumstances from nonowner sources. It includes all changes in equity during a period except those resulting from investments by owners and distributions to owners.'

_____ is the sum of net income and other items that must bypass the income statement because they have not been realized, including items like an unrealized holding gain or loss from available for sale securities and foreign currency translation gains or losses.

a. 3M Company
b. BMC Software, Inc.
c. BNSF Railway
d. Comprehensive income

26. _____ are the earnings returned on the initial investment amount.

In the US, the Financial Accounting Standards Board (FASB) requires companies' income statements to report _____ for each of the major categories of the income statement: continuing operations, discontinued operations, extraordinary items, and net income.

The _____ formula does not include preferred dividends for categories outside of continued operations and net income.

a. Earnings per share
b. Earnings yield
c. Invested capital
d. Average accounting return

27. _____s are goods that have completed the manufacturing process but have not yet been sold or distributed to the end user.

Chapter 9. Production Cycle

Manufacturing has three classes of inventory:

1. Raw material
2. Work in process
3. _____s

A good purchased as a 'raw material' goes into the manufacture of a product. A good only partially completed during the manufacturing process is called 'work in process'. When the good is completed as to manufacturing but not yet sold or distributed to the end-user is called a '_____'.

a. 3M Company
c. Finished good
b. Reorder point
d. FIFO and LIFO accounting

28. The _____ is the national, professional association of CPAs in the United States, with more than 330,000 members, including CPAs in business and industry, public practice, government, and education; student affiliates; and international associates. It sets ethical standards for the profession and U.S. auditing standards for audits of private companies; federal, state and local governments; and non-profit organizations.

Approximately 40% of its members are engaged in the practice of public accounting, in areas such as auditing, accounting, taxation, general business consulting, business valuation, personal financial planning and business technology.

a. Other postemployment benefits
c. AIG
b. American Institute of Certified Public Accountants
d. ABC Television Network

29. _____, commonly abbreviated as SAS, provide guidance to external auditors on generally accepted auditing standards in regards to auditing an entity and issuing a report. They are usually issued by the certified public accountant authoritative body in the region where the standards apply, such as the American Institute of Certified Public Accountants in the United States.

- _____
- _____ (Taiwan)

a. GASB 45
c. Financial Instruments and Exchange Law
b. RSM International
d. Statements on Auditing Standards

30. _____ is one of financial audit skill which help an auditor understand the client's business and changes in the business, to identify potential risk areas and to plan other audit procedures.

Chapter 9. Production Cycle

_____ include comparison of financial information (data in financial statement) with

1. prior periods
2. budgets
3. forecasts
4. similar industries and so on.

It also includes consideration of predictable relationships, such as:

1. gross profit to sales,
2. payroll costs to employees,
3. financial information and non-financial information, for examples the CEO's reports and the industry news.

possible sources of information about the client include:

1. interim financial information
2. Budgets
3. Management accounts
4. Non-Financial information
5. Bank and cash records
6. VAT returns
7. Board minutes
8. Discussion or correspondance with the client at they year-end

a. Assurance service

c. External auditor

b. International Federation of Audit Bureaux of Circulations

d. Analytical procedures

31. _____, Gross profit margin or Gross Profit Rate can be defined as the amount of contribution to the business enterprise, after paying for direct-fixed and direct-variable unit costs, required to cover overheads (fixed commitments) and provide a buffer for unknown items. It expresses the relationship between gross profit and sales revenue.

It can be expressed in absolute terms:

Gross Profit = Revenue − Cost of Goods Sold

or as the ratio of gross profit to sales revenue, usually in the form of a percentage:

_____ Percentage = (Revenue-Cost of Goods Sold)/Revenue

Cost of goods sold includes variable costs and fixed costs directly linked to the product, such as material and labor.

Chapter 9. Production Cycle

a. Gross margin
b. BMC Software, Inc.
c. 3M Company
d. BNSF Railway

32. The _____ is an equation that equals the cost of goods sold divided by the average inventory. Average inventory equals beginning inventory plus ending inventory divided by 2.

The formula for _____:

$$\text{Inventory Turnover} = \frac{\text{Cost of Goods Sold}}{\text{Average Inventory}}$$

The formula for average inventory:

$$\text{Average Inventory} = \frac{\text{Beginning inventory} + \text{Ending inventory}}{2}$$

A low turnover rate may point to overstocking, obsolescence, or deficiencies in the product line or marketing effort.

a. Inventory turnover
b. Enterprise Value/Sales
c. Earnings per share
d. Upside potential ratio

33. _____ is one of the Accounting Liquidity ratios, a financial ratio. This ratio measures the number of times, on average, the inventory is sold during the period. Its purpose is to measure the liquidity of the inventory.
   a. ABC Television Network
   b. Ending inventory
   c. Inventory turnover ratio
   d. AIG

34. The term '_____' refers to the concept of collecting information and attempting to spot a pattern in the information. In some fields of study, the term '_____' has more formally-defined meanings.

In project management _____ is a mathematical technique that uses historical results to predict future outcome.

a. Multicollinearity
b. 3M Company
c. Regression analysis
d. Trend analysis

35. _____ is a process where a business physically counts its entire inventory. A _____ may be mandated by financial accounting rules or the tax regulations to place an accurate value on the inventory, or the business may need to count inventory so component parts or raw materials can be restocked. Businesses may use several different tactics to minimize the disruption caused by _____.
   a. BNSF Railway
   b. Physical inventory
   c. 3M Company
   d. BMC Software, Inc.

36. _____ is one of the four Ps of the marketing mix. The other three aspects are product, promotion, and place. It is also a key variable in microeconomic price allocation theory.
   a. Target costing
   b. Price
   c. Cost-plus pricing
   d. Pricing

37. _____ means the giving out of information, either voluntarily or to be in compliance with legal regulations or workplace rules.

   - In Computer security, full _____ means disclosing full information about vulnerabilities.
   - In computing, _____ widget
   - Journalism, full _____ refers to disclosing the interests of the writer which may bear on the subject being written about, for example, if the writer has worked with an interview subject in the past.

   - In law:
     - The law of England and Wales, _____ refers to a process that may form part of legal proceedings, whereby parties inform to other parties the existence of any relevant documents that are, or have been, in their control. This compares with the process known as discovery in the course of legal proceedings in the United States.
     - In U.S. civil procedure (litigation rules for civil cases), _____ is a stage prior to trial. In civil cases, each party must disclose to the opposing party the following: names of witnesses which it may use to support its side, copies of documents (or mere description of these documents) in its control which it may use to support its side, computation of damages claimed, and certain insurance information. _____ is related to, but technically prior to, the discovery stage.
     - In Company law (known as 'corporate law' in the United States), _____ refers to giving out information about public or limited companies or their officers, which might be kept secret if the company was a private company or a partnership.

   - In real property transactions, _____ refers to providing to a buyer information known to the seller or broker/agent concerning the condition or other aspects of real property that would affect the property's value or desirability. These rules regarding what information must be disclosed, and whether the information must be disclosed even if a buyer does not ask, vary from one jurisdiction to the next.

   a. Trailing
   b. Tax harmonisation
   c. Controlled Foreign Corporations
   d. Disclosure

38. _____ is a term that is commonly used in relation to the audit of the financial statements of an entity. (.
   a. Audit working paper
   b. Engagement Letter
   c. Auditor independence
   d. Audit risk

Chapter 10. Finance and Investment Cycle

1. _____ LLP, based in Chicago, was once one of the 'Big Five' accounting firms among PricewaterhouseCoopers, Deloitte Touche Tohmatsu, Ernst ' Young and KPMG, providing auditing, tax, and consulting services to large corporations. In 2002, the firm voluntarily surrendered its licenses to practice as Certified Public Accountants in the United States after being found guilty of criminal charges relating to the firm's handling of the auditing of Enron, the energy corporation, resulting in the loss of 85,000 jobs. Although the verdict was subsequently overturned by the Supreme Court of the United States, it has not returned as a viable business.
   a. ABC Television Network
   b. Arthur Andersen
   c. AIG
   d. AMEX

2. The _____ is the highest judicial body in the United States, and leads the federal judiciary. It consists of the Chief Justice of the United States and eight Associate Justices, who are nominated by the President and confirmed with the 'advice and consent' (majority vote) of the Senate. Once appointed, Justices effectively have life tenure, serving 'during good Behaviour', which terminates only upon death, resignation, retirement, or conviction on impeachment.
   a. Supreme Court of the United States
   b. BNSF Railway
   c. 3M Company
   d. BMC Software, Inc.

3. The Federal National Mortgage Association (FNMA) (NYSE: FNM), commonly known as _____, is a stockholder-owned corporation chartered by Congress in 1968 as a government sponsored enterprise (GSE), but founded in 1938 during the Great Depression. The corporation's purpose is to purchase and securitize mortgages in order to ensure that funds are consistently available to the institutions that lend money to home buyers.

   On September 7, 2008, James Lockhart, director of the Federal Housing Finance Agency (FHFA), announced that _____ and Freddie Mac were being placed into conservatorship of the FHFA.

   a. Fannie Mae
   b. Freddie Mac
   c. National Conference of Commissioners on Uniform State Laws
   d. Public company

4. The Federal Home Loan Mortgage Corporation (FHLMC) (NYSE: FRE) is an insolvent government sponsored enterprise (GSE) of the United States federal government.

   The FHLMC was created in 1970 to expand the secondary market for mortgages in the US. Along with other GSEs, _____ buys mortgages on the secondary market, pools them, and sells them as mortgage-backed securities to investors on the open market.

   a. Freddie Mac
   b. Butterfield Bank
   c. Limited liability partnership
   d. MicroStrategy

5. A _____ is the transfer of an interest in property (or the equivalent in law - a charge) to a lender as a security for a debt - usually a loan of money. While a _____ in itself is not a debt, it is the lender's security for a debt. It is a transfer of an interest in land (or the equivalent) from the owner to the _____ lender, on the condition that this interest will be returned to the owner when the terms of the _____ have been satisfied or performed.
   a. BMC Software, Inc.
   b. BNSF Railway
   c. 3M Company
   d. Mortgage

6. _____ is a concept that denotes the precise probability of specific eventualities. Technically, the notion of _____ is independent from the notion of value and, as such, eventualities may have both beneficial and adverse consequences. However, in general usage the convention is to focus only on potential negative impact to some characteristic of value that may arise from a future event.

   a. Risk
   c. Discounting
   b. Risk adjusted return on capital
   d. Discount factor

7. _____ are ten auditing standards, developed by the AICPA, consisting of general standards, standards of field work, and standards of reporting, along with interpretations. They were developed by the AICPA in 1947 and have undergone minor changes since then.

The _____ are as follows:

1. The auditor must have adequate technical training and proficiency to perform the audit
2. The auditor must maintain independence in mental attitude in all matters related to the audit.
3. The auditor must use due professional care during the performance of the audit and the preparation of the report.

1. The auditor must adequately plan the work and must properly supervise any assistants.
2. The auditor must obtain a sufficient understanding of the entity and its environment, including its internal control, to assess the risk of material misstatement of the financial statements whether due to error or fraud, and to design the nature, timing, and extent of further audit procedures.
3. The auditor must obtain sufficient appropriate audit evidence by performing audit procedures to afford a reasonable basis for an opinion regarding the financial statements under audit.

The new standards are in effect for audits of financial statements for periods beginning on or after December 15, 2006.

1. The auditor must state in the auditor's report whether the financial statements are in accordance with generally accepted accounting principles (GAAP.)
2. The auditor must identify in the auditor's report those circumstances in which such principles have not been consistently observed in the current period in relation to the preceding period.
3. When the auditor determines that informative disclosures are not reasonably adequate, the auditor must so state in the auditor's report.
4. The auditor must either express an opinion regarding the financial statements, taken as a whole the auditor should state the reasons therefore in the auditor's report. In all cases where the auditor's name is associated with the financial statements, the auditor should clearly indicate the character of the auditor's work, if any, and the degree of responsibility the auditor is taking, in the auditor's report.

   a. Negative assurance
   c. Joint audit
   b. Generally accepted auditing standards
   d. Continuous auditing

8. _____, in auditing, is the risk that the account or section being audited is materially misstated without considering internal controls due to error; _____ does not include an assessment of the risk of material misstatement due to fraud. The assessment of _____ depends on the professional judgement of the auditor, and it is done after assessing the business environment of the entity being audited.

_____ is typically assessed using a scale, with assessments being either low, medium, or high.

   a. ABC Television Network   b. AMEX
   c. AIG   d. Inherent risk

9. A _____ is a contract conferring a right on one person to possess property belonging to another person (called a landlord or lessor) to the exclusion of the owner landlord. It is a rental agreement between landlord and tenant. The relationship between the tenant and the landlord is called a tenancy, and the right to possession by the tenant is sometimes called a leasehold interest.

   a. Lease   b. Model Code of Professional Responsibility
   c. Robinson-Patman Act   d. Federal Sentencing Guidelines

10. A _____ is a type of debt Like all debt instruments, a _____ entails the redistribution of financial assets over time, between the lender and the borrower.

   a. Lender   b. Loan to value
   c. Loan   d. Debenture

11. An _____ is the buying of one company by another. An _____ may be friendly or hostile. In the former case, the companies cooperate in negotiations; in the latter case, the takeover target is unwilling to be bought or the target's board has no prior knowledge of the offer. _____ usually refers to a purchase of a smaller firm by a larger one. Sometimes, however, a smaller firm will acquire management control of a larger or longer established company and keep its name for the combined entity. This is known as a reverse takeover.

   a. ABC Television Network   b. AMEX
   c. AIG   d. Acquisition

12. Title _____s serve as guarantees to the recipient of property, ensuring that the recipient receives what he or she bargained for. The English _____s of title, sometimes included in deeds to real property, are that the grantor is lawfully seized (in fee simple) of the property, (2) that the grantor has the right to convey the property to the grantee, (3) that the property is conveyed without encumbrances (this _____ is frequently modified to allow for certain encumbrances), (4) that the grantor has done no act to encumber the property, (5) that the grantee shall have quiet possession of the property, and (6) that the grantor will execute such further assurances of the land as may be requisite (Nos. 3 and 4, which overlap significantly, are sometimes treated as one item.)

   a. Liability   b. Tax patent
   c. Patent   d. Covenant

13. _____ is the acquisition of goods and/or services at the best possible total cost of ownership, in the right quantity and quality, at the right time, in the right place and from the right source for the direct benefit or use of corporations or individuals, generally via a contract. Simple _____ may involve nothing more than repeat purchasing. Complex _____ could involve finding long term partners - or even 'co-destiny' suppliers that might fundamentally commit one organization to another.

a. Customer satisfaction
b. Time to market
c. Free cash flow
d. Procurement

14. _____ means the giving out of information, either voluntarily or to be in compliance with legal regulations or workplace rules.

- In Computer security, full _____ means disclosing full information about vulnerabilities.
- In computing, _____ widget
- Journalism, full _____ refers to disclosing the interests of the writer which may bear on the subject being written about, for example, if the writer has worked with an interview subject in the past.

- In law:
    - The law of England and Wales, _____ refers to a process that may form part of legal proceedings, whereby parties inform to other parties the existence of any relevant documents that are, or have been, in their control. This compares with the process known as discovery in the course of legal proceedings in the United States.
    - In U.S. civil procedure (litigation rules for civil cases), _____ is a stage prior to trial. In civil cases, each party must disclose to the opposing party the following: names of witnesses which it may use to support its side, copies of documents (or mere description of these documents) in its control which it may use to support its side, computation of damages claimed, and certain insurance information. _____ is related to, but technically prior to, the discovery stage.
    - In Company law (known as 'corporate law' in the United States), _____ refers to giving out information about public or limited companies or their officers, which might be kept secret if the company was a private company or a partnership.

- In real property transactions, _____ refers to providing to a buyer information known to the seller or broker/agent concerning the condition or other aspects of real property that would affect the property's value or desirability. These rules regarding what information must be disclosed, and whether the information must be disclosed even if a buyer does not ask, vary from one jurisdiction to the next.

a. Controlled Foreign Corporations
b. Trailing
c. Tax harmonisation
d. Disclosure

15. An _____ is a tax levied on the financial income of people, corporations, or other legal entities. Various _____ systems exist, with varying degrees of tax incidence. Income taxation can be progressive, proportional, or regressive.
a. Individual Retirement Arrangement
b. Ordinary income
c. Implied level of government service
d. Income tax

16. The general definition of an _____ is an evaluation of a person, organization, system, process, project or product. _____s are performed to ascertain the validity and reliability of information; also to provide an assessment of a system's internal control. The goal of an _____ is to express an opinion on the person/organization/system (etc) in question, under evaluation based on work done on a test basis.
a. Institute of Chartered Accountants of India
b. Audit regime
c. Assurance service
d. Audit

Chapter 10. Finance and Investment Cycle

17. A _____ is a fungible, negotiable instrument representing financial value. they are broadly categorized into debt securities (such as banknotes, bonds and debentures), and equity securities; e.g., common stocks. The company or other entity issuing the _____ is called the issuer.
    a. BMC Software, Inc.
    b. Security
    c. 3M Company
    d. Tracking stock

18. In economics, _____ or _____ goods or real _____ refers to factors of production used to create goods or services that are not themselves significantly consumed (though they may depreciate) in the production process. _____ goods may be acquired with money or financial _____. In finance and accounting, _____ generally refers to financial wealth, especially that used to start or maintain a business.
    a. Screening
    b. Capital
    c. Vyborg Appeal
    d. Disclosure

19. _____ is that which is owed; usually referencing assets owed, but the term can also cover moral obligations and other interactions not requiring money. In the case of assets, _____ is a means of using future purchasing power in the present before a summation has been earned. Some companies and corporations use _____ as a part of their overall corporate finance strategy.
    a. Lender
    b. Debt
    c. Debenture
    d. Loan

20. In financial accounting, a _____ is defined as an obligation of an entity arising from past transactions or events, the settlement of which may result in the transfer or use of assets, provision of services or other yielding of economic benefits in the future.
    a. Liability
    b. Vested
    c. Corporate governance
    d. False Claims Act

21. In economic models, the _____ time frame assumes no fixed factors of production. Firms can enter or leave the marketplace, and the cost (and availability) of land, labor, raw materials, and capital goods can be assumed to vary. In contrast, in the short-run time frame, certain factors are assumed to be fixed, because there is not sufficient time for them to change.
    a. BMC Software, Inc.
    b. 3M Company
    c. Short-run
    d. Long-run

22. _____ are liabilities with a future benefit over one year, such as notes payable that mature greater than one year.

In accounting, the _____ are shown on the right wing of the balance-sheet representing the sources of funds, which are generally bounded in form of capital assets.

Examples of _____ are debentures, mortgage loans and other bank loans (note: not all bank loans are long term as not all are paid over a period greater than a year, the example is bridging loan.)

   a. Gross sales
   b. Long-term liabilities
   c. Cash basis accounting
   d. Book value

Chapter 10. Finance and Investment Cycle

23. Companies that have publicly traded securities typically use _____s to keep track of the individuals and entities that own their stocks and bonds. Most _____s are banks or trust companies, but sometimes a company acts as its own _____.

_____s perform three main functions:

1. Issue and cancel certificates to reflect changes in ownership. For example, when a company declares a stock dividend or stock split, the _____ issues new shares. _____s keep records of who owns a company's stocks and bonds and how those stocks and bonds are held--whether by the owner in certificate form, by the company in book-entry form, or by the investor's brokerage firm in street name. They also keep records of how many shares or bonds each investor owns.
2. Act as an intermediary for the company. A _____ may also serve as the company's paying agent to pay out interest, cash and stock dividends, or other distributions to stock- and bondholders. In addition, _____s act as proxy agent (sending out proxy materials), exchange agent (exchanging a company's stock or bonds in a merger), tender agent (tendering shares in a tender offer), and mailing agent (mailing the company's quarterly, annual, and other reports.)
3. Handle lost, destroyed, or stolen certificates. _____s help shareholders and bondholders when a stock or bond certificate has been lost, destroyed, or stolen.

In many cases, you can find out which _____ a company uses by visiting the investor relations section of the companye;s website.

   a. Transfer agent   b. Financial market
   c. Mark-to-market   d. Market price

24. A _____ is a bond which is worth a certain monetary value and which may only be spent for specific reasons or on specific goods. Examples include -- but are not limited to -- housing, travel and food _____s. The term _____ is also a synonym for receipt, and is often used to refer to receipts used as evidence of, for example, the declaration that a service has been performed or that an expenditure has been made.

   a. BMC Software, Inc.   b. 3M Company
   c. Voucher   d. Source document

25. _____ is a legal term that refers to a holder of property on behalf of a beneficiary. A trust can be set up either to benefit particular persons, or for any charitable purposes (but not generally for non-charitable purposes): typical examples are a will trust for the testator's children and family, a pension trust (to confer benefits on employees and their families), and a charitable trust. In all cases, the _____ may be a person or company, whether or not they are a prospective beneficiary.

   a. Cash cow   b. Performance measurement
   c. Trustee   d. Management by exception

26. _____ is one of a series of accounting transactions dealing with the billing of customers who owe money to a person, company or organization for goods and services that have been provided to the customer. In most business entities this is typically done by generating an invoice and mailing or electronically delivering it to the customer, who in turn must pay it within an established timeframe called credit or payment terms.

An example of a common payment term is Net 30, meaning payment is due in the amount of the invoice 30 days from the date of invoice.

a. Accrued revenue
b. Adjusting entries
c. Accrual
d. Accounts receivable

27. In business and accounting, _____ are everything of value that is owned by a person or company. It is a claim on the property your income of a borrower. The balance sheet of a firm records the monetary value of the _____ owned by the firm.

a. Earnings before interest, taxes, depreciation and amortization
b. Accounts receivable
c. Accrual basis accounting
d. Assets

28. _____ are defined as identifiable non-monetary assets that cannot be seen, touched or physically measured, which are created through time and/or effort and that are identifiable as a separate asset. There are two primary forms of intangibles - legal intangibles (such as trade secrets (e.g., customer lists), copyrights, patents, trademarks, and goodwill) and competitive intangibles (such as knowledge activities (know-how, knowledge), collaboration activities, leverage activities, and structural activities.) Legal intangibles are known under the generic term intellectual property and generate legal property rights defensible in a court of law.

a. Overhead
b. AIG
c. ABC Television Network
d. Intangible assets

29. A _____ is a set of exclusive rights granted by a state to an inventor or his assignee for a limited period of time in exchange for a disclosure of an invention.

The procedure for granting _____s, the requirements placed on the _____ee and the extent of the exclusive rights vary widely between countries according to national laws and international agreements. Typically, however, a _____ application must include one or more claims defining the invention which must be new, inventive, and useful or industrially applicable.

a. Negligence
b. FLSA
c. Trust indenture
d. Patent

30. A _____ or trade mark, identified by the symbols â„¢ (not yet registered) and Â® (registered), is a distinctive sign or indicator used by an individual, business organization or other legal entity to identify that the products and/or services to consumers with which the _____ appears originate from a unique source, and to distinguish its products or services from those of other entities. A _____ is a type of intellectual property, and typically a name, word, phrase, logo, symbol, design, image, or a combination of these elements. There is also a range of non-conventional _____s comprising marks which do not fall into these standard categories.

a. Kanban
b. FIFO
c. Trademark
d. Risk management

31. _____, in auditing, is the risk that a company's internal controls are insufficient to mitigate or detect errors or fraud.

a. 3M Company
c. BMC Software, Inc.
b. BNSF Railway
d. Control risk

32. An _____ is a term used in behavioral economics to describe those types of behaviors that impose costs on a person in the long-run that are not taken into account when making decisions in the present. Classical Economics discourages government from creating legislation that targets internalities, because it is assumed that the consumer takes these personal costs into account when paying for the good that causes the _____. For example, cigarettes should be taxed because of the negative consumption externalities that they impose, such as second-hand smoke, not because the smoker harms him or herself by smoking.
   a. Authorised capital
   c. Internality
   b. Inventory turnover ratio
   d. Operating budget

33. In accounting and organizational theory, _____ is defined as a process effected by an organization's structure, work and authority flows, people and management information systems, designed to help the organization accomplish specific goals or objectives. It is a means by which an organization's resources are directed, monitored, and measured. It plays an important role in preventing and detecting fraud and protecting the organization's resources, both physical (e.g., machinery and property) and intangible (e.g., reputation or intellectual property such as trademarks.)
   a. Auditor independence
   c. Internal control
   b. Audit risk
   d. Audit committee

34. _____ is a step in a risk management process. _____ is the determination of quantitative or qualitative value of risk related to a concrete situation and a recognized threat (also called hazard.) Quantitative _____ requires calculations of two components of risk: R, the magnitude of the potential loss L, and the probability p that the loss will occur.
   a. BMC Software, Inc.
   c. BNSF Railway
   b. 3M Company
   d. Risk assessment

35. _____ is the calculated approximation of a result which is usable even if input data may be incomplete or uncertain.

In statistics, see _____ theory, estimator.

In mathematics, approximation or _____ typically means finding upper or lower bounds of a quantity that cannot readily be computed precisely and is also an educated guess .

   a. AMEX
   c. Estimation
   b. ABC Television Network
   d. AIG

36. An _____ is quite usually a standard guarantee from the seller of a product that specifies the extent to which the quality or performance of the product is assured and states the conditions under which the product can be returned, replaced, or repaired. It is often given in the form of a specific, written 'Warranty' document. However, a warranty may also arise by operation of law based upon the seller's description of the goods, and perhaps their source and quality, and any material deviation from that specification would violate the guarantee.
   a. Escheat
   c. Express warranty
   b. Operating Lease
   d. Exclusive right

Chapter 10. Finance and Investment Cycle

37. A _____ has several related meanings:

- a daily record of events or business; a private _____ is usually referred to as a diary.
- a newspaper or other periodical, in the literal sense of one published each day;
- many publications issued at stated intervals, such as magazines, or scholarly academic _____s, or the record of the transactions of a society, are often called _____s. Although _____ is sometimes used, erroneously, as a synonym for 'magazine,' in academic use, a _____ refers to a serious, scholarly publication, most often peer-reviewed. A non-scholarly magazine written for an educated audience about an industry or an area of professional activity is usually called a professional magazine.

The word 'journalist' for one whose business is writing for the public press has been in use since the end of the 17th century.

Open access _____s are scholarly _____s that are available to the reader without financial or other barrier other than access to the internet itself. Some are subsidized, and some require payment on behalf of the author. Subsidized _____s are financed by an academic institution or a government information center.

a. BMC Software, Inc.
b. Journal
c. 3M Company
d. BNSF Railway

38. _____ is that part of statistical practice concerned with the selection of individual observations intended to yield some knowledge about a population of concern, especially for the purposes of statistical inference. Each observation measures one or more properties (weight, location, etc.) of an observable entity enumerated to distinguish objects or individuals.
a. Abby Joseph Cohen
b. Arthur Betz Laffer
c. Alan Greenspan
d. Sampling

39. In finance, _____ is the process of estimating the potential market value of a financial asset or liability. They can be done on assets (for example, investments in marketable securities such as stocks, options, business enterprises, or intangible assets such as patents and trademarks) or on liabilities (e.g., Bonds issued by a company.) A _____ is required in many contexts including investment analysis, capital budgeting, merger and acquisition transactions, financial reporting, taxable events to determine the proper tax liability, and in litigation.
a. Valuation
b. Disclosure
c. Daybook
d. Vyborg Appeal

40. _____ are payments made by a corporation to its shareholder members. It is the portion of corporate profits paid out to stockholders. When a corporation earns a profit or surplus, that money can be put to two uses: it can either be re-invested in the business (called retained earnings), or it can be paid to the shareholders as a dividend.
a. Dividends
b. Dividend stripping
c. Dividend yield
d. Dividend payout ratio

Chapter 10. Finance and Investment Cycle

41. _____, also called fair price (in a commonplace conflation of the two distinct concepts), is a concept used in finance and economics, defined as a rational and unbiased estimate of the potential market price of a good, service, or asset, taking into account such objective factors as:

- acquisition/production/distribution costs, replacement costs, or costs of close substitutes
- actual utility at a given level of development of social productive capability
- supply vs. demand

and subjective factors such as

- risk characteristics
- cost of capital
- individually perceived utility

In accounting, _____ is used as an estimate of the market value of an asset (or liability) for which a market price cannot be determined (usually because there is no established market for the asset.) Under GAAP (FAS 157), _____ is the amount at which the asset could be bought or sold in a current transaction between willing parties, or transferred to an equivalent party, other than in a liquidation sale. This is used for assets whose carrying value is based on mark-to-market valuations; for assets carried at historical cost, the _____ of the asset is not used. One example of where _____ is an issue is a College kitchen with a cost of $2 million which was built 5 years ago.

a. BNSF Railway
c. Fair value
b. BMC Software, Inc.
d. 3M Company

42. _____, also known as property, plant, and equipment (PP&E), is a term used in accountancy for assets and property which cannot easily be converted into cash. This can be compared with current assets such as cash or bank accounts, which are described as liquid assets. In most cases, only tangible assets are referred to as fixed.
a. Bankruptcy prediction
c. Subledger
b. Minority interest
d. Fixed asset

Chapter 11. Completing the Audit

1. The _____ (sometimes called 'Peekaboo') is a private-sector, non-profit corporation created by the Sarbanes-Oxley Act, a 2002 United States federal law, to oversee the auditors of public companies. Its stated purpose is to 'protect the interests of investors and further the public interest in the preparation of informative, fair, and independent audit reports'. Although a private entity, the _____ has many government-like regulatory functions, making it in some ways similar to the private Self Regulatory Organizations (SROs) that regulate stock markets and other aspects of the financial markets in the United States.
   a. 3M Company
   b. Financial Crimes Enforcement Network
   c. Pension Benefit Guaranty Corporation
   d. Public Company Accounting Oversight Board

2. The term _____ usually refers to a company that is permitted to offer its registered securities (stock, bonds, etc.) for sale to the general public, typically through a stock exchange, or occasionally a company whose stock is traded over the counter (OTC) via market makers who use non-exchange quotation services.

   The term '_____' may also refer to a company owned by the government.

   a. Governmental Accounting Standards Board
   b. MicroStrategy
   c. Professional association
   d. Public Company

3. An _____ is the buying of one company by another. An _____ may be friendly or hostile. In the former case, the companies cooperate in negotiations; in the latter case, the takeover target is unwilling to be bought or the target's board has no prior knowledge of the offer. _____ usually refers to a purchase of a smaller firm by a larger one. Sometimes, however, a smaller firm will acquire management control of a larger or longer established company and keep its name for the combined entity. This is known as a reverse takeover.
   a. AMEX
   b. AIG
   c. ABC Television Network
   d. Acquisition

4. An _____ is a term used in behavioral economics to describe those types of behaviors that impose costs on a person in the long-run that are not taken into account when making decisions in the present. Classical Economics discourages government from creating legislation that targets internalities, because it is assumed that the consumer takes these personal costs into account when paying for the good that causes the _____. For example, cigarettes should be taxed because of the negative consumption externalities that they impose, such as second-hand smoke, not because the smoker harms him or herself by smoking.
   a. Internality
   b. Inventory turnover ratio
   c. Operating budget
   d. Authorised capital

5. In accounting and organizational theory, _____ is defined as a process effected by an organization's structure, work and authority flows, people and management information systems, designed to help the organization accomplish specific goals or objectives. It is a means by which an organization's resources are directed, monitored, and measured. It plays an important role in preventing and detecting fraud and protecting the organization's resources, both physical (e.g., machinery and property) and intangible (e.g., reputation or intellectual property such as trademarks.)
   a. Internal control
   b. Audit risk
   c. Auditor independence
   d. Audit committee

6. The general definition of an _____ is an evaluation of a person, organization, system, process, project or product. _____s are performed to ascertain the validity and reliability of information; also to provide an assessment of a system's internal control. The goal of an _____ is to express an opinion on the person/organization/system (etc) in question, under evaluation based on work done on a test basis.

Chapter 11. Completing the Audit

a. Assurance service
c. Institute of Chartered Accountants of India
b. Audit regime
d. Audit

7. In accounting, _____ has a very specific meaning. It is an outflow of cash or other valuable assets from a person or company to another person or company. This outflow of cash is generally one side of a trade for products or services that have equal or better current or future value to the buyer than to the seller.
   a. AMEX
   c. ABC Television Network
   b. Expense
   d. AIG

8. A _____ is an annual report required by the U.S. Securities and Exchange Commission (SEC), that gives a comprehensive summary of a public company's performance. Although similarly named, the annual report on _____ is distinct from the often glossy 'annual report to shareholders', which a company must send to its shareholders when it holds an annual meeting to elect directors (though some companies combine the annual report and the 10-K into one document.) The 10-K includes information such as company history, organizational structure, executive compensation, equity, subsidiaries, and audited financial statements, among other information.
   a. Form 8-K
   c. Form 10-K
   b. Form 10-Q
   d. 3M Company

9. _____ that may or may not be incurred by an entity depending on the outcome of a future event such as a court case. These liabilities are recorded in a company's accounts and shown in the balance sheet when both probable and reasonably estimable. A footnote to the balance sheet describes the nature and extent of the _____.
   a. Nonacquiescence
   c. Headnote
   b. Tangible
   d. Contingent liabilities

10. The _____ is the United States federal government agency that collects taxes and enforces the internal revenue laws. It is an agency within the U.S. Dept of the treasury responsible for interpretation and application of Federal tax law. The official U.S. Treasury regulations provide (in part):

The _____ is a bureau of the Department of the Treasury under the immediate direction of the Commissioner of Internal Revenue.

   a. Indirect tax
   c. Income tax
   b. Use tax
   d. Internal Revenue Service

11. In financial accounting, a _____ is defined as an obligation of an entity arising from past transactions or events, the settlement of which may result in the transfer or use of assets, provision of services or other yielding of economic benefits in the future.
   a. False Claims Act
   c. Corporate governance
   b. Liability
   d. Vested

12. _____ are ten auditing standards, developed by the AICPA, consisting of general standards, standards of field work, and standards of reporting, along with interpretations. They were developed by the AICPA in 1947 and have undergone minor changes since then.

Chapter 11. Completing the Audit

The _____ are as follows:

1. The auditor must have adequate technical training and proficiency to perform the audit
2. The auditor must maintain independence in mental attitude in all matters related to the audit.
3. The auditor must use due professional care during the performance of the audit and the preparation of the report.

1. The auditor must adequately plan the work and must properly supervise any assistants.
2. The auditor must obtain a sufficient understanding of the entity and its environment, including its internal control, to assess the risk of material misstatement of the financial statements whether due to error or fraud, and to design the nature, timing, and extent of further audit procedures.
3. The auditor must obtain sufficient appropriate audit evidence by performing audit procedures to afford a reasonable basis for an opinion regarding the financial statements under audit.

The new standards are in effect for audits of financial statements for periods beginning on or after December 15, 2006.

1. The auditor must state in the auditor's report whether the financial statements are in accordance with generally accepted accounting principles (GAAP.)
2. The auditor must identify in the auditor's report those circumstances in which such principles have not been consistently observed in the current period in relation to the preceding period.
3. When the auditor determines that informative disclosures are not reasonably adequate, the auditor must so state in the auditor's report.
4. The auditor must either express an opinion regarding the financial statements, taken as a whole the auditor should state the reasons therefore in the auditor's report. In all cases where the auditor's name is associated with the financial statements, the auditor should clearly indicate the character of the auditor's work, if any, and the degree of responsibility the auditor is taking, in the auditor's report.

a. Negative assurance
b. Joint audit
c. Continuous auditing
d. Generally accepted auditing standards

13. A _____ or chief executive is one of the highest-ranking corporate officer (executive) or administrator in charge of total management. An individual selected as President and _____ of a corporation, company, organization, or agency, reports to the board of directors. In internal communication and press releases, many companies capitalize the term and those of other high positions, even when they are not proper nouns.
a. Kohlberg Kravis Roberts ' Co
b. Return on assets
c. Return on equity
d. Chief executive officer

14. _____ is a letter issued by an auditor's client to the auditor in writing as one of audit evidences. The date of the document must not be later than the date of audit work completion. It is used to let the client's management declare in writing that the financial statements and other presentations to the auditor are sufficient and appropriate and without omission of material facts to the financial statements, to the best of the management's knowledge.

Chapter 11. Completing the Audit

a. Management assertions
b. Joint audit
c. Statements on Auditing Standards
d. Management representation

15. _____ refers to the confirmation of certain characteristics of an object, person, or organization. This confirmation is often, but not always, provided by some form of external review, education, or assessment. One of the most common types of _____ in modern society is professional _____, where a person is certified as being able to competently complete a job or task, usually by the passing of an examination.

a. BMC Software, Inc.
b. BNSF Railway
c. 3M Company
d. Certification

16. A _____ has several related meanings:

- a daily record of events or business; a private _____ is usually referred to as a diary.
- a newspaper or other periodical, in the literal sense of one published each day;
- many publications issued at stated intervals, such as magazines, or scholarly academic _____s, or the record of the transactions of a society, are often called _____s. Although _____ is sometimes used, erroneously, as a synonym for 'magazine,' in academic use, a _____ refers to a serious, scholarly publication, most often peer-reviewed. A non-scholarly magazine written for an educated audience about an industry or an area of professional activity is usually called a professional magazine.

The word 'journalist' for one whose business is writing for the public press has been in use since the end of the 17th century.

Open access _____s are scholarly _____s that are available to the reader without financial or other barrier other than access to the internet itself. Some are subsidized, and some require payment on behalf of the author. Subsidized _____s are financed by an academic institution or a government information center.

a. BNSF Railway
b. BMC Software, Inc.
c. Journal
d. 3M Company

17. _____ are formal records of a business' financial activities.

In British English, including United Kingdom company law, _____ are often referred to as accounts, although the term _____ is also used, particularly by accountants.

_____ provide an overview of a business' financial condition in both short and long term.

a. 3M Company
b. Statement of retained earnings
c. Notes to the financial statements
d. Financial statements

18. _____ is the world's largest professional services firm. It was formed in 1998 from a merger between Price Waterhouse and Coopers ' Lybrand, both formed in London.

_____ earned aggregated worldwide revenues of $28 billion for fiscal 2008, and employed over 146,000 people in 150 countries.

Chapter 11. Completing the Audit

a. Daybook
c. Serial bonds
b. Total-factor productivity
d. PricewaterhouseCoopers

19. The term _____ is a term applied to practices that are perfunctory, or seek to satisfy the minimum requirements or to conform to a convention or doctrine. It has different meanings in different fields.

In accounting, _____ earnings are those earnings of companies in addition to actual earnings calculated under the Generally Accepted Accounting Principles (GAAP) in their quarterly and yearly financial reports.

a. Bottom line
c. Treasury stock
b. Payroll
d. Pro forma

20. An _____ is a practitioner of accountancy, which is the measurement, disclosure or provision of assurance about financial information that helps managers, investors, tax authorities and other decision makers make resource allocation decisions.

The word '_____' is derived from the French 'Compter' which took its origin from the Latin 'Computare'. The word was formerly written in English as 'Accomptant', but in process of time the word, which was always pronounced by dropping the 'p', became gradually changed both in pronunciation and in orthography to its present form.

a. AMEX
c. AIG
b. ABC Television Network
d. Accountant

21. _____ LLP, based in Chicago, was once one of the 'Big Five' accounting firms among PricewaterhouseCoopers, Deloitte Touche Tohmatsu, Ernst ' Young and KPMG, providing auditing, tax, and consulting services to large corporations. In 2002, the firm voluntarily surrendered its licenses to practice as Certified Public Accountants in the United States after being found guilty of criminal charges relating to the firm's handling of the auditing of Enron, the energy corporation, resulting in the loss of 85,000 jobs. Although the verdict was subsequently overturned by the Supreme Court of the United States, it has not returned as a viable business.

a. ABC Television Network
c. Arthur Andersen
b. AMEX
d. AIG

22. The _____ is the national, professional association of CPAs in the United States, with more than 330,000 members, including CPAs in business and industry, public practice, government, and education; student affiliates; and international associates. It sets ethical standards for the profession and U.S. auditing standards for audits of private companies; federal, state and local governments; and non-profit organizations.

Approximately 40% of its members are engaged in the practice of public accounting, in areas such as auditing, accounting, taxation, general business consulting, business valuation, personal financial planning and business technology.

a. Other postemployment benefits
c. American Institute of Certified Public Accountants
b. AIG
d. ABC Television Network

23. In accounting/accountancy, _____ are journal entries usually made at the end of an accounting period to allocate income and expenditure to the period in which they actually occurred. The revenue recognition principle is the basis of making _____ that pertain to unearned and accrued revenues under accrual-basis accounting. They are sometimes called Balance Day adjustments because they are made on balance day.

a. Earnings before interest, taxes, depreciation and amortization

b. Accrued expense

c. Adjusting entries

d. Accrual

24. _____ means the giving out of information, either voluntarily or to be in compliance with legal regulations or workplace rules.

- In Computer security, full _____ means disclosing full information about vulnerabilities.
- In computing, _____ widget
- Journalism, full _____ refers to disclosing the interests of the writer which may bear on the subject being written about, for example, if the writer has worked with an interview subject in the past.

- In law:
    - The law of England and Wales, _____ refers to a process that may form part of legal proceedings, whereby parties inform to other parties the existence of any relevant documents that are, or have been, in their control. This compares with the process known as discovery in the course of legal proceedings in the United States.
    - In U.S. civil procedure (litigation rules for civil cases), _____ is a stage prior to trial. In civil cases, each party must disclose to the opposing party the following: names of witnesses which it may use to support its side, copies of documents (or mere description of these documents) in its control which it may use to support its side, computation of damages claimed, and certain insurance information. _____ is related to, but technically prior to, the discovery stage.
    - In Company law (known as 'corporate law' in the United States), _____ refers to giving out information about public or limited companies or their officers, which might be kept secret if the company was a private company or a partnership.

- In real property transactions, _____ refers to providing to a buyer information known to the seller or broker/agent concerning the condition or other aspects of real property that would affect the property's value or desirability. These rules regarding what information must be disclosed, and whether the information must be disclosed even if a buyer does not ask, vary from one jurisdiction to the next.

a. Disclosure

b. Controlled Foreign Corporations

c. Tax harmonisation

d. Trailing

25. A _____ is a business that functions without the intention or threat of liquidation for the foreseeable future, usually regarded as at least within 12 months.

In accounting, '_____' refers to a company's ability to continue functioning as a business entity. It is the responsibility of the directors to assess whether the _____ assumption is appropriate when preparing the financial statements.

Chapter 11. Completing the Audit

a. 3M Company
c. Payment
b. BMC Software, Inc.
d. Going concern

26. _____ is that part of statistical practice concerned with the selection of individual observations intended to yield some knowledge about a population of concern, especially for the purposes of statistical inference. Each observation measures one or more properties (weight, location, etc.) of an observable entity enumerated to distinguish objects or individuals.

a. Abby Joseph Cohen
c. Arthur Betz Laffer
b. Sampling
d. Alan Greenspan

27. In a publicly-held company, an _____ is an operating committee of the Board of Directors, typically charged with oversight of financial reporting and disclosure. Committee members are drawn from members of the Company's board of directors, with a Chairperson selected from among the members. An _____ of a publicly-traded company in the United States is composed of independent and outside directors referred to as non-executive directors, at least one of which is typically a financial expert.

a. Event data
c. External auditor
b. Audit working paper
d. Audit committee

28. The _____ of 2002 (Pub.L. 107-204, 116 Stat. 745, enacted July 30, 2002), also known as the Public Company Accounting Reform and Investor Protection Act of 2002, is a United States federal law enacted on July 30, 2002 in response to a number of major corporate and accounting scandals including those affecting Enron, Tyco International, Adelphia, Peregrine Systems and WorldCom. The legislation establishes new or enhanced standards for all U.S. public company boards, management, and public accounting firms. It does not apply to privately held companies.

a. Fair Labor Standards Act
c. FCPA
b. Lease
d. Sarbanes-Oxley Act

Chapter 12. Reports on Audited Financial Statements

1. _____ are formal records of a business' financial activities.

In British English, including United Kingdom company law, _____ are often referred to as accounts, although the term _____ is also used, particularly by accountants.

_____ provide an overview of a business' financial condition in both short and long term.

   a. 3M Company
   c. Notes to the financial statements
   b. Statement of retained earnings
   d. Financial statements

2. The general definition of an _____ is an evaluation of a person, organization, system, process, project or product. _____s are performed to ascertain the validity and reliability of information; also to provide an assessment of a system's internal control. The goal of an _____ is to express an opinion on the person/organization/system (etc) in question, under evaluation based on work done on a test basis.

   a. Assurance service
   c. Audit regime
   b. Institute of Chartered Accountants of India
   d. Audit

3. A _____ is an annual report required by the U.S. Securities and Exchange Commission (SEC), that gives a comprehensive summary of a public company's performance. Although similarly named, the annual report on _____ is distinct from the often glossy 'annual report to shareholders', which a company must send to its shareholders when it holds an annual meeting to elect directors (though some companies combine the annual report and the 10-K into one document.) The 10-K includes information such as company history, organizational structure, executive compensation, equity, subsidiaries, and audited financial statements, among other information.

   a. Form 8-K
   c. 3M Company
   b. Form 10-Q
   d. Form 10-K

4. The _____ is the national, professional association of CPAs in the United States, with more than 330,000 members, including CPAs in business and industry, public practice, government, and education; student affiliates; and international associates. It sets ethical standards for the profession and U.S. auditing standards for audits of private companies; federal, state and local governments; and non-profit organizations.

Approximately 40% of its members are engaged in the practice of public accounting, in areas such as auditing, accounting, taxation, general business consulting, business valuation, personal financial planning and business technology.

   a. AIG
   c. ABC Television Network
   b. American Institute of Certified Public Accountants
   d. Other postemployment benefits

5. A _____ or chief executive is one of the highest-ranking corporate officer (executive) or administrator in charge of total management. An individual selected as President and _____ of a corporation, company, organization, or agency, reports to the board of directors. In internal communication and press releases, many companies capitalize the term and those of other high positions, even when they are not proper nouns.

   a. Return on equity
   c. Kohlberg Kravis Roberts ' Co
   b. Return on assets
   d. Chief executive officer

Chapter 12. Reports on Audited Financial Statements

6. _____ means the giving out of information, either voluntarily or to be in compliance with legal regulations or workplace rules.

- In Computer security, full _____ means disclosing full information about vulnerabilities.
- In computing, _____ widget
- Journalism, full _____ refers to disclosing the interests of the writer which may bear on the subject being written about, for example, if the writer has worked with an interview subject in the past.

- In law:
    - The law of England and Wales, _____ refers to a process that may form part of legal proceedings, whereby parties inform to other parties the existence of any relevant documents that are, or have been, in their control. This compares with the process known as discovery in the course of legal proceedings in the United States.
    - In U.S. civil procedure (litigation rules for civil cases), _____ is a stage prior to trial. In civil cases, each party must disclose to the opposing party the following: names of witnesses which it may use to support its side, copies of documents (or mere description of these documents) in its control which it may use to support its side, computation of damages claimed, and certain insurance information. _____ is related to, but technically prior to, the discovery stage.
    - In Company law (known as 'corporate law' in the United States), _____ refers to giving out information about public or limited companies or their officers, which might be kept secret if the company was a private company or a partnership.

- In real property transactions, _____ refers to providing to a buyer information known to the seller or broker/agent concerning the condition or other aspects of real property that would affect the property's value or desirability. These rules regarding what information must be disclosed, and whether the information must be disclosed even if a buyer does not ask, vary from one jurisdiction to the next.

a. Controlled Foreign Corporations
b. Trailing
c. Disclosure
d. Tax harmonisation

7. The _____ of 2002 (Pub.L. 107-204, 116 Stat. 745, enacted July 30, 2002), also known as the Public Company Accounting Reform and Investor Protection Act of 2002, is a United States federal law enacted on July 30, 2002 in response to a number of major corporate and accounting scandals including those affecting Enron, Tyco International, Adelphia, Peregrine Systems and WorldCom. The legislation establishes new or enhanced standards for all U.S. public company boards, management, and public accounting firms. It does not apply to privately held companies.

a. Fair Labor Standards Act
b. FCPA
c. Lease
d. Sarbanes-Oxley Act

8. _____ refers to the confirmation of certain characteristics of an object, person, or organization. This confirmation is often, but not always, provided by some form of external review, education, or assessment. One of the most common types of _____ in modern society is professional _____, where a person is certified as being able to competently complete a job or task, usually by the passing of an examination.

a. 3M Company
b. BMC Software, Inc.
c. BNSF Railway
d. Certification

Chapter 12. Reports on Audited Financial Statements

9. An _____ is a term used in behavioral economics to describe those types of behaviors that impose costs on a person in the long-run that are not taken into account when making decisions in the present. Classical Economics discourages government from creating legislation that targets internalities, because it is assumed that the consumer takes these personal costs into account when paying for the good that causes the _____. For example, cigarettes should be taxed because of the negative consumption externalities that they impose, such as second-hand smoke, not because the smoker harms him or herself by smoking.
   a. Authorised capital
   b. Operating budget
   c. Inventory turnover ratio
   d. Internality

10. In accounting and organizational theory, _____ is defined as a process effected by an organization's structure, work and authority flows, people and management information systems, designed to help the organization accomplish specific goals or objectives. It is a means by which an organization's resources are directed, monitored, and measured. It plays an important role in preventing and detecting fraud and protecting the organization's resources, both physical (e.g., machinery and property) and intangible (e.g., reputation or intellectual property such as trademarks.)
    a. Auditor independence
    b. Audit risk
    c. Audit committee
    d. Internal control

11. The _____ is a 'voluntary organization of persons interested in accounting education and research'. It was formed in 1916. Its main publication, the The Accounting Review, was first published in 1926.
    a. Institute of Management Accountants
    b. Australian Accounting Standards Board
    c. International Accounting Standards Board
    d. American Accounting Association

12. _____, commonly abbreviated as SAS, provide guidance to external auditors on generally accepted auditing standards in regards to auditing an entity and issuing a report. They are usually issued by the certified public accountant authoritative body in the region where the standards apply, such as the American Institute of Certified Public Accountants in the United States.

    - _____
    - _____ (Taiwan)

    a. Financial Instruments and Exchange Law
    b. Statements on Auditing Standards
    c. GASB 45
    d. RSM International

13. _____ is the term used to refer to the standard framework of guidelines for financial accounting used in any given jurisdiction. _____ includes the standards, conventions, and rules accountants follow in recording and summarizing transactions, and in the preparation of financial statements.

    Financial accounting information must be assembled and reported objectively.

    a. Current asset
    b. Generally accepted accounting principles
    c. General ledger
    d. Long-term liabilities

Chapter 12. Reports on Audited Financial Statements

14. _____, Quarterly Report Pursuant to Section 13 or 15(d) of the Securities Exchange Act of 1934, is an SEC filing that must be filed quarterly with the US Securities and Exchange Commission. It contains similar information to the annual form 10-K, however the information is generally less detailed, and the financial statements are generally unaudited. Information for the final quarter of a firm's fiscal year is included in the 10-K, so only three 10-Q filings are made each year.

a. Form 20-F
b. Form 8-K
c. 3M Company
d. Form 10-Q

15. _____ are ten auditing standards, developed by the AICPA, consisting of general standards, standards of field work, and standards of reporting, along with interpretations. They were developed by the AICPA in 1947 and have undergone minor changes since then.

The _____ are as follows:

1. The auditor must have adequate technical training and proficiency to perform the audit
2. The auditor must maintain independence in mental attitude in all matters related to the audit.
3. The auditor must use due professional care during the performance of the audit and the preparation of the report.

1. The auditor must adequately plan the work and must properly supervise any assistants.
2. The auditor must obtain a sufficient understanding of the entity and its environment, including its internal control, to assess the risk of material misstatement of the financial statements whether due to error or fraud, and to design the nature, timing, and extent of further audit procedures.
3. The auditor must obtain sufficient appropriate audit evidence by performing audit procedures to afford a reasonable basis for an opinion regarding the financial statements under audit.

The new standards are in effect for audits of financial statements for periods beginning on or after December 15, 2006.

1. The auditor must state in the auditor's report whether the financial statements are in accordance with generally accepted accounting principles (GAAP.)
2. The auditor must identify in the auditor's report those circumstances in which such principles have not been consistently observed in the current period in relation to the preceding period.
3. When the auditor determines that informative disclosures are not reasonably adequate, the auditor must so state in the auditor's report.
4. The auditor must either express an opinion regarding the financial statements, taken as a whole the auditor should state the reasons therefore in the auditor's report. In all cases where the auditor's name is associated with the financial statements, the auditor should clearly indicate the character of the auditor's work, if any, and the degree of responsibility the auditor is taking, in the auditor's report.

a. Negative assurance
b. Joint audit
c. Continuous auditing
d. Generally accepted auditing standards

Chapter 12. Reports on Audited Financial Statements

16. _____ refers to the independence of the auditor from parties, that have an interest in the financial statements of an entity. It is essentially an attitude of mind characterized by integrity and an objective approach to the audit process. The concept requires the auditor to carry out his work freely and in an objective manner.

 a. Audit
 b. Information audit
 c. Internal Auditing
 d. Auditor independence

17. A _____ proof is a mathematical proof that a particular theory is consistent. The early development of mathematical proof theory was driven by the desire to provide finitary _____ proofs for all of mathematics as part of Hilbert's program. Hilbert's program was strongly impacted by incompleteness theorems, which showed that sufficiently strong proof theories cannot prove their own _____

 a. Daybook
 b. Monte Carlo methods
 c. Consumption
 d. Consistency

18. A _____ is a business that functions without the intention or threat of liquidation for the foreseeable future, usually regarded as at least within 12 months.

In accounting, '_____' refers to a company's ability to continue functioning as a business entity. It is the responsibility of the directors to assess whether the _____ assumption is appropriate when preparing the financial statements.

 a. Payment
 b. 3M Company
 c. BMC Software, Inc.
 d. Going concern

19. _____ is a legally declared inability or impairment of ability of an individual or organization to pay its creditors. Creditors may file a _____ petition against a debtor ('involuntary _____') in an effort to recoup a portion of what they are owed or initiate a restructuring. In the majority of cases, however, _____ is initiated by the debtor (a 'voluntary _____' that is filed by the bankrupt individual or organization.)

 a. 3M Company
 b. Bankruptcy protection
 c. BMC Software, Inc.
 d. Bankruptcy

20. A _____ has several related meanings:

- a daily record of events or business; a private _____ is usually referred to as a diary.
- a newspaper or other periodical, in the literal sense of one published each day;
- many publications issued at stated intervals, such as magazines, or scholarly academic _____s, or the record of the transactions of a society, are often called _____s. Although _____ is sometimes used, erroneously, as a synonym for 'magazine,' in academic use, a _____ refers to a serious, scholarly publication, most often peer-reviewed. A non-scholarly magazine written for an educated audience about an industry or an area of professional activity is usually called a professional magazine.

The word 'journalist' for one whose business is writing for the public press has been in use since the end of the 17th century.

Open access _____s are scholarly _____s that are available to the reader without financial or other barrier other than access to the internet itself. Some are subsidized, and some require payment on behalf of the author. Subsidized _____s are financed by an academic institution or a government information center.

a. BNSF Railway
c. BMC Software, Inc.
b. 3M Company
d. Journal

21. In mathematics _____s are numbers or other things that get multiplied. In particular, see:

- Factorization, the decomposition of an object into a product of other objects
- Integer factorization, the process of breaking down a composite number into smaller non-trivial divisors
- A coefficient
- A divisor of a particular number, or of an element of a monoid
- A von Neumann algebra with a trivial center

In statistics

- _____ analysis is the study of how _____s or certain variables affect variables.

In technology:

- Human _____s, a profession that focuses on how people interact with products, tools, or procedures
- 'Functionality, Application domain, Conditions, Technology, Objects and Responsibility;', In object-oriented programming

In computer science and information technology:

- Authentication _____, a piece of information used to verify a person's identity for security purposes
- _____, a Unix command for numbers factorization
- _____ (programming language), an experimental Forth-like programming language

In television:

- The O'Reilly _____, an American talk show hosted by Bill O'Reilly on Fox News.
- The Krypton _____, a British game show hosted by Gordon Burns, formally on ITV. Also had an American version.

a. The Goodyear Tire ' Rubber Company
c. Merck ' Co., Inc.
b. Valuation
d. Factor

22. The _____ is a private, not-for-profit organization whose primary purpose is to develop generally accepted accounting principles (GAAP) within the United States in the public's interest. The Securities and Exchange Commission (SEC) designated the _____ as the organization responsible for setting accounting standards for public companies in the U.S. It was created in 1973, replacing the Accounting Principles Board and the Committee on Accounting Procedure of the American Institute of Certified Public Accountants. The _____'s mission is 'to establish and improve standards of financial accounting and reporting for the guidance and education of the public, including issuers, auditors, and users of financial information.'

Chapter 12. Reports on Audited Financial Statements

The _____ is not a governmental body.

a. Governmental Accounting Standards Board
b. Fannie Mae
c. Public company
d. Financial Accounting Standards Board

23. _____ LLP, based in Chicago, was once one of the 'Big Five' accounting firms among PricewaterhouseCoopers, Deloitte Touche Tohmatsu, Ernst ' Young and KPMG, providing auditing, tax, and consulting services to large corporations. In 2002, the firm voluntarily surrendered its licenses to practice as Certified Public Accountants in the United States after being found guilty of criminal charges relating to the firm's handling of the auditing of Enron, the energy corporation, resulting in the loss of 85,000 jobs. Although the verdict was subsequently overturned by the Supreme Court of the United States, it has not returned as a viable business.

a. AMEX
b. Arthur Andersen
c. AIG
d. ABC Television Network

24. An _____ is a comprehensive report on a company's activities throughout the preceding year. _____s are intended to give shareholders and other interested persons information about the company's activities and financial performance. Most jurisdictions require companies to prepare and disclose _____s, and many require the _____ to be filed at the company's registry.

a. AIG
b. AMEX
c. ABC Television Network
d. Annual report

25. _____ is a specific term used in companies' financial reporting from the company-whole point of view. Because that use excludes the effects of changing ownership interest, an economic measure of _____ is necessary for financial analysis from the shareholders' point of view

_____ is defined by the Financial Accounting Standards Board, or FASB, as 'the change in equity [net assets] of a business enterprise during a period from transactions and other events and circumstances from nonowner sources. It includes all changes in equity during a period except those resulting from investments by owners and distributions to owners.'

_____ is the sum of net income and other items that must bypass the income statement because they have not been realized, including items like an unrealized holding gain or loss from available for sale securities and foreign currency translation gains or losses.

a. 3M Company
b. Comprehensive income
c. BNSF Railway
d. BMC Software, Inc.

26. _____ are the earnings returned on the initial investment amount.

In the US, the Financial Accounting Standards Board (FASB) requires companies' income statements to report _____ for each of the major categories of the income statement: continuing operations, discontinued operations, extraordinary items, and net income.

The _____ formula does not include preferred dividends for categories outside of continued operations and net income.

a. Earnings yield
b. Average accounting return
c. Invested capital
d. Earnings per share

Chapter 13. Other Public Accounting Services

1. An _____ is a practitioner of accountancy, which is the measurement, disclosure or provision of assurance about financial information that helps managers, investors, tax authorities and other decision makers make resource allocation decisions.

The word '_____' is derived from the French 'Compter' which took its origin from the Latin 'Computare'. The word was formerly written in English as 'Accomptant', but in process of time the word, which was always pronounced by dropping the 'p', became gradually changed both in pronunciation and in orthography to its present form.

   a. AMEX
   c. ABC Television Network
   b. AIG
   d. Accountant

2. The _____ is the national, professional association of CPAs in the United States, with more than 330,000 members, including CPAs in business and industry, public practice, government, and education; student affiliates; and international associates. It sets ethical standards for the profession and U.S. auditing standards for audits of private companies; federal, state and local governments; and non-profit organizations.

Approximately 40% of its members are engaged in the practice of public accounting, in areas such as auditing, accounting, taxation, general business consulting, business valuation, personal financial planning and business technology.

   a. AIG
   c. Other postemployment benefits
   b. ABC Television Network
   d. American Institute of Certified Public Accountants

3. _____ is the statutory title of qualified accountants in the United States who have passed the Uniform _____ Examination and have met additional state education and experience requirements for certification as a _____. Individuals who have passed the Exam but have not either accomplished the required on-the-job experience or have previously met it but in the meantime have lapsed their continuing professional education are, in many states, permitted the designation '_____ Inactive' or an equivalent phrase. In most U.S. states, only _____s who are licensed are able to provide to the public attestation (including auditing) opinions on financial statements.
   a. Chartered Accountant
   c. Certified General Accountant
   b. Chartered Certified Accountant
   d. Certified Public Accountant

4. _____s have been defined by the American Institute of Certified Public Accountants (AICPA) as 'Independent Professional Services that improve information quality or its context'. _____s reduce the information risk; risk that the information provided is incorrect, on more than just financial data. The major purpose of _____s is to provide independent and professional opinions that improve the quality of information to management as well as other decision makers within a given firm.
   a. Assurance service
   c. ITGCs
   b. Institute of Chartered Accountants of India
   d. Auditor independence

5. _____ is subcontracting a process, such as product design or manufacturing, to a third-party company. The decision to outsource is often made in the interest of lowering cost or making better use of time and energy costs, redirecting or conserving energy directed at the competencies of a particular business, or to make more efficient use of land, labor, capital, (information) technology and resources. _____ became part of the business lexicon during the 1980s.

Chapter 13. Other Public Accounting Services 119

a. USA Today

b. US Airways, Inc.

c. Economic Growth and Tax Relief Reconciliation Act of 2001

d. Outsourcing

6. A _____ is a fungible, negotiable instrument representing financial value. they are broadly categorized into debt securities (such as banknotes, bonds and debentures), and equity securities; e.g., common stocks. The company or other entity issuing the _____ is called the issuer.

a. Tracking stock

b. Security

c. 3M Company

d. BMC Software, Inc.

7. _____ in the United States currently refers to the federal Old-Age, Survivors, and Disability Insurance (OASDI) program.

The original _____ Act and the current version of the Act, as amended encompass several social welfare and social insurance programs. The larger and better known programs are:

- Federal Old-Age, Survivors, and Disability Insurance
- Unemployment benefits
- Temporary Assistance for Needy Families
- Health Insurance for Aged and Disabled (Medicare)
- Grants to States for Medical Assistance Programs (Medicaid)
- State Children's Health Insurance Program (SCHIP)
- Supplemental Security Income (Social SecurityI)

U.S. _____ is a social insurance program funded through dedicated payroll taxes called Federal Insurance Contributions Act (FICA.) Tax deposits are formally entrusted to Federal Old-Age and Survivors Insurance Trust Fund, or Federal Disability Insurance Trust Fund, Federal Hospital Insurance Trust Fund or the Federal Supplementary Medical Insurance Trust Fund.

a. Sale

b. Price-to-sales ratio

c. Social Security

d. Comparable

8. The United States _____ is an independent agency of the United States federal government that administers Social Security, a social insurance program consisting of retirement, disability, and survivors' benefits. To qualify for these benefits, most American workers pay Social Security taxes on their earnings; future benefits are based on the employees' contributions.

The _____ was established by a law currently codified at 42 U.S.C.

a. Minority interest

b. Return on assets

c. Social Security Administration

d. Time value of money

9. The _____ is the umbrella body for the Chartered Accountant profession in Canada and Bermuda. Membership of the CICA totals 70,000 Chartered Accountants and 8,500 students.

Canadian chartered accountants use the designation CA.

a. BNSF Railway
b. 3M Company
c. Canadian Institute of Chartered Accountants
d. BMC Software, Inc.

10. _____ is the title used by members of certain professional accountancy associations in the British Commonwealth countries and Ireland. The term chartered comes from the Royal Charter granted to the world's first professional body of accountants upon their establishment in 1854. The Edinburgh Society of Accountants (formed 1854), the Glasgow Institute of Accountants and Actuaries (1854) and the Aberdeen Society of Accountants (1867) were each granted a royal charter almost from their inception.

a. Certified General Accountant
b. Certified public accountant
c. Chartered Certified Accountant
d. Chartered Accountant

11. _____, commonly known as e-commerce or eCommerce, consists of the buying and selling of products or services over electronic systems such as the Internet and other computer networks. The amount of trade conducted electronically has grown extraordinarily since the spread of the Internet. A wide variety of commerce is conducted in this way, spurring and drawing on innovations in electronic funds transfer, supply chain management, Internet marketing, online transaction processing, electronic data interchange (EDI), inventory management systems, and automated data collection systems.

a. AIG
b. ABC Television Network
c. Electronic data interchange
d. Electronic commerce

12. _____ refers to the computer-based systems used to perform financial transactions electronically.

The term is used for a number of different concepts:

- Cardholder-initiated transactions, where a cardholder makes use of a payment card
- Direct deposit payroll payments for a business to its employees, possibly via a payroll services company
- Direct debit payments from customer to business, where the transaction is initiated by the business with customer permission
- Electronic bill payment in online banking, which may be delivered by _____ or paper check
- Transactions involving stored value of electronic money, possibly in a private currency
- Wire transfer via an international banking network (generally carries a higher fee)
- Electronic Benefit Transfer

electronic funds transferPOS (short for _____ at Point of Sale) is an Australian and New Zealand electronic processing system for credit cards, debit cards and charge cards.

European banks and card companies also sometimes reference 'electronic funds transferPOS' as the system used for processing card transactions through terminals on points of sale, though the system is not the trademarked Australian/New Zealand variant.

Credit cards

Chapter 13. Other Public Accounting Services

_____ may be initiated by a cardholder when a payment card such as a credit card or debit card is used.

a. ABC Television Network
c. AMEX
b. AIG
d. Electronic funds transfer

13. _____ are formal records of a business' financial activities.

In British English, including United Kingdom company law, _____ are often referred to as accounts, although the term _____ is also used, particularly by accountants.

_____ provide an overview of a business' financial condition in both short and long term.

a. Statement of retained earnings
c. Notes to the financial statements
b. 3M Company
d. Financial statements

14. _____ is the process of estimation in unknown situations. Prediction is a similar, but more general term. Both can refer to estimation of time series, cross-sectional or longitudinal data.

a. 3M Company
c. BMC Software, Inc.
b. Forecasting
d. BNSF Railway

15. _____ are ten auditing standards, developed by the AICPA, consisting of general standards, standards of field work, and standards of reporting, along with interpretations. They were developed by the AICPA in 1947 and have undergone minor changes since then.

The _____ are as follows:

1. The auditor must have adequate technical training and proficiency to perform the audit
2. The auditor must maintain independence in mental attitude in all matters related to the audit.
3. The auditor must use due professional care during the performance of the audit and the preparation of the report.

1. The auditor must adequately plan the work and must properly supervise any assistants.
2. The auditor must obtain a sufficient understanding of the entity and its environment, including its internal control, to assess the risk of material misstatement of the financial statements whether due to error or fraud, and to design the nature, timing, and extent of further audit procedures.
3. The auditor must obtain sufficient appropriate audit evidence by performing audit procedures to afford a reasonable basis for an opinion regarding the financial statements under audit.

The new standards are in effect for audits of financial statements for periods beginning on or after December 15, 2006.

1. The auditor must state in the auditor's report whether the financial statements are in accordance with generally accepted accounting principles (GAAP.)
2. The auditor must identify in the auditor's report those circumstances in which such principles have not been consistently observed in the current period in relation to the preceding period.
3. When the auditor determines that informative disclosures are not reasonably adequate, the auditor must so state in the auditor's report.
4. The auditor must either express an opinion regarding the financial statements, taken as a whole the auditor should state the reasons therefore in the auditor's report. In all cases where the auditor's name is associated with the financial statements, the auditor should clearly indicate the character of the auditor's work, if any, and the degree of responsibility the auditor is taking, in the auditor's report.

a. Negative assurance
c. Joint audit
b. Continuous auditing
d. Generally accepted auditing standards

16. _____ is the world's largest professional services firm. It was formed in 1998 from a merger between Price Waterhouse and Coopers ' Lybrand, both formed in London.

_____ earned aggregated worldwide revenues of $28 billion for fiscal 2008, and employed over 146,000 people in 150 countries.

a. Serial bonds
c. Daybook
b. Total-factor productivity
d. PricewaterhouseCoopers

17. The term _____ is a term applied to practices that are perfunctory, or seek to satisfy the minimum requirements or to conform to a convention or doctrine. It has different meanings in different fields.

In accounting, _____ earnings are those earnings of companies in addition to actual earnings calculated under the Generally Accepted Accounting Principles (GAAP) in their quarterly and yearly financial reports.

a. Treasury stock
c. Bottom line
b. Payroll
d. Pro forma

18. The general definition of an _____ is an evaluation of a person, organization, system, process, project or product. _____s are performed to ascertain the validity and reliability of information; also to provide an assessment of a system's internal control. The goal of an _____ is to express an opinion on the person/organization/system (etc) in question, under evaluation based on work done on a test basis.

a. Audit regime
c. Assurance service
b. Institute of Chartered Accountants of India
d. Audit

Chapter 13. Other Public Accounting Services

19. _____, commonly abbreviated as SAS, provide guidance to external auditors on generally accepted auditing standards in regards to auditing an entity and issuing a report. They are usually issued by the certified public accountant authoritative body in the region where the standards apply, such as the American Institute of Certified Public Accountants in the United States.

- _____
- _____ (Taiwan)

a. RSM International
b. GASB 45
c. Statements on Auditing Standards
d. Financial Instruments and Exchange Law

20. Accounting _____ define the basic standards for representing attestation engagements. Attestation is defined as an engagement in which a practitioner is hired to issue written communication that expresses a conclusion about the reliability of written assertions prepared by a separate party. The American Institute of Certified Public Accountants identified a number of different engagements that fall under the scope of _____, including: examining financial forecasts and projections, examining pro forma financial statements, evaluating internal control, assessing compliance with rules, regulations, and contractual obligations, as well as evaluating management discussions and analysis of financial results.

a. Institute of Chartered Accountants of India
b. Audit working paper
c. Audit management
d. Attestation standards

21. _____ LLP, based in Chicago, was once one of the 'Big Five' accounting firms among PricewaterhouseCoopers, Deloitte Touche Tohmatsu, Ernst ' Young and KPMG, providing auditing, tax, and consulting services to large corporations. In 2002, the firm voluntarily surrendered its licenses to practice as Certified Public Accountants in the United States after being found guilty of criminal charges relating to the firm's handling of the auditing of Enron, the energy corporation, resulting in the loss of 85,000 jobs. Although the verdict was subsequently overturned by the Supreme Court of the United States, it has not returned as a viable business.

a. AIG
b. ABC Television Network
c. AMEX
d. Arthur Andersen

22. An _____ is a term used in behavioral economics to describe those types of behaviors that impose costs on a person in the long-run that are not taken into account when making decisions in the present. Classical Economics discourages government from creating legislation that targets internalities, because it is assumed that the consumer takes these personal costs into account when paying for the good that causes the _____. For example, cigarettes should be taxed because of the negative consumption externalities that they impose, such as second-hand smoke, not because the smoker harms him or herself by smoking.

a. Operating budget
b. Inventory turnover ratio
c. Authorised capital
d. Internality

23. In accounting and organizational theory, _____ is defined as a process effected by an organization's structure, work and authority flows, people and management information systems, designed to help the organization accomplish specific goals or objectives. It is a means by which an organization's resources are directed, monitored, and measured. It plays an important role in preventing and detecting fraud and protecting the organization's resources, both physical (e.g., machinery and property) and intangible (e.g., reputation or intellectual property such as trademarks.)

a. Auditor independence
b. Audit committee
c. Audit risk
d. Internal control

24. A _____ or chief executive is one of the highest-ranking corporate officer (executive) or administrator in charge of total management. An individual selected as President and _____ of a corporation, company, organization, or agency, reports to the board of directors. In internal communication and press releases, many companies capitalize the term and those of other high positions, even when they are not proper nouns.
   a. Kohlberg Kravis Roberts ' Co
   b. Return on assets
   c. Chief executive officer
   d. Return on equity

25. A _____ has several related meanings:

   - a daily record of events or business; a private _____ is usually referred to as a diary.
   - a newspaper or other periodical, in the literal sense of one published each day;
   - many publications issued at stated intervals, such as magazines, or scholarly academic _____s, or the record of the transactions of a society, are often called _____s. Although _____ is sometimes used, erroneously, as a synonym for 'magazine,' in academic use, a _____ refers to a serious, scholarly publication, most often peer-reviewed. A non-scholarly magazine written for an educated audience about an industry or an area of professional activity is usually called a professional magazine.

The word 'journalist' for one whose business is writing for the public press has been in use since the end of the 17th century.

Open access _____s are scholarly _____s that are available to the reader without financial or other barrier other than access to the internet itself. Some are subsidized, and some require payment on behalf of the author. Subsidized _____s are financed by an academic institution or a government information center.

   a. Journal
   b. 3M Company
   c. BNSF Railway
   d. BMC Software, Inc.

26. _____ refers to the confirmation of certain characteristics of an object, person, or organization. This confirmation is often, but not always, provided by some form of external review, education, or assessment. One of the most common types of _____ in modern society is professional _____, where a person is certified as being able to competently complete a job or task, usually by the passing of an examination.
   a. BNSF Railway
   b. Certification
   c. 3M Company
   d. BMC Software, Inc.

Chapter 13. Other Public Accounting Services

27. _____ means the giving out of information, either voluntarily or to be in compliance with legal regulations or workplace rules.

- In Computer security, full _____ means disclosing full information about vulnerabilities.
- In computing, _____ widget
- Journalism, full _____ refers to disclosing the interests of the writer which may bear on the subject being written about, for example, if the writer has worked with an interview subject in the past.

- In law:
    - The law of England and Wales, _____ refers to a process that may form part of legal proceedings, whereby parties inform to other parties the existence of any relevant documents that are, or have been, in their control. This compares with the process known as discovery in the course of legal proceedings in the United States.
    - In U.S. civil procedure (litigation rules for civil cases), _____ is a stage prior to trial. In civil cases, each party must disclose to the opposing party the following: names of witnesses which it may use to support its side, copies of documents (or mere description of these documents) in its control which it may use to support its side, computation of damages claimed, and certain insurance information. _____ is related to, but technically prior to, the discovery stage.
    - In Company law (known as 'corporate law' in the United States), _____ refers to giving out information about public or limited companies or their officers, which might be kept secret if the company was a private company or a partnership.

- In real property transactions, _____ refers to providing to a buyer information known to the seller or broker/agent concerning the condition or other aspects of real property that would affect the property's value or desirability. These rules regarding what information must be disclosed, and whether the information must be disclosed even if a buyer does not ask, vary from one jurisdiction to the next.

a. Tax harmonisation
c. Controlled Foreign Corporations
b. Trailing
d. Disclosure

28. Established in 1988 the _____ is the professional organization that governs professional fraud examiners. Its activities include producing fraud information, tools and training. It also governs the professional designation of Certified Fraud Examiner.
a. AIG
c. ABC Television Network
b. AMEX
d. Association of Certified Fraud Examiners

29. _____ is a designation awarded by the Association of _____s (ACertified Fraud Examiner.) The ACertified Fraud Examiner is a 41,000 member-based global association dedicated to providing anti-fraud education and training.

In order to become a _____ one must meet the following requirements:

- Be an Associate Member of the ACertified Fraud Examiner in good standing
- Meet minimum academic and professional requirements
- Be of high moral character
- Agree to abide by the Bylaws and Code of Professional Ethics of the Association of _____s

Generally, applicants for _____ certification have a minimum of a bachelor's degree or equivalent from an institution of higher education. Two years of professional experience related to fraud can be substituted for each year of college.

a. Certified Fraud Examiner
b. Chartered Accountant
c. Chartered Certified Accountant
d. Certified public accountant

30. _____ is the term used to refer to the standard framework of guidelines for financial accounting used in any given jurisdiction. _____ includes the standards, conventions, and rules accountants follow in recording and summarizing transactions, and in the preparation of financial statements.

Financial accounting information must be assembled and reported objectively.

a. Long-term liabilities
b. Current asset
c. General ledger
d. Generally accepted accounting principles

31. _____ is a method of accounting whereby cash flow of financial events is considered. The method recognizes revenues when cash is received and recognizes expenses when cash is paid out. In cash accounting, revenues and expenses are also called cash receipts and cash payments respectively.

a. Closing entries
b. Treasury stock
c. Net sales
d. Cash basis accounting

Chapter 14. Professional Ethics

1. _____ is the set of processes, customs, policies, laws, and institutions affecting the way a corporation is directed, administered or controlled. _____ also includes the relationships among the many stakeholders involved and the goals for which the corporation is governed. The principal stakeholders are the shareholders/members, management, and the board of directors.
   a. Patent
   b. FLSA
   c. Corporate Governance
   d. Trust indenture

2. The _____ is the national, professional association of CPAs in the United States, with more than 330,000 members, including CPAs in business and industry, public practice, government, and education; student affiliates; and international associates. It sets ethical standards for the profession and U.S. auditing standards for audits of private companies; federal, state and local governments; and non-profit organizations.

   Approximately 40% of its members are engaged in the practice of public accounting, in areas such as auditing, accounting, taxation, general business consulting, business valuation, personal financial planning and business technology.

   a. AIG
   b. ABC Television Network
   c. Other postemployment benefits
   d. American Institute of Certified Public Accountants

3. An _____ is a practitioner of accountancy, which is the measurement, disclosure or provision of assurance about financial information that helps managers, investors, tax authorities and other decision makers make resource allocation decisions.

   The word '_____' is derived from the French 'Compter' which took its origin from the Latin 'Computare'. The word was formerly written in English as 'Accomptant', but in process of time the word, which was always pronounced by dropping the 'p', became gradually changed both in pronunciation and in orthography to its present form.

   a. ABC Television Network
   b. Accountant
   c. AMEX
   d. AIG

4. _____ is the statutory title of qualified accountants in the United States who have passed the Uniform _____ Examination and have met additional state education and experience requirements for certification as a _____. Individuals who have passed the Exam but have not either accomplished the required on-the-job experience or have previously met it but in the meantime have lapsed their continuing professional education are, in many states, permitted the designation '_____ Inactive' or an equivalent phrase. In most U.S. states, only _____s who are licensed are able to provide to the public attestation (including auditing) opinions on financial statements.
   a. Chartered Certified Accountant
   b. Certified Public Accountant
   c. Certified General Accountant
   d. Chartered Accountant

5. A _____ is a body of elected or appointed members who jointly oversee the activities of a company or organization. The body sometimes has a different name, such as board of trustees, board of governors, board of managers, or executive board. It is often simply referred to as 'the board.'

   A board's activities are determined by the powers, duties, and responsibilities delegated to it or conferred on it by an authority outside itself.

a. Consumer protection laws
c. Board of directors
b. Chief Financial Officers Act of 1990
d. Hospital Survey and Construction Act

6. _____ LLP, based in Chicago, was once one of the 'Big Five' accounting firms among PricewaterhouseCoopers, Deloitte Touche Tohmatsu, Ernst ' Young and KPMG, providing auditing, tax, and consulting services to large corporations. In 2002, the firm voluntarily surrendered its licenses to practice as Certified Public Accountants in the United States after being found guilty of criminal charges relating to the firm's handling of the auditing of Enron, the energy corporation, resulting in the loss of 85,000 jobs. Although the verdict was subsequently overturned by the Supreme Court of the United States, it has not returned as a viable business.
   a. AMEX
   b. ABC Television Network
   c. AIG
   d. Arthur Andersen

7. Established in 1988 the _____ is the professional organization that governs professional fraud examiners. Its activities include producing fraud information, tools and training. It also governs the professional designation of Certified Fraud Examiner.
   a. ABC Television Network
   b. AIG
   c. AMEX
   d. Association of Certified Fraud Examiners

8. _____ is a designation awarded by the Association of _____s (ACertified Fraud Examiner.) The ACertified Fraud Examiner is a 41,000 member-based global association dedicated to providing anti-fraud education and training.

In order to become a _____ one must meet the following requirements:

- Be an Associate Member of the ACertified Fraud Examiner in good standing
- Meet minimum academic and professional requirements
- Be of high moral character
- Agree to abide by the Bylaws and Code of Professional Ethics of the Association of _____s

Generally, applicants for _____ certification have a minimum of a bachelor's degree or equivalent from an institution of higher education. Two years of professional experience related to fraud can be substituted for each year of college.

   a. Chartered Certified Accountant
   b. Certified public accountant
   c. Certified Fraud Examiner
   d. Chartered Accountant

9. A _____ is a fungible, negotiable instrument representing financial value. they are broadly categorized into debt securities (such as banknotes, bonds and debentures), and equity securities; e.g., common stocks. The company or other entity issuing the _____ is called the issuer.
   a. BMC Software, Inc.
   b. Tracking stock
   c. Security
   d. 3M Company

10. The U.S. _____ is an independent agency of the United States government which holds primary responsibility for enforcing the federal securities laws and regulating the securities industry, the nation's stock and options exchanges, and other electronic securities markets. The SEC was created by section 4 of the Securities Exchange Act of 1934 (now codified as 15 U.S.C. ÂÂ§ 78d and commonly referred to as the 1934 Act.)

Chapter 14. Professional Ethics

a. BMC Software, Inc.
c. BNSF Railway
b. Securities and Exchange Commission
d. 3M Company

11. _____s have been defined by the American Institute of Certified Public Accountants (AICPA) as 'Independent Professional Services that improve information quality or its context'. _____s reduce the information risk; risk that the information provided is incorrect, on more than just financial data. The major purpose of _____s is to provide independent and professional opinions that improve the quality of information to management as well as other decision makers within a given firm.
   a. ITGCs
   c. Institute of Chartered Accountants of India
   b. Auditor independence
   d. Assurance service

12. _____ refers to the independence of the auditor from parties, that have an interest in the financial statements of an entity. It is essentially an attitude of mind characterized by integrity and an objective approach to the audit process. The concept requires the auditor to carry out his work freely and in an objective manner.
   a. Internal Auditing
   c. Information audit
   b. Auditor independence
   d. Audit

13. _____ is a fee paid on borrowed assets. It is the price paid for the use of borrowed money , or, money earned by deposited funds .Assets that are sometimes lent with _____ include money, shares, consumer goods through hire purchase, major assets such as aircraft, and even entire factories in finance lease arrangements. The _____ is calculated upon the value of the assets in the same manner as upon money.
   a. ABC Television Network
   c. Insolvency
   b. Interest
   d. AIG

14. A _____ is a type of debt Like all debt instruments, a _____ entails the redistribution of financial assets over time, between the lender and the borrower.
   a. Lender
   c. Debenture
   b. Loan to value
   d. Loan

15. The _____ (sometimes called 'Peekaboo') is a private-sector, non-profit corporation created by the Sarbanes-Oxley Act, a 2002 United States federal law, to oversee the auditors of public companies. Its stated purpose is to 'protect the interests of investors and further the public interest in the preparation of informative, fair, and independent audit reports'. Although a private entity, the _____ has many government-like regulatory functions, making it in some ways similar to the private Self Regulatory Organizations (SROs) that regulate stock markets and other aspects of the financial markets in the United States.
   a. 3M Company
   c. Financial Crimes Enforcement Network
   b. Pension Benefit Guaranty Corporation
   d. Public Company Accounting Oversight Board

16. The term _____ usually refers to a company that is permitted to offer its registered securities (stock, bonds, etc.) for sale to the general public, typically through a stock exchange, or occasionally a company whose stock is traded over the counter (OTC) via market makers who use non-exchange quotation services.

The term '_____' may also refer to a company owned by the government.

a. Professional association
c. MicroStrategy
b. Public Company
d. Governmental Accounting Standards Board

17. _____ is the recording of the value of assets, liabilities, income, and expenses in the daybooks, journals, and ledgers, in which debit and credit entries are chronologically posted to record changes in value. _____ is often mistaken for accounting, which is the system of recording, verifying, and reporting such information. Practitioners of accounting are called accountants.
   a. Controlling account
   b. Debit and credit
   c. Double-entry bookkeeping
   d. Bookkeeping

18. _____, Quarterly Report Pursuant to Section 13 or 15(d) of the Securities Exchange Act of 1934, is an SEC filing that must be filed quarterly with the US Securities and Exchange Commission. It contains similar information to the annual form 10-K, however the information is generally less detailed, and the financial statements are generally unaudited. Information for the final quarter of a firm's fiscal year is included in the 10-K, so only three 10-Q filings are made each year.
   a. Form 10-Q
   b. 3M Company
   c. Form 8-K
   d. Form 20-F

19. A _____ has several related meanings:

   - a daily record of events or business; a private _____ is usually referred to as a diary.
   - a newspaper or other periodical, in the literal sense of one published each day;
   - many publications issued at stated intervals, such as magazines, or scholarly academic _____s, or the record of the transactions of a society, are often called _____s. Although _____ is sometimes used, erroneously, as a synonym for 'magazine,' in academic use, a _____ refers to a serious, scholarly publication, most often peer-reviewed. A non-scholarly magazine written for an educated audience about an industry or an area of professional activity is usually called a professional magazine.

The word 'journalist' for one whose business is writing for the public press has been in use since the end of the 17th century.

Open access _____s are scholarly _____s that are available to the reader without financial or other barrier other than access to the internet itself. Some are subsidized, and some require payment on behalf of the author. Subsidized _____s are financed by an academic institution or a government information center.

   a. 3M Company
   b. BMC Software, Inc.
   c. BNSF Railway
   d. Journal

20. _____ is the world's largest professional services firm. It was formed in 1998 from a merger between Price Waterhouse and Coopers ' Lybrand, both formed in London.

_____ earned aggregated worldwide revenues of $28 billion for fiscal 2008, and employed over 146,000 people in 150 countries.

   a. Serial bonds
   b. Total-factor productivity
   c. Daybook
   d. PricewaterhouseCoopers

Chapter 14. Professional Ethics

21. _____ is an increasingly broadening term with which an organization knowledge and experience, Employee Relations and resource planning at various levels. The field draws upon concepts developed in Industrial/Organizational Psychology and System Theory. _____ has at least two related interpretations depending on context.
   a. Human resources
   b. BMC Software, Inc.
   c. 3M Company
   d. Separation of duties

22. The general definition of an _____ is an evaluation of a person, organization, system, process, project or product. _____s are performed to ascertain the validity and reliability of information; also to provide an assessment of a system's internal control. The goal of an _____ is to express an opinion on the person/organization/system (etc) in question, under evaluation based on work done on a test basis.
   a. Institute of Chartered Accountants of India
   b. Audit
   c. Audit regime
   d. Assurance service

23. In a publicly-held company, an _____ is an operating committee of the Board of Directors, typically charged with oversight of financial reporting and disclosure. Committee members are drawn from members of the Company's board of directors, with a Chairperson selected from among the members. An _____ of a publicly-traded company in the United States is composed of independent and outside directors referred to as non-executive directors, at least one of which is typically a financial expert.
   a. Audit working paper
   b. External auditor
   c. Event data
   d. Audit committee

Chapter 14. Professional Ethics

24. _____ means the giving out of information, either voluntarily or to be in compliance with legal regulations or workplace rules.

- In Computer security, full _____ means disclosing full information about vulnerabilities.
- In computing, _____ widget
- Journalism, full _____ refers to disclosing the interests of the writer which may bear on the subject being written about, for example, if the writer has worked with an interview subject in the past.

- In law:
    - The law of England and Wales, _____ refers to a process that may form part of legal proceedings, whereby parties inform to other parties the existence of any relevant documents that are, or have been, in their control. This compares with the process known as discovery in the course of legal proceedings in the United States.
    - In U.S. civil procedure (litigation rules for civil cases), _____ is a stage prior to trial. In civil cases, each party must disclose to the opposing party the following: names of witnesses which it may use to support its side, copies of documents (or mere description of these documents) in its control which it may use to support its side, computation of damages claimed, and certain insurance information. _____ is related to, but technically prior to, the discovery stage.
    - In Company law (known as 'corporate law' in the United States), _____ refers to giving out information about public or limited companies or their officers, which might be kept secret if the company was a private company or a partnership.

- In real property transactions, _____ refers to providing to a buyer information known to the seller or broker/agent concerning the condition or other aspects of real property that would affect the property's value or desirability. These rules regarding what information must be disclosed, and whether the information must be disclosed even if a buyer does not ask, vary from one jurisdiction to the next.

a. Trailing
b. Tax harmonisation
c. Controlled Foreign Corporations
d. Disclosure

25. The _____ of 2002 (Pub.L. 107-204, 116 Stat. 745, enacted July 30, 2002), also known as the Public Company Accounting Reform and Investor Protection Act of 2002, is a United States federal law enacted on July 30, 2002 in response to a number of major corporate and accounting scandals including those affecting Enron, Tyco International, Adelphia, Peregrine Systems and WorldCom. The legislation establishes new or enhanced standards for all U.S. public company boards, management, and public accounting firms. It does not apply to privately held companies.

a. Fair Labor Standards Act
b. Lease
c. FCPA
d. Sarbanes-Oxley Act

26. A _____ or chief executive is one of the highest-ranking corporate officer (executive) or administrator in charge of total management. An individual selected as President and _____ of a corporation, company, organization, or agency, reports to the board of directors. In internal communication and press releases, many companies capitalize the term and those of other high positions, even when they are not proper nouns.

a. Chief executive officer
b. Return on equity
c. Return on assets
d. Kohlberg Kravis Roberts ' Co

Chapter 14. Professional Ethics

27. Employment is a contract between two parties, one being the employer and the other being the _____. An _____ may be defined as: 'A person in the service of another under any contract of hire, express or implied, oral or written, where the employer has the power or right to control and direct the _____ in the material details of how the work is to be performed.' Black's Law Dictionary page 471 (5th ed. 1979.)
   a. AMEX
   b. Employee
   c. ABC Television Network
   d. AIG

28. A _____ is a professionally managed type of collective investment scheme that pools money from many investors and invests it in stocks, bonds, short-term money market instruments, and/or other securities. The _____ will have a fund manager that trades the pooled money on a regular basis. As of early 2008, the worldwide value of all _____s totals more than $26 trillion.
   a. Laffer curve
   b. Competition law
   c. Mutual fund
   d. Moving average

29. _____ refers to the confirmation of certain characteristics of an object, person, or organization. This confirmation is often, but not always, provided by some form of external review, education, or assessment. One of the most common types of _____ in modern society is professional _____, where a person is certified as being able to competently complete a job or task, usually by the passing of an examination.
   a. BMC Software, Inc.
   b. BNSF Railway
   c. 3M Company
   d. Certification

30. _____ is that part of statistical practice concerned with the selection of individual observations intended to yield some knowledge about a population of concern, especially for the purposes of statistical inference. Each observation measures one or more properties (weight, location, etc.) of an observable entity enumerated to distinguish objects or individuals.
   a. Arthur Betz Laffer
   b. Alan Greenspan
   c. Abby Joseph Cohen
   d. Sampling

31. The _____ is the former authoritative body of the American Institute of Certified Public Accountants (AICPA.) It was created by the American Institute of Certified Public Accountants in 1959 and issued pronouncements on accounting principles until 1973, when it was replaced by the Financial Accounting Standards Board (FASB.)

The _____ was disbanded in the hopes that the smaller, fully-independent FASB could more effectively create accounting standards.

   a. Institute of Management Accountants
   b. Accounting Principles Board
   c. International Federation of Accountants
   d. American Payroll Association

32. _____ were documents issued by the Committee on Accounting Procedure between 1938 and 1959 on various accounting problems. They were discontinued with the dissolution of the Committee in 1959 under a recommendation from the Special Committee on Research Program. In all, 51 bulletins were issued, however, the lack of binding authority over AICPA's membership reduced the influence of, and compliance with the content of the bulletins.
   a. ABC Television Network
   b. AIG
   c. Other postemployment benefits
   d. Accounting Research Bulletins

33. The _____ was a predecessor of the Accounting Principles Board, itself a predecessor to the Financial Accounting Standards Board in the United States. Its formation and activities were early efforts to rationalize and legitimize the reporting of business performance. However, it is widely regarded as having failed.

   a. Price variance
   b. Consolidated financial statements
   c. Lump sum
   d. Committee on Accounting Procedure

34. The _____ is a private, not-for-profit organization whose primary purpose is to develop generally accepted accounting principles (GAAP) within the United States in the public's interest. The Securities and Exchange Commission (SEC) designated the _____ as the organization responsible for setting accounting standards for public companies in the U.S. It was created in 1973, replacing the Accounting Principles Board and the Committee on Accounting Procedure of the American Institute of Certified Public Accountants. The _____'s mission is 'to establish and improve standards of financial accounting and reporting for the guidance and education of the public, including issuers, auditors, and users of financial information.'

The _____ is not a governmental body.

   a. Governmental Accounting Standards Board
   b. Public company
   c. Fannie Mae
   d. Financial Accounting Standards Board

35. The _____ is an independent agency of the United States government, established in 1914 by the _____ Act. Its principal mission is the promotion of 'consumer protection' and the elimination and prevention of what regulators perceive to be harmfully 'anti-competitive' business practices, such as coercive monopoly.

The _____ Act was one of President Wilson's major acts against trusts.

   a. Federal Trade Commission
   b. BNSF Railway
   c. 3M Company
   d. BMC Software, Inc.

36. An _____ is the buying of one company by another. An _____ may be friendly or hostile. In the former case, the companies cooperate in negotiations; in the latter case, the takeover target is unwilling to be bought or the target's board has no prior knowledge of the offer. _____ usually refers to a purchase of a smaller firm by a larger one. Sometimes, however, a smaller firm will acquire management control of a larger or longer established company and keep its name for the combined entity. This is known as a reverse takeover.

   a. AIG
   b. Acquisition
   c. AMEX
   d. ABC Television Network

37. Literally, _____ means: 'urgently asking'. It is the action or instance of soliciting; petition; proposal.

In England and Wales, the term soliciting refers to: 'for a common prostitute to loiter or solicit in a street or public place for the purpose of prostitution', under the Street Offences Act 1959.

   a. Solicitation
   b. BNSF Railway
   c. 3M Company
   d. BMC Software, Inc.

Chapter 14. Professional Ethics

38. The _____ is the highest judicial body in the United States, and leads the federal judiciary. It consists of the Chief Justice of the United States and eight Associate Justices, who are nominated by the President and confirmed with the 'advice and consent' (majority vote) of the Senate. Once appointed, Justices effectively have life tenure, serving 'during good Behaviour', which terminates only upon death, resignation, retirement, or conviction on impeachment.
   a. BMC Software, Inc.
   b. BNSF Railway
   c. 3M Company
   d. Supreme Court of the United States

39. _____ is a concept whereby a person's financial liability is limited to a fixed sum, most commonly the value of a person's investment in a company or partnership with _____. A shareholder in a limited company is not personally liable for any of the debts of the company, other than for the value of his investment in that company. The same is true for the members of a _____ partnership and the limited partners in a limited partnership.
   a. Joint venture
   b. Burden of proof
   c. Limited liability
   d. Due diligence

40. A _____ is a partnership in which some or all partners (depending on the jurisdiction) have limited liability. It therefore exhibits elements of partnerships and corporations. In an _____ one partner is not responsible or liable for another partner's misconduct or negligence.
   a. Financial Accounting Standards Board
   b. Privately held
   c. Dow Jones ' Company
   d. Limited liability partnership

41. A _____ is a form of partnership similar to a general partnership, except that in addition to one or more general partners (GPs), there are one or more limited partners (_____s.) It is a partnership in which only one partner is required to be a general partner.

The GPs are, in all major respects, in the same legal position as partners in a conventional firm, i.e. they have management control, share the right to use partnership property, share the profits of the firm in predefined proportions, and have joint and several liability for the debts of the partnership.

   a. Minority interest
   b. Debenture
   c. Limited partnership
   d. Dow Jones ' Company

42. A _____ is a type of business entity in which partners (owners) share with each other the profits or losses of the business undertaking in which all have invested. _____s are often favored over corporations for taxation purposes, as the _____ structure does not generally incur a tax on profits before it is distributed to the partners (i.e. there is no dividend tax levied.) However, depending on the _____ structure and the jurisdiction in which it operates, owners of a _____ may be exposed to greater personal liability than they would as shareholders of a corporation.
   a. Partnership
   b. Resource Conservation and Recovery Act
   c. Corporate governance
   d. National Information Infrastructure Protection Act

43. A _____, or simply proprietorship is a type of business entity which legally has no separate existence from its owner. Hence, the limitations of liability enjoyed by a corporation and limited liability partnerships do not apply to sole proprietors. All debts of the business are debts of the owner.
   a. Customer satisfaction
   b. Free cash flow
   c. Time to market
   d. Sole proprietorship

44. In financial accounting, a _____ is defined as an obligation of an entity arising from past transactions or events, the settlement of which may result in the transfer or use of assets, provision of services or other yielding of economic benefits in the future.
   a. False Claims Act
   b. Corporate governance
   c. Vested
   d. Liability

45. A sole _____, or simply _____ is a type of business entity which legally has no separate existence from its owner. Hence, the limitations of liability enjoyed by a corporation and limited liability partnerships do not apply to sole proprietors. All debts of the business are debts of the owner.
   a. Pre-determined overhead rate
   b. Safety stock
   c. Free cash flow
   d. Proprietorship

46. An _____ is a term used in behavioral economics to describe those types of behaviors that impose costs on a person in the long-run that are not taken into account when making decisions in the present. Classical Economics discourages government from creating legislation that targets internalities, because it is assumed that the consumer takes these personal costs into account when paying for the good that causes the _____. For example, cigarettes should be taxed because of the negative consumption externalities that they impose, such as second-hand smoke, not because the smoker harms him or herself by smoking.
   a. Authorised capital
   b. Inventory turnover ratio
   c. Internality
   d. Operating budget

47. The _____ is the United States federal government agency that collects taxes and enforces the internal revenue laws. It is an agency within the U.S. Dept of the treasury responsible for interpretation and application of Federal tax law. The official U.S. Treasury regulations provide (in part):

The _____ is a bureau of the Department of the Treasury under the immediate direction of the Commissioner of Internal Revenue.

   a. Indirect tax
   b. Internal Revenue Service
   c. Use tax
   d. Income tax

48. _____ in economics and business is the result of an exchange and from that trade we assign a numerical monetary value to a good, service or asset. If Alice trades Bob 4 apples for an orange, the _____ of an orange is 4 apples. Inversely, the _____ of an apple is 1/4 oranges.
   a. Discounts and allowances
   b. Transactional Net Margin Method
   c. Price discrimination
   d. Price

Chapter 15. Legal Liability

1. In financial accounting, a _____ is defined as an obligation of an entity arising from past transactions or events, the settlement of which may result in the transfer or use of assets, provision of services or other yielding of economic benefits in the future.
   - a. Vested
   - b. Liability
   - c. False Claims Act
   - d. Corporate governance

2. The Federal National Mortgage Association (FNMA) (NYSE: FNM), commonly known as _____, is a stockholder-owned corporation chartered by Congress in 1968 as a government sponsored enterprise (GSE), but founded in 1938 during the Great Depression. The corporation's purpose is to purchase and securitize mortgages in order to ensure that funds are consistently available to the institutions that lend money to home buyers.

   On September 7, 2008, James Lockhart, director of the Federal Housing Finance Agency (FHFA), announced that _____ and Freddie Mac were being placed into conservatorship of the FHFA.

   - a. Fannie Mae
   - b. National Conference of Commissioners on Uniform State Laws
   - c. Public company
   - d. Freddie Mac

3. A _____ has several related meanings:
   - a daily record of events or business; a private _____ is usually referred to as a diary.
   - a newspaper or other periodical, in the literal sense of one published each day;
   - many publications issued at stated intervals, such as magazines, or scholarly academic _____s, or the record of the transactions of a society, are often called _____s. Although _____ is sometimes used, erroneously, as a synonym for 'magazine,' in academic use, a _____ refers to a serious, scholarly publication, most often peer-reviewed. A non-scholarly magazine written for an educated audience about an industry or an area of professional activity is usually called a professional magazine.

   The word 'journalist' for one whose business is writing for the public press has been in use since the end of the 17th century.

   Open access _____s are scholarly _____s that are available to the reader without financial or other barrier other than access to the internet itself. Some are subsidized, and some require payment on behalf of the author. Subsidized _____s are financed by an academic institution or a government information center.

   - a. BNSF Railway
   - b. Journal
   - c. 3M Company
   - d. BMC Software, Inc.

4. A _____ is the transfer of an interest in property (or the equivalent in law - a charge) to a lender as a security for a debt - usually a loan of money. While a _____ in itself is not a debt, it is the lender's security for a debt. It is a transfer of an interest in land (or the equivalent) from the owner to the _____ lender, on the condition that this interest will be returned to the owner when the terms of the _____ have been satisfied or performed.
   - a. BMC Software, Inc.
   - b. BNSF Railway
   - c. 3M Company
   - d. Mortgage

5. The _____ (sometimes called 'Peekaboo') is a private-sector, non-profit corporation created by the Sarbanes-Oxley Act, a 2002 United States federal law, to oversee the auditors of public companies. Its stated purpose is to 'protect the interests of investors and further the public interest in the preparation of informative, fair, and independent audit reports'. Although a private entity, the _____ has many government-like regulatory functions, making it in some ways similar to the private Self Regulatory Organizations (SROs) that regulate stock markets and other aspects of the financial markets in the United States.
   a. Financial Crimes Enforcement Network
   b. Pension Benefit Guaranty Corporation
   c. 3M Company
   d. Public Company Accounting Oversight Board

6. A _____ is a fungible, negotiable instrument representing financial value. they are broadly categorized into debt securities (such as banknotes, bonds and debentures), and equity securities; e.g., common stocks. The company or other entity issuing the _____ is called the issuer.
   a. 3M Company
   b. BMC Software, Inc.
   c. Security
   d. Tracking stock

7. The U.S. _____ is an independent agency of the United States government which holds primary responsibility for enforcing the federal securities laws and regulating the securities industry, the nation's stock and options exchanges, and other electronic securities markets. The SEC was created by section 4 of the Securities Exchange Act of 1934 (now codified as 15 U.S.C. ÂÂ§ 78d and commonly referred to as the 1934 Act.)
   a. Securities and Exchange Commission
   b. BNSF Railway
   c. 3M Company
   d. BMC Software, Inc.

8. _____s are any method of reducing taxable income resulting in a reduction of the payments to tax collecting entities, including state and federal governments. The methodology can vary depending on local and international tax laws.

In North America, a _____ is generally defined as any method that recovers more than $1 in tax for every $1 spent, within 4 years.

   a. Tax avoidance
   b. Tax protester
   c. Corporate tax
   d. Tax shelter

9. Congress enacted the _____, in the aftermath of the stock market crash of 1929 and during the ensuing Great Depression.
   a. Bookkeeping
   b. Monte Carlo methods
   c. Sustainability measurement
   d. Securities Act of 1933

10. _____ is a legal concept in the common law legal systems usually used to achieve compensation for injuries (not accidents.) _____ is a type of tort or delict (also known as a civil wrong.)
   a. Letter of credit
   b. Robinson-Patman Act
   c. Negligence
   d. Hospital Survey and Construction Act

Chapter 15. Legal Liability

11. _____ LLP, based in Chicago, was once one of the 'Big Five' accounting firms among PricewaterhouseCoopers, Deloitte Touche Tohmatsu, Ernst ' Young and KPMG, providing auditing, tax, and consulting services to large corporations. In 2002, the firm voluntarily surrendered its licenses to practice as Certified Public Accountants in the United States after being found guilty of criminal charges relating to the firm's handling of the auditing of Enron, the energy corporation, resulting in the loss of 85,000 jobs. Although the verdict was subsequently overturned by the Supreme Court of the United States, it has not returned as a viable business.

a. AIG
c. AMEX
b. Arthur Andersen
d. ABC Television Network

12. In mathematics _____s are numbers or other things that get multiplied. In particular, see:

- Factorization, the decomposition of an object into a product of other objects
- Integer factorization, the process of breaking down a composite number into smaller non-trivial divisors
- A coefficient
- A divisor of a particular number, or of an element of a monoid
- A von Neumann algebra with a trivial center

In statistics

- _____ analysis is the study of how _____s or certain variables affect variables.

In technology:

- Human _____s, a profession that focuses on how people interact with products, tools, or procedures
- 'Functionality, Application domain, Conditions, Technology, Objects and Responsibility;', In object-oriented programming

In computer science and information technology:

- Authentication _____, a piece of information used to verify a person's identity for security purposes
- _____, a Unix command for numbers factorization
- _____ (programming language), an experimental Forth-like programming language

In television:

- The O'Reilly _____, an American talk show hosted by Bill O'Reilly on Fox News.
- The Krypton _____, a British game show hosted by Gordon Burns, formally on ITV. Also had an American version.

a. The Goodyear Tire ' Rubber Company
c. Merck ' Co., Inc.
b. Valuation
d. Factor

13. The general definition of an _____ is an evaluation of a person, organization, system, process, project or product. _____s are performed to ascertain the validity and reliability of information; also to provide an assessment of a system's internal control. The goal of an _____ is to express an opinion on the person/organization/system (etc) in question, under evaluation based on work done on a test basis.
   a. Assurance service
   b. Institute of Chartered Accountants of India
   c. Audit regime
   d. Audit

14. _____ is a term that is commonly used in relation to the audit of the financial statements of an entity. (.
   a. Auditor independence
   b. Audit working paper
   c. Engagement Letter
   d. Audit risk

15. _____, in auditing, is the risk that a company's internal controls are insufficient to mitigate or detect errors or fraud.
   a. BMC Software, Inc.
   b. 3M Company
   c. BNSF Railway
   d. Control risk

16. _____, in auditing, is the risk that the account or section being audited is materially misstated without considering internal controls due to error; _____ does not include an assessment of the risk of material misstatement due to fraud. The assessment of _____ depends on the professional judgement of the auditor, and it is done after assessing the business environment of the entity being audited.

   _____ is typically assessed using a scale, with assessments being either low, medium, or high.

   a. AIG
   b. AMEX
   c. ABC Television Network
   d. Inherent risk

17. An _____ is a term used in behavioral economics to describe those types of behaviors that impose costs on a person in the long-run that are not taken into account when making decisions in the present. Classical Economics discourages government from creating legislation that targets internalities, because it is assumed that the consumer takes these personal costs into account when paying for the good that causes the _____. For example, cigarettes should be taxed because of the negative consumption externalities that they impose, such as second-hand smoke, not because the smoker harms him or herself by smoking.
   a. Operating budget
   b. Authorised capital
   c. Internality
   d. Inventory turnover ratio

18. In accounting and organizational theory, _____ is defined as a process effected by an organization's structure, work and authority flows, people and management information systems, designed to help the organization accomplish specific goals or objectives. It is a means by which an organization's resources are directed, monitored, and measured. It plays an important role in preventing and detecting fraud and protecting the organization's resources, both physical (e.g., machinery and property) and intangible (e.g., reputation or intellectual property such as trademarks.)
   a. Audit committee
   b. Audit risk
   c. Internal control
   d. Auditor independence

Chapter 15. Legal Liability

19. _____ is a concept that denotes the precise probability of specific eventualities. Technically, the notion of _____ is independent from the notion of value and, as such, eventualities may have both beneficial and adverse consequences. However, in general usage the convention is to focus only on potential negative impact to some characteristic of value that may arise from a future event.
   a. Risk
   b. Risk adjusted return on capital
   c. Discounting
   d. Discount factor

20. _____ is that part of statistical practice concerned with the selection of individual observations intended to yield some knowledge about a population of concern, especially for the purposes of statistical inference. Each observation measures one or more properties (weight, location, etc.) of an observable entity enumerated to distinguish objects or individuals.
   a. Abby Joseph Cohen
   b. Arthur Betz Laffer
   c. Sampling
   d. Alan Greenspan

21. A _____ or chief executive is one of the highest-ranking corporate officer (executive) or administrator in charge of total management. An individual selected as President and _____ of a corporation, company, organization, or agency, reports to the board of directors. In internal communication and press releases, many companies capitalize the term and those of other high positions, even when they are not proper nouns.
   a. Kohlberg Kravis Roberts ' Co
   b. Return on equity
   c. Chief executive officer
   d. Return on assets

22. A _____ is an annual report required by the U.S. Securities and Exchange Commission (SEC), that gives a comprehensive summary of a public company's performance. Although similarly named, the annual report on _____ is distinct from the often glossy 'annual report to shareholders', which a company must send to its shareholders when it holds an annual meeting to elect directors (though some companies combine the annual report and the 10-K into one document.) The 10-K includes information such as company history, organizational structure, executive compensation, equity, subsidiaries, and audited financial statements, among other information.
   a. Form 10-K
   b. Form 8-K
   c. Form 10-Q
   d. 3M Company

23. _____, Quarterly Report Pursuant to Section 13 or 15(d) of the Securities Exchange Act of 1934, is an SEC filing that must be filed quarterly with the US Securities and Exchange Commission. It contains similar information to the annual form 10-K, however the information is generally less detailed, and the financial statements are generally unaudited. Information for the final quarter of a firm's fiscal year is included in the 10-K, so only three 10-Q filings are made each year.
   a. 3M Company
   b. Form 8-K
   c. Form 20-F
   d. Form 10-Q

24. _____ refers to the confirmation of certain characteristics of an object, person, or organization. This confirmation is often, but not always, provided by some form of external review, education, or assessment. One of the most common types of _____ in modern society is professional _____, where a person is certified as being able to competently complete a job or task, usually by the passing of an examination.
   a. 3M Company
   b. BNSF Railway
   c. BMC Software, Inc.
   d. Certification

Chapter 15. Legal Liability

25. _____, also referred to simply as a 'public offering' or 'flotation,' is when a company issues common stock or shares to the public for the first time. They are often issued by smaller, younger companies seeking capital to expand, but can also be done by large privately-owned companies looking to become publicly traded.

In an _____ the issuer may obtain the assistance of an underwriting firm, which helps it determine what type of security to issue (common or preferred), best offering price and time to bring it to market.

a. Intergenerational equity
c. AT'T Wireless Services, Inc.
b. Insolvency
d. Initial public offering

26. Initial _____, also referred to simply as a '_____' or 'flotation,' is when a company issues common stock or shares to the public for the first time. They are often issued by smaller, younger companies seeking capital to expand, but can also be done by large privately-owned companies looking to become publicly traded.

In an Ipublic offering the issuer may obtain the assistance of an underwriting firm, which helps it determine what type of security to issue (common or preferred), best offering price and time to bring it to market.

a. Restricted stock
c. Commercial paper
b. Gross income
d. Public offering

27. The _____ is the national, professional association of CPAs in the United States, with more than 330,000 members, including CPAs in business and industry, public practice, government, and education; student affiliates; and international associates. It sets ethical standards for the profession and U.S. auditing standards for audits of private companies; federal, state and local governments; and non-profit organizations.

Approximately 40% of its members are engaged in the practice of public accounting, in areas such as auditing, accounting, taxation, general business consulting, business valuation, personal financial planning and business technology.

a. AIG
c. Other postemployment benefits
b. ABC Television Network
d. American Institute of Certified Public Accountants

28. _____, commonly abbreviated as SAS, provide guidance to external auditors on generally accepted auditing standards in regards to auditing an entity and issuing a report. They are usually issued by the certified public accountant authoritative body in the region where the standards apply, such as the American Institute of Certified Public Accountants in the United States.

- _____
- _____ (Taiwan)

a. Financial Instruments and Exchange Law
c. RSM International
b. GASB 45
d. Statements on Auditing Standards

Chapter 15. Legal Liability

29. A _____ is a statute in a common law legal system that sets forth the maximum period of time, after certain events, that legal proceedings based on those events may be initiated. In civil law systems, similar provisions are usually part of the civil code or criminal code and are often known collectively as 'periods of prescription' or 'prescriptive periods.'

A common law legal system might have a statute limiting the time for prosecution of crimes called misdemeanors to two years after the offense occurred. In that statute, if a person is discovered to have committed a misdemeanor three years ago, the time has expired for the prosecution of the misdemeanor.

a. Statute of limitations
b. 3M Company
c. BNSF Railway
d. BMC Software, Inc.

30. _____ is a report required to be filed by public companies with the United States Securities and Exchange Commission pursuant to the Securities Exchange Act of 1934, as amended. After a significant event like bankruptcy or departure of a CEO, a public company generally must file a Current Report on _____ within four business days to provide an update to previously filed quartely reports on Form 10-Q and/or Annual Reports on Form 10-K. _____ is a very broad form used to notify investors of any unscheduled material event that is important to shareholders or the SEC.

a. 3M Company
b. Form 10-Q
c. Form 20-F
d. Form 8-K

31. The _____ of 1934 is a law governing the secondary trading of securities (stocks, bonds, and debentures) in the United States of America. The Act, 48 Stat. 881 (enacted June 6, 1934), codified at 15 U.S.C.

a. BNSF Railway
b. BMC Software, Inc.
c. 3M Company
d. Securities Exchange Act

32. The _____ is a law governing the secondary trading of securities (stocks, bonds, and debentures) in the United States of America. The Act, 48 Stat. 881 (enacted June 6, 1934), codified at 15 U.S.C.

a. BNSF Railway
b. 3M Company
c. BMC Software, Inc.
d. Securities Exchange Act of 1934

33. _____ is the world's largest professional services firm. It was formed in 1998 from a merger between Price Waterhouse and Coopers ' Lybrand, both formed in London.

_____ earned aggregated worldwide revenues of $28 billion for fiscal 2008, and employed over 146,000 people in 150 countries.

a. PricewaterhouseCoopers
b. Total-factor productivity
c. Daybook
d. Serial bonds

34. The _____ is the highest judicial body in the United States, and leads the federal judiciary. It consists of the Chief Justice of the United States and eight Associate Justices, who are nominated by the President and confirmed with the 'advice and consent' (majority vote) of the Senate. Once appointed, Justices effectively have life tenure, serving 'during good Behaviour', which terminates only upon death, resignation, retirement, or conviction on impeachment.

a. Supreme Court of the United States
b. BNSF Railway
c. 3M Company
d. BMC Software, Inc.

35. The _____ is the obligation to shift the assumed conclusion away from an oppositional opinion to one's own position. The _____ may only be fulfilled by evidence.

The _____ is often associated with the Latin maxim semper necessitas probandi incumbit ei qui agit, the best translation of which seems to be: 'the necessity of proof always lies with the person who lays charges.' This is a statement of a version of the presumption of innocence which underpins the assessment of evidence in some legal systems, and is not a general statement of when one takes on the _____.

a. Covenant
c. Partnership
b. Primary authority
d. Burden of proof

36. The _____ of 1977 (15 U.S.C. §§ 78dd-1, et seq.) is a United States federal law known primarily for two of its main provisions, one that addresses accounting transparency requirements under the Securities Exchange Act of 1934 and another concerning bribery of foreign officials.

a. Foreign Corrupt Practices Act
c. Competition law
b. Lease
d. Pre-emption right

37. The _____ of 2002 (Pub.L. 107-204, 116 Stat. 745, enacted July 30, 2002), also known as the Public Company Accounting Reform and Investor Protection Act of 2002, is a United States federal law enacted on July 30, 2002 in response to a number of major corporate and accounting scandals including those affecting Enron, Tyco International, Adelphia, Peregrine Systems and WorldCom. The legislation establishes new or enhanced standards for all U.S. public company boards, management, and public accounting firms. It does not apply to privately held companies.

a. Sarbanes-Oxley Act
c. Lease
b. Fair Labor Standards Act
d. FCPA

38. The _____ are rules that set out a uniform sentencing policy for convicted felons in the United States federal courts system.

The Guidelines are the product of the United States Sentencing Commission and are part of an overall federal sentencing reform package that took effect in the mid-1960s. The implementation of this reform package was the result of bipartisan cooperation, led chiefly by Senator Edward Kennedy, as Chair of the Senate Judiciary Committee, and Attorney General Edwin Meese.

a. Hospital Survey and Construction Act
c. Letter of credit
b. Primary authority
d. Federal sentencing guidelines

39. _____ is a concept whereby a person's financial liability is limited to a fixed sum, most commonly the value of a person's investment in a company or partnership with _____. A shareholder in a limited company is not personally liable for any of the debts of the company, other than for the value of his investment in that company. The same is true for the members of a _____ partnership and the limited partners in a limited partnership.

a. Burden of proof
c. Due diligence
b. Joint venture
d. Limited liability

40. A _____ is a partnership in which some or all partners (depending on the jurisdiction) have limited liability. It therefore exhibits elements of partnerships and corporations. In an _____ one partner is not responsible or liable for another partner's misconduct or negligence.

a. Financial Accounting Standards Board
b. Limited liability partnership
c. Privately held
d. Dow Jones ' Company

41. A _____ is a type of business entity in which partners (owners) share with each other the profits or losses of the business undertaking in which all have invested. _____s are often favored over corporations for taxation purposes, as the _____ structure does not generally incur a tax on profits before it is distributed to the partners (i.e. there is no dividend tax levied.) However, depending on the _____ structure and the jurisdiction in which it operates, owners of a _____ may be exposed to greater personal liability than they would as shareholders of a corporation.
   a. Resource Conservation and Recovery Act
   b. National Information Infrastructure Protection Act
   c. Corporate governance
   d. Partnership

42. _____, in law and economics, is a form of risk management primarily used to hedge against the risk of a contingent loss. _____ is defined as the equitable transfer of the risk of a loss, from one entity to another, in exchange for a premium, and can be thought of as a guaranteed small loss to prevent a large, possibly devastating loss. An insurer is a company selling the _____; an insured is the person or entity buying the _____.
   a. AIG
   b. ABC Television Network
   c. Insurance
   d. AMEX

43. In economics, _____ or _____ goods or real _____ refers to factors of production used to create goods or services that are not themselves significantly consumed (though they may depreciate) in the production process. _____ goods may be acquired with money or financial _____. In finance and accounting, _____ generally refers to financial wealth, especially that used to start or maintain a business.
   a. Disclosure
   b. Vyborg Appeal
   c. Screening
   d. Capital

44. A _____ is any one of a variety of different systems, institutions, procedures, social relations and infrastructures whereby persons trade, and goods and services are exchanged, forming part of the economy. It is an arrangement that allows buyers and sellers to exchange things. _____s vary in size, range, geographic scale, location, types and variety of human communities, as well as the types of goods and services traded.
   a. Market Failure
   b. Market
   c. Perfect competition
   d. Recession

Chapter 16. Internal, Governmental, and Fraud Audits

1. An _____ is a term used in behavioral economics to describe those types of behaviors that impose costs on a person in the long-run that are not taken into account when making decisions in the present. Classical Economics discourages government from creating legislation that targets internalities, because it is assumed that the consumer takes these personal costs into account when paying for the good that causes the _____. For example, cigarettes should be taxed because of the negative consumption externalities that they impose, such as second-hand smoke, not because the smoker harms him or herself by smoking.

   a. Operating budget
   c. Inventory turnover ratio
   b. Authorised capital
   d. Internality

2. _____ is a profession and activity involved in helping organisations achieve their stated objectives. It does this by using a systematic methodology for analyzing business processes, procedures and activities with the goal of highlighting organizational problems and recommending solutions. Professionals called internal auditors are employed by organizations to perform the _____ activity.

   a. Internal auditing
   c. Assurance service
   b. ITGCs
   d. Information audit

3. The general definition of an _____ is an evaluation of a person, organization, system, process, project or product. _____s are performed to ascertain the validity and reliability of information; also to provide an assessment of a system's internal control. The goal of an _____ is to express an opinion on the person/organization/system (etc) in question, under evaluation based on work done on a test basis.

   a. Assurance service
   c. Institute of Chartered Accountants of India
   b. Audit regime
   d. Audit

4. Established in 1941, The _____ is internationally recognized as a trustworthy guidance-setting body. Serving members in 165 countries, The IIA is the internal audit profession's global voice, chief advocate, recognized authority, acknowledged leader, and principal educator, with global headquarters in Altamonte Springs, Fla., United States.

   The stated mission of The _____ is to provide dynamic leadership for the global profession of internal auditing.

   a. Auditor independence
   c. Institute of Internal Auditors
   b. Audit regime
   d. Event data

5. Internal auditing is a profession and activity involved in helping organisations achieve their stated objectives. It does this by utilizing a systematic methodology for analyzing business processes, procedures and activities with the goal of highlighting organizational problems and recommending solutions. Professionals called _____ are employed by organizations to perform the internal auditing activity.

   a. Auditor independence
   c. Internal Auditing
   b. Internal auditors
   d. Auditing Standards Board

6. The _____ (sometimes called 'Peekaboo') is a private-sector, non-profit corporation created by the Sarbanes-Oxley Act, a 2002 United States federal law, to oversee the auditors of public companies. Its stated purpose is to 'protect the interests of investors and further the public interest in the preparation of informative, fair, and independent audit reports'. Although a private entity, the _____ has many government-like regulatory functions, making it in some ways similar to the private Self Regulatory Organizations (SROs) that regulate stock markets and other aspects of the financial markets in the United States.

Chapter 16. Internal, Governmental, and Fraud Audits

a. 3M Company
b. Pension Benefit Guaranty Corporation
c. Public Company Accounting Oversight Board
d. Financial Crimes Enforcement Network

7. The U.S. _____ is an independent agency of the United States government which holds primary responsibility for enforcing the federal securities laws and regulating the securities industry, the nation's stock and options exchanges, and other electronic securities markets. The SEC was created by section 4 of the Securities Exchange Act of 1934 (now codified as 15 U.S.C. ÂÂ§ 78d and commonly referred to as the 1934 Act.)
a. BMC Software, Inc.
b. Securities and Exchange Commission
c. BNSF Railway
d. 3M Company

8. _____ refers to the additional value of a commodity over the cost of commodities used to produce it from the previous stage of production. An example is the price of gasoline at the pump over the price of the oil in it. In national accounts used in macroeconomics, it refers to the contribution of the factors of production, i.e., land, labor, and capital goods, to raising the value of a product and corresponds to the incomes received by the owners of these factors.
a. Supply-side economics
b. 3M Company
c. Minimum wage
d. Value added

9. _____ is a term that is commonly used in relation to the audit of the financial statements of an entity. (.
a. Audit working paper
b. Auditor independence
c. Engagement Letter
d. Audit risk

10. _____, in auditing, is the risk that a company's internal controls are insufficient to mitigate or detect errors or fraud.
a. 3M Company
b. BNSF Railway
c. Control risk
d. BMC Software, Inc.

11. _____, in auditing, is the risk that the account or section being audited is materially misstated without considering internal controls due to error; _____ does not include an assessment of the risk of material misstatement due to fraud. The assessment of _____ depends on the professional judgement of the auditor, and it is done after assessing the business environment of the entity being audited.

_____ is typically assessed using a scale, with assessments being either low, medium, or high.

a. AMEX
b. AIG
c. ABC Television Network
d. Inherent risk

12. In accounting and organizational theory, _____ is defined as a process effected by an organization's structure, work and authority flows, people and management information systems, designed to help the organization accomplish specific goals or objectives. It is a means by which an organization's resources are directed, monitored, and measured. It plays an important role in preventing and detecting fraud and protecting the organization's resources, both physical (e.g., machinery and property) and intangible (e.g., reputation or intellectual property such as trademarks.)
a. Audit committee
b. Internal control
c. Auditor independence
d. Audit risk

Chapter 16. Internal, Governmental, and Fraud Audits

13. _____ is a concept that denotes the precise probability of specific eventualities. Technically, the notion of _____ is independent from the notion of value and, as such, eventualities may have both beneficial and adverse consequences. However, in general usage the convention is to focus only on potential negative impact to some characteristic of value that may arise from a future event.
    a. Risk adjusted return on capital
    b. Discounting
    c. Discount factor
    d. Risk

14. _____ is that part of statistical practice concerned with the selection of individual observations intended to yield some knowledge about a population of concern, especially for the purposes of statistical inference. Each observation measures one or more properties (weight, location, etc.) of an observable entity enumerated to distinguish objects or individuals.
    a. Arthur Betz Laffer
    b. Alan Greenspan
    c. Abby Joseph Cohen
    d. Sampling

15. A _____ an audit of financial statements, is the review of the financial statements of a company or any other legal entity (including governments), resulting in the publication of an independent opinion on whether or not those financial statements are relevant, accurate, complete, and fairly presented. _____s are typically performed by firms of practicing accountants due to the specialist financial reporting knowledge they require. The _____ is one of many assurance or attestation functions provided by accounting and auditing firms, whereby the firm provides an independent opinion on published information.
    a. Management representation
    b. Financial audit
    c. Mainframe audit
    d. Lead Auditor

16. A _____ has several related meanings:

    - a daily record of events or business; a private _____ is usually referred to as a diary.
    - a newspaper or other periodical, in the literal sense of one published each day;
    - many publications issued at stated intervals, such as magazines, or scholarly academic _____s, or the record of the transactions of a society, are often called _____s. Although _____ is sometimes used, erroneously, as a synonym for 'magazine,' in academic use, a _____ refers to a serious, scholarly publication, most often peer-reviewed. A non-scholarly magazine written for an educated audience about an industry or an area of professional activity is usually called a professional magazine.

The word 'journalist' for one whose business is writing for the public press has been in use since the end of the 17th century.

Open access _____s are scholarly _____s that are available to the reader without financial or other barrier other than access to the internet itself. Some are subsidized, and some require payment on behalf of the author. Subsidized _____s are financed by an academic institution or a government information center.

   a. BNSF Railway
   b. BMC Software, Inc.
   c. Journal
   d. 3M Company

17. _____ is a demonstration of a process -- such as a variable, term, or object -- relative in terms of the specific process or set of validation tests used to determine its presence and quantity. Properties described in this manner must be sufficiently accessible, so that persons other than the definer may independently measure or test for them at will. An _____ is generally designed to model a conceptual definition.

   a. ABC Television Network   b. Operational definition
   c. AMEX   d. AIG

18. _____ is the process of systematic examination of a quality system carried out by an internal or external quality auditor or an audit team. It is an important part of organization's quality management system and is a key element in the ISO quality system standard, ISO 9001.

_____s are typically performed at predefined time intervals and ensure that the institution has clearly-defined internal quality monitoring procedures linked to effective action.

   a. BMC Software, Inc.   b. Quality audit
   c. BNSF Railway   d. 3M Company

19. _____ is the recording of the value of assets, liabilities, income, and expenses in the daybooks, journals, and ledgers, in which debit and credit entries are chronologically posted to record changes in value. _____ is often mistaken for accounting, which is the system of recording, verifying, and reporting such information. Practitioners of accounting are called accountants.

   a. Bookkeeping   b. Debit and credit
   c. Controlling account   d. Double-entry bookkeeping

20. In probability theory and statistics, the _____ (or expectation value or mean and for continuous random variables with a density function it is the probability density -weighted integral of the possible values.

The term '_____' can be misleading.

   a. AMEX   b. ABC Television Network
   c. AIG   d. Expected value

21. _____ refers to an examination of a program, function, operation or the management systems and procedures of a governmental or non-profit entity to assess whether the entity is achieving economy, efficiency and effectiveness in the employment of available resources. The examination is objective and systematic, generally using structured and professionally adopted methodologies.

In most countries, _____s of governmental activities are carried out by the external audit bodies at federal or state level.

   a. Statements on Auditing Standards   b. Performance audit
   c. Mainframe audit   d. Trustworthy Repositories Audit ' Certification

Chapter 16. Internal, Governmental, and Fraud Audits

22. _____s have been defined by the American Institute of Certified Public Accountants (AICPA) as 'Independent Professional Services that improve information quality or its context'. _____s reduce the information risk; risk that the information provided is incorrect, on more than just financial data. The major purpose of _____s is to provide independent and professional opinions that improve the quality of information to management as well as other decision makers within a given firm.

    a. Assurance service
    b. Auditor independence
    c. Institute of Chartered Accountants of India
    d. ITGCs

23. Established in 1988 the _____ is the professional organization that governs professional fraud examiners. Its activities include producing fraud information, tools and training. It also governs the professional designation of Certified Fraud Examiner.

    a. AMEX
    b. Association of Certified Fraud Examiners
    c. ABC Television Network
    d. AIG

24. _____ is a designation awarded by the Association of _____s (ACertified Fraud Examiner.) The ACertified Fraud Examiner is a 41,000 member-based global association dedicated to providing anti-fraud education and training.

In order to become a _____ one must meet the following requirements:

- Be an Associate Member of the ACertified Fraud Examiner in good standing
- Meet minimum academic and professional requirements
- Be of high moral character
- Agree to abide by the Bylaws and Code of Professional Ethics of the Association of _____s

Generally, applicants for _____ certification have a minimum of a bachelor's degree or equivalent from an institution of higher education. Two years of professional experience related to fraud can be substituted for each year of college.

    a. Certified public accountant
    b. Chartered Certified Accountant
    c. Chartered Accountant
    d. Certified Fraud Examiner

Chapter 17. Overview of Sampling

1. _____ is that part of statistical practice concerned with the selection of individual observations intended to yield some knowledge about a population of concern, especially for the purposes of statistical inference. Each observation measures one or more properties (weight, location, etc.) of an observable entity enumerated to distinguish objects or individuals.

   a. Abby Joseph Cohen
   b. Alan Greenspan
   c. Arthur Betz Laffer
   d. Sampling

2. _____ are ten auditing standards, developed by the AICPA, consisting of general standards, standards of field work, and standards of reporting, along with interpretations. They were developed by the AICPA in 1947 and have undergone minor changes since then.

   The _____ are as follows:

   1. The auditor must have adequate technical training and proficiency to perform the audit
   2. The auditor must maintain independence in mental attitude in all matters related to the audit.
   3. The auditor must use due professional care during the performance of the audit and the preparation of the report.

   1. The auditor must adequately plan the work and must properly supervise any assistants.
   2. The auditor must obtain a sufficient understanding of the entity and its environment, including its internal control, to assess the risk of material misstatement of the financial statements whether due to error or fraud, and to design the nature, timing, and extent of further audit procedures.
   3. The auditor must obtain sufficient appropriate audit evidence by performing audit procedures to afford a reasonable basis for an opinion regarding the financial statements under audit.

   The new standards are in effect for audits of financial statements for periods beginning on or after December 15, 2006.

   1. The auditor must state in the auditor's report whether the financial statements are in accordance with generally accepted accounting principles (GAAP.)
   2. The auditor must identify in the auditor's report those circumstances in which such principles have not been consistently observed in the current period in relation to the preceding period.
   3. When the auditor determines that informative disclosures are not reasonably adequate, the auditor must so state in the auditor's report.
   4. The auditor must either express an opinion regarding the financial statements, taken as a whole the auditor should state the reasons therefore in the auditor's report. In all cases where the auditor's name is associated with the financial statements, the auditor should clearly indicate the character of the auditor's work, if any, and the degree of responsibility the auditor is taking, in the auditor's report.

   a. Continuous auditing
   b. Negative assurance
   c. Joint audit
   d. Generally accepted auditing standards

Chapter 17. Overview of Sampling

3. _____ refers to a business or organization attempting to acquire goods or services to accomplish the goals of the enterprise. Though there are several organizations that attempt to set standards in the _____ process, processes can vary greatly between organizations. Typically the word e;_____e; is not used interchangeably with the word e;procuremente;, since procurement typically includes Expediting, Supplier Quality, and Traffic and Logistics (T'L) in addition to _____.

   a. Free port   b. Consignor
   c. Supply chain   d. Purchasing

4. In mathematics _____s are numbers or other things that get multiplied. In particular, see:

- Factorization, the decomposition of an object into a product of other objects
- Integer factorization, the process of breaking down a composite number into smaller non-trivial divisors
- A coefficient
- A divisor of a particular number, or of an element of a monoid
- A von Neumann algebra with a trivial center

In statistics

- _____ analysis is the study of how _____s or certain variables affect variables.

In technology:

- Human _____s, a profession that focuses on how people interact with products, tools, or procedures
- 'Functionality, Application domain, Conditions, Technology, Objects and Responsibility;', In object-oriented programming

In computer science and information technology:

- Authentication _____, a piece of information used to verify a person's identity for security purposes
- _____, a Unix command for numbers factorization
- _____ (programming language), an experimental Forth-like programming language

In television:

- The O'Reilly _____, an American talk show hosted by Bill O'Reilly on Fox News.
- The Krypton _____, a British game show hosted by Gordon Burns, formally on ITV. Also had an American version.

   a. Factor   b. Valuation
   c. Merck ' Co., Inc.   d. The Goodyear Tire ' Rubber Company

Chapter 17. Overview of Sampling
153

5. _____ is a concept that denotes the precise probability of specific eventualities. Technically, the notion of _____ is independent from the notion of value and, as such, eventualities may have both beneficial and adverse consequences. However, in general usage the convention is to focus only on potential negative impact to some characteristic of value that may arise from a future event.
   a. Risk
   b. Discounting
   c. Discount factor
   d. Risk adjusted return on capital

6. _____, in auditing, is the risk that a company's internal controls are insufficient to mitigate or detect errors or fraud.
   a. Control risk
   b. BNSF Railway
   c. 3M Company
   d. BMC Software, Inc.

7. An _____ is a term used in behavioral economics to describe those types of behaviors that impose costs on a person in the long-run that are not taken into account when making decisions in the present. Classical Economics discourages government from creating legislation that targets internalities, because it is assumed that the consumer takes these personal costs into account when paying for the good that causes the _____. For example, cigarettes should be taxed because of the negative consumption externalities that they impose, such as second-hand smoke, not because the smoker harms him or herself by smoking.
   a. Operating budget
   b. Inventory turnover ratio
   c. Authorised capital
   d. Internality

8. In accounting and organizational theory, _____ is defined as a process effected by an organization's structure, work and authority flows, people and management information systems, designed to help the organization accomplish specific goals or objectives. It is a means by which an organization's resources are directed, monitored, and measured. It plays an important role in preventing and detecting fraud and protecting the organization's resources, both physical (e.g., machinery and property) and intangible (e.g., reputation or intellectual property such as trademarks.)
   a. Audit committee
   b. Auditor independence
   c. Audit risk
   d. Internal control

9. An _____ is the buying of one company by another. An _____ may be friendly or hostile. In the former case, the companies cooperate in negotiations; in the latter case, the takeover target is unwilling to be bought or the target's board has no prior knowledge of the offer. _____ usually refers to a purchase of a smaller firm by a larger one. Sometimes, however, a smaller firm will acquire management control of a larger or longer established company and keep its name for the combined entity. This is known as a reverse takeover.
   a. AIG
   b. Acquisition
   c. AMEX
   d. ABC Television Network

10. The general definition of an _____ is an evaluation of a person, organization, system, process, project or product. _____s are performed to ascertain the validity and reliability of information; also to provide an assessment of a system's internal control. The goal of an _____ is to express an opinion on the person/organization/system (etc) in question, under evaluation based on work done on a test basis.
    a. Institute of Chartered Accountants of India
    b. Audit
    c. Assurance service
    d. Audit regime

11. _____ is a term that is commonly used in relation to the audit of the financial statements of an entity. (.

Chapter 17. Overview of Sampling

a. Engagement Letter
b. Auditor independence
c. Audit working paper
d. Audit risk

12. _____, in auditing, is the risk that the auditing procedures used will not find a material misstatement in the financial statements of the company being audited. .

a. BNSF Railway
b. Detection risk
c. 3M Company
d. BMC Software, Inc.

13. _____, in auditing, is the risk that the account or section being audited is materially misstated without considering internal controls due to error; _____ does not include an assessment of the risk of material misstatement due to fraud. The assessment of _____ depends on the professional judgement of the auditor, and it is done after assessing the business environment of the entity being audited.

_____ is typically assessed using a scale, with assessments being either low, medium, or high.

a. AIG
b. ABC Television Network
c. AMEX
d. Inherent risk

14. _____ is the calculated approximation of a result which is usable even if input data may be incomplete or uncertain.

In statistics, see _____ theory, estimator.

In mathematics, approximation or _____ typically means finding upper or lower bounds of a quantity that cannot readily be computed precisely and is also an educated guess .

a. AMEX
b. Estimation
c. AIG
d. ABC Television Network

15. In probability theory and statistics, _____ is a measure of the variability or dispersion of a population, a data set, or a probability distribution. A low _____ indicates that the data points tend to be very close to the same value (the mean), while high _____ indicates that the data are 'spread out' over a large range of values.

For example, the average height for adult men in the United States is about 70 inches, with a _____ of around 3 inches.

a. Standard deviation
b. Variance
c. Moving average
d. Probability distribution

Chapter 18. Attribute Sampling 155

1. _____ is that part of statistical practice concerned with the selection of individual observations intended to yield some knowledge about a population of concern, especially for the purposes of statistical inference. Each observation measures one or more properties (weight, location, etc.) of an observable entity enumerated to distinguish objects or individuals.
  a. Alan Greenspan
  b. Abby Joseph Cohen
  c. Sampling
  d. Arthur Betz Laffer

2. The _____ is the national, professional association of CPAs in the United States, with more than 330,000 members, including CPAs in business and industry, public practice, government, and education; student affiliates; and international associates. It sets ethical standards for the profession and U.S. auditing standards for audits of private companies; federal, state and local governments; and non-profit organizations.

Approximately 40% of its members are engaged in the practice of public accounting, in areas such as auditing, accounting, taxation, general business consulting, business valuation, personal financial planning and business technology.

  a. Other postemployment benefits
  b. ABC Television Network
  c. AIG
  d. American Institute of Certified Public Accountants

3. An _____ is the buying of one company by another. An _____ may be friendly or hostile. In the former case, the companies cooperate in negotiations; in the latter case, the takeover target is unwilling to be bought or the target's board has no prior knowledge of the offer. _____ usually refers to a purchase of a smaller firm by a larger one. Sometimes, however, a smaller firm will acquire management control of a larger or longer established company and keep its name for the combined entity. This is known as a reverse takeover.
  a. ABC Television Network
  b. AIG
  c. AMEX
  d. Acquisition

4. The general definition of an _____ is an evaluation of a person, organization, system, process, project or product. _____s are performed to ascertain the validity and reliability of information; also to provide an assessment of a system's internal control. The goal of an _____ is to express an opinion on the person/organization/system (etc) in question, under evaluation based on work done on a test basis.
  a. Audit regime
  b. Audit
  c. Institute of Chartered Accountants of India
  d. Assurance service

5. _____ is a term that is commonly used in relation to the audit of the financial statements of an entity. (.
  a. Auditor independence
  b. Audit risk
  c. Audit working paper
  d. Engagement Letter

6. _____, in auditing, is the risk that a company's internal controls are insufficient to mitigate or detect errors or fraud.
  a. BNSF Railway
  b. Control risk
  c. 3M Company
  d. BMC Software, Inc.

7. _____, in auditing, is the risk that the account or section being audited is materially misstated without considering internal controls due to error; _____ does not include an assessment of the risk of material misstatement due to fraud. The assessment of _____ depends on the professional judgement of the auditor, and it is done after assessing the business environment of the entity being audited.

_____ is typically assessed using a scale, with assessments being either low, medium, or high.

    a. Inherent risk
    b. AIG
    c. ABC Television Network
    d. AMEX

8. An _____ is a term used in behavioral economics to describe those types of behaviors that impose costs on a person in the long-run that are not taken into account when making decisions in the present. Classical Economics discourages government from creating legislation that targets internalities, because it is assumed that the consumer takes these personal costs into account when paying for the good that causes the _____. For example, cigarettes should be taxed because of the negative consumption externalities that they impose, such as second-hand smoke, not because the smoker harms him or herself by smoking.

    a. Operating budget
    b. Inventory turnover ratio
    c. Internality
    d. Authorised capital

9. In accounting and organizational theory, _____ is defined as a process effected by an organization's structure, work and authority flows, people and management information systems, designed to help the organization accomplish specific goals or objectives. It is a means by which an organization's resources are directed, monitored, and measured. It plays an important role in preventing and detecting fraud and protecting the organization's resources, both physical (e.g., machinery and property) and intangible (e.g., reputation or intellectual property such as trademarks.)

    a. Auditor independence
    b. Audit committee
    c. Audit risk
    d. Internal control

10. _____ refers to a business or organization attempting to acquire goods or services to accomplish the goals of the enterprise. Though there are several organizations that attempt to set standards in the _____ process, processes can vary greatly between organizations. Typically the word e;_____e; is not used interchangeably with the word e;procuremente;, since procurement typically includes Expediting, Supplier Quality, and Traffic and Logistics (T'L) in addition to _____.

    a. Supply chain
    b. Purchasing
    c. Consignor
    d. Free port

11. _____ is a concept that denotes the precise probability of specific eventualities. Technically, the notion of _____ is independent from the notion of value and, as such, eventualities may have both beneficial and adverse consequences. However, in general usage the convention is to focus only on potential negative impact to some characteristic of value that may arise from a future event.

    a. Risk adjusted return on capital
    b. Discounting
    c. Discount factor
    d. Risk

12. _____ are ten auditing standards, developed by the AICPA, consisting of general standards, standards of field work, and standards of reporting, along with interpretations. They were developed by the AICPA in 1947 and have undergone minor changes since then.

The _____ are as follows:

1. The auditor must have adequate technical training and proficiency to perform the audit
2. The auditor must maintain independence in mental attitude in all matters related to the audit.
3. The auditor must use due professional care during the performance of the audit and the preparation of the report.

1. The auditor must adequately plan the work and must properly supervise any assistants.
2. The auditor must obtain a sufficient understanding of the entity and its environment, including its internal control, to assess the risk of material misstatement of the financial statements whether due to error or fraud, and to design the nature, timing, and extent of further audit procedures.
3. The auditor must obtain sufficient appropriate audit evidence by performing audit procedures to afford a reasonable basis for an opinion regarding the financial statements under audit.

The new standards are in effect for audits of financial statements for periods beginning on or after December 15, 2006.

1. The auditor must state in the auditor's report whether the financial statements are in accordance with generally accepted accounting principles (GAAP.)
2. The auditor must identify in the auditor's report those circumstances in which such principles have not been consistently observed in the current period in relation to the preceding period.
3. When the auditor determines that informative disclosures are not reasonably adequate, the auditor must so state in the auditor's report.
4. The auditor must either express an opinion regarding the financial statements, taken as a whole the auditor should state the reasons therefore in the auditor's report. In all cases where the auditor's name is associated with the financial statements, the auditor should clearly indicate the character of the auditor's work, if any, and the degree of responsibility the auditor is taking, in the auditor's report.

a. Generally accepted auditing standards
b. Joint audit
c. Negative assurance
d. Continuous auditing

Chapter 19. Variables Sampling

1. _____ is that part of statistical practice concerned with the selection of individual observations intended to yield some knowledge about a population of concern, especially for the purposes of statistical inference. Each observation measures one or more properties (weight, location, etc.) of an observable entity enumerated to distinguish objects or individuals.
   a. Arthur Betz Laffer
   b. Sampling
   c. Alan Greenspan
   d. Abby Joseph Cohen

2. In finance, _____ is the process of estimating the potential market value of a financial asset or liability. They can be done on assets (for example, investments in marketable securities such as stocks, options, business enterprises, or intangible assets such as patents and trademarks) or on liabilities (e.g., Bonds issued by a company.) A _____ is required in many contexts including investment analysis, capital budgeting, merger and acquisition transactions, financial reporting, taxable events to determine the proper tax liability, and in litigation.
   a. Daybook
   b. Valuation
   c. Disclosure
   d. Vyborg Appeal

3. A _____ has several related meanings:

   - a daily record of events or business; a private _____ is usually referred to as a diary.
   - a newspaper or other periodical, in the literal sense of one published each day;
   - many publications issued at stated intervals, such as magazines, or scholarly academic _____s, or the record of the transactions of a society, are often called _____s. Although _____ is sometimes used, erroneously, as a synonym for 'magazine,' in academic use, a _____ refers to a serious, scholarly publication, most often peer-reviewed. A non-scholarly magazine written for an educated audience about an industry or an area of professional activity is usually called a professional magazine.

   The word 'journalist' for one whose business is writing for the public press has been in use since the end of the 17th century.

   Open access _____s are scholarly _____s that are available to the reader without financial or other barrier other than access to the internet itself. Some are subsidized, and some require payment on behalf of the author. Subsidized _____s are financed by an academic institution or a government information center.

   a. BNSF Railway
   b. Journal
   c. 3M Company
   d. BMC Software, Inc.

4. The general definition of an _____ is an evaluation of a person, organization, system, process, project or product. _____s are performed to ascertain the validity and reliability of information; also to provide an assessment of a system's internal control. The goal of an _____ is to express an opinion on the person/organization/system (etc) in question, under evaluation based on work done on a test basis.
   a. Audit regime
   b. Institute of Chartered Accountants of India
   c. Audit
   d. Assurance service

5. _____ is a term that is commonly used in relation to the audit of the financial statements of an entity. (.
   a. Audit working paper
   b. Auditor independence
   c. Engagement Letter
   d. Audit risk

6. _____, in auditing, is the risk that a company's internal controls are insufficient to mitigate or detect errors or fraud.

Chapter 19. Variables Sampling

a. 3M Company
c. BNSF Railway
b. BMC Software, Inc.
d. Control risk

7. _____, in auditing, is the risk that the auditing procedures used will not find a material misstatement in the financial statements of the company being audited. .

a. Detection risk
c. 3M Company
b. BNSF Railway
d. BMC Software, Inc.

8. _____ are ten auditing standards, developed by the AICPA, consisting of general standards, standards of field work, and standards of reporting, along with interpretations. They were developed by the AICPA in 1947 and have undergone minor changes since then.

The _____ are as follows:

1. The auditor must have adequate technical training and proficiency to perform the audit
2. The auditor must maintain independence in mental attitude in all matters related to the audit.
3. The auditor must use due professional care during the performance of the audit and the preparation of the report.

1. The auditor must adequately plan the work and must properly supervise any assistants.
2. The auditor must obtain a sufficient understanding of the entity and its environment, including its internal control, to assess the risk of material misstatement of the financial statements whether due to error or fraud, and to design the nature, timing, and extent of further audit procedures.
3. The auditor must obtain sufficient appropriate audit evidence by performing audit procedures to afford a reasonable basis for an opinion regarding the financial statements under audit.

The new standards are in effect for audits of financial statements for periods beginning on or after December 15, 2006.

1. The auditor must state in the auditor's report whether the financial statements are in accordance with generally accepted accounting principles (GAAP.)
2. The auditor must identify in the auditor's report those circumstances in which such principles have not been consistently observed in the current period in relation to the preceding period.
3. When the auditor determines that informative disclosures are not reasonably adequate, the auditor must so state in the auditor's report.
4. The auditor must either express an opinion regarding the financial statements, taken as a whole the auditor should state the reasons therefore in the auditor's report. In all cases where the auditor's name is associated with the financial statements, the auditor should clearly indicate the character of the auditor's work, if any, and the degree of responsibility the auditor is taking, in the auditor's report.

a. Joint audit
c. Negative assurance
b. Generally accepted auditing standards
d. Continuous auditing

9. _____, in auditing, is the risk that the account or section being audited is materially misstated without considering internal controls due to error; _____ does not include an assessment of the risk of material misstatement due to fraud. The assessment of _____ depends on the professional judgement of the auditor, and it is done after assessing the business environment of the entity being audited.

_____ is typically assessed using a scale, with assessments being either low, medium, or high.

   a. AIG   b. ABC Television Network
   c. AMEX   d. Inherent risk

10. An _____ is a term used in behavioral economics to describe those types of behaviors that impose costs on a person in the long-run that are not taken into account when making decisions in the present. Classical Economics discourages government from creating legislation that targets internalities, because it is assumed that the consumer takes these personal costs into account when paying for the good that causes the _____. For example, cigarettes should be taxed because of the negative consumption externalities that they impose, such as second-hand smoke, not because the smoker harms him or herself by smoking.

   a. Inventory turnover ratio   b. Operating budget
   c. Internality   d. Authorised capital

11. In accounting and organizational theory, _____ is defined as a process effected by an organization's structure, work and authority flows, people and management information systems, designed to help the organization accomplish specific goals or objectives. It is a means by which an organization's resources are directed, monitored, and measured. It plays an important role in preventing and detecting fraud and protecting the organization's resources, both physical (e.g., machinery and property) and intangible (e.g., reputation or intellectual property such as trademarks.)

   a. Internal control   b. Audit committee
   c. Audit risk   d. Auditor independence

12. An _____ is the buying of one company by another. An _____ may be friendly or hostile. In the former case, the companies cooperate in negotiations; in the latter case, the takeover target is unwilling to be bought or the target's board has no prior knowledge of the offer. _____ usually refers to a purchase of a smaller firm by a larger one. Sometimes, however, a smaller firm will acquire management control of a larger or longer established company and keep its name for the combined entity. This is known as a reverse takeover.

   a. AMEX   b. ABC Television Network
   c. AIG   d. Acquisition

13. _____ refers to a business or organization attempting to acquire goods or services to accomplish the goals of the enterprise. Though there are several organizations that attempt to set standards in the _____ process, processes can vary greatly between organizations. Typically the word e;_____e; is not used interchangeably with the word e;procuremente;, since procurement typically includes Expediting, Supplier Quality, and Traffic and Logistics (T'L) in addition to _____.

   a. Consignor   b. Supply chain
   c. Free port   d. Purchasing

Chapter 19. Variables Sampling

14. _____ is a concept that denotes the precise probability of specific eventualities. Technically, the notion of _____ is independent from the notion of value and, as such, eventualities may have both beneficial and adverse consequences. However, in general usage the convention is to focus only on potential negative impact to some characteristic of value that may arise from a future event.

   a. Risk adjusted return on capital
   b. Discounting
   c. Discount factor
   d. Risk

15. _____ is one of financial audit skill which help an auditor understand the client's business and changes in the business, to identify potential risk areas and to plan other audit procedures.

   _____ include comparison of financial information (data in financial statement) with

   1. prior periods
   2. budgets
   3. forecasts
   4. similar industries and so on.

   It also includes consideration of predictable relationships, such as:

   1. gross profit to sales,
   2. payroll costs to employees,
   3. financial information and non-financial information, for examples the CEO's reports and the industry news.

   possible sources of information about the client include:

   1. interim financial information
   2. Budgets
   3. Management accounts
   4. Non-Financial information
   5. Bank and cash records
   6. VAT returns
   7. Board minutes
   8. Discussion or correspondance with the client at they year-end

   a. External auditor
   b. Assurance service
   c. International Federation of Audit Bureaux of Circulations
   d. Analytical procedures

16. _____ is systematic determination of merit, worth, and significance of something or someone using criteria against a set of standards. _____ often is used to characterize and appraise subjects of interest in a wide range of human enterprises, including the arts, criminal justice, foundations and non-profit organizations, government, health care, and other human services.

Depending on the topic of interest, there are professional groups which look to the quality and rigor of the _____ process.

    a. ABC Television Network   b. AIG
    c. Evaluation   d. AMEX

17. _____ is the calculated approximation of a result which is usable even if input data may be incomplete or uncertain.

In statistics, see _____ theory, estimator.

In mathematics, approximation or _____ typically means finding upper or lower bounds of a quantity that cannot readily be computed precisely and is also an educated guess .

    a. Estimation   b. AIG
    c. ABC Television Network   d. AMEX

18. In mathematics _____s are numbers or other things that get multiplied. In particular, see:

- Factorization, the decomposition of an object into a product of other objects
- Integer factorization, the process of breaking down a composite number into smaller non-trivial divisors
- A coefficient
- A divisor of a particular number, or of an element of a monoid
- A von Neumann algebra with a trivial center

In statistics

- _____ analysis is the study of how _____s or certain variables affect variables.

In technology:

- Human _____s, a profession that focuses on how people interact with products, tools, or procedures
- 'Functionality, Application domain, Conditions, Technology, Objects and Responsibility;', In object-oriented programming

In computer science and information technology:

- Authentication _____, a piece of information used to verify a person's identity for security purposes
- _____, a Unix command for numbers factorization
- _____ (programming language), an experimental Forth-like programming language

In television:

- The O'Reilly _____, an American talk show hosted by Bill O'Reilly on Fox News.
- The Krypton _____, a British game show hosted by Gordon Burns, formally on ITV. Also had an American version.

a. Factor
c. The Goodyear Tire ' Rubber Company
b. Merck ' Co., Inc.
d. Valuation

19. In probability theory and statistics, _____ is a measure of the variability or dispersion of a population, a data set, or a probability distribution. A low _____ indicates that the data points tend to be very close to the same value (the mean), while high _____ indicates that the data are 'spread out' over a large range of values.

For example, the average height for adult men in the United States is about 70 inches, with a _____ of around 3 inches.

a. Variance
c. Standard deviation
b. Moving average
d. Probability distribution

Chapter 20. Information Systems Auditing

1. The Federal National Mortgage Association (FNMA) (NYSE: FNM), commonly known as _____, is a stockholder-owned corporation chartered by Congress in 1968 as a government sponsored enterprise (GSE), but founded in 1938 during the Great Depression. The corporation's purpose is to purchase and securitize mortgages in order to ensure that funds are consistently available to the institutions that lend money to home buyers.

On September 7, 2008, James Lockhart, director of the Federal Housing Finance Agency (FHFA), announced that _____ and Freddie Mac were being placed into conservatorship of the FHFA.

   a. Fannie Mae
   b. Public company
   c. National Conference of Commissioners on Uniform State Laws
   d. Freddie Mac

2. _____ are ten auditing standards, developed by the AICPA, consisting of general standards, standards of field work, and standards of reporting, along with interpretations. They were developed by the AICPA in 1947 and have undergone minor changes since then.

The _____ are as follows:

1. The auditor must have adequate technical training and proficiency to perform the audit
2. The auditor must maintain independence in mental attitude in all matters related to the audit.
3. The auditor must use due professional care during the performance of the audit and the preparation of the report.

1. The auditor must adequately plan the work and must properly supervise any assistants.
2. The auditor must obtain a sufficient understanding of the entity and its environment, including its internal control, to assess the risk of material misstatement of the financial statements whether due to error or fraud, and to design the nature, timing, and extent of further audit procedures.
3. The auditor must obtain sufficient appropriate audit evidence by performing audit procedures to afford a reasonable basis for an opinion regarding the financial statements under audit.

The new standards are in effect for audits of financial statements for periods beginning on or after December 15, 2006.

1. The auditor must state in the auditor's report whether the financial statements are in accordance with generally accepted accounting principles (GAAP.)
2. The auditor must identify in the auditor's report those circumstances in which such principles have not been consistently observed in the current period in relation to the preceding period.
3. When the auditor determines that informative disclosures are not reasonably adequate, the auditor must so state in the auditor's report.
4. The auditor must either express an opinion regarding the financial statements, taken as a whole the auditor should state the reasons therefore in the auditor's report. In all cases where the auditor's name is associated with the financial statements, the auditor should clearly indicate the character of the auditor's work, if any, and the degree of responsibility the auditor is taking, in the auditor's report.

Chapter 20. Information Systems Auditing

a. Negative assurance
c. Continuous auditing
b. Generally accepted auditing standards
d. Joint audit

3. A _____ is the transfer of an interest in property (or the equivalent in law - a charge) to a lender as a security for a debt - usually a loan of money. While a _____ in itself is not a debt, it is the lender's security for a debt. It is a transfer of an interest in land (or the equivalent) from the owner to the _____ lender, on the condition that this interest will be returned to the owner when the terms of the _____ have been satisfied or performed.
   a. BNSF Railway
   c. 3M Company
   b. BMC Software, Inc.
   d. Mortgage

4. A _____ or chief executive is one of the highest-ranking corporate officer (executive) or administrator in charge of total management. An individual selected as President and _____ of a corporation, company, organization, or agency, reports to the board of directors. In internal communication and press releases, many companies capitalize the term and those of other high positions, even when they are not proper nouns.
   a. Chief executive officer
   c. Return on equity
   b. Return on assets
   d. Kohlberg Kravis Roberts ' Co

5. _____ refers to the confirmation of certain characteristics of an object, person, or organization. This confirmation is often, but not always, provided by some form of external review, education, or assessment. One of the most common types of _____ in modern society is professional _____, where a person is certified as being able to competently complete a job or task, usually by the passing of an examination.
   a. BMC Software, Inc.
   c. BNSF Railway
   b. Certification
   d. 3M Company

6. The general definition of an _____ is an evaluation of a person, organization, system, process, project or product. _____s are performed to ascertain the validity and reliability of information; also to provide an assessment of a system's internal control. The goal of an _____ is to express an opinion on the person/organization/system (etc) in question, under evaluation based on work done on a test basis.
   a. Assurance service
   c. Institute of Chartered Accountants of India
   b. Audit
   d. Audit regime

7. An _____ is an examination of the controls within an Information technology (IT) infrastructure. An IT audit is the process of collecting and evaluating evidence of an organization's information systems, practices, and operations. The evaluation of obtained evidence determines if the information systems are safeguarding assets, maintaining data integrity, and operating effectively and efficiently to achieve the organization's goals or objectives.
   a. Information technology audit
   c. Information technology audit process
   b. AIG
   d. ABC Television Network

8. ISACA is an international professional association that deals with IT Governance. It is an affiliate member of IFAC. Previously known as the _____, ISACA now goes by its acronym only, to reflect the broad range of IT governance professionals it serves.
   a. East Asia Economic Caucus
   c. Amoco
   b. American Accounting Association
   d. Information Systems Audit and Control Association

9. _____ is a company-wide computer software system used to manage and coordinate all the resources, information, and functions of a business from shared data stores.

An _____ system has a service-oriented architecture with modular hardware and software units or 'services' that communicate on a local area network. The modular design allows a business to add or reconfigure modules (perhaps from different vendors) while preserving data integrity in one shared database that may be centralized or distributed.

a. AIG
b. AMEX
c. ABC Television Network
d. Enterprise resource planning

10. _____ is that part of statistical practice concerned with the selection of individual observations intended to yield some knowledge about a population of concern, especially for the purposes of statistical inference. Each observation measures one or more properties (weight, location, etc.) of an observable entity enumerated to distinguish objects or individuals.
a. Alan Greenspan
b. Abby Joseph Cohen
c. Arthur Betz Laffer
d. Sampling

11. A _____ is a fungible, negotiable instrument representing financial value. they are broadly categorized into debt securities (such as banknotes, bonds and debentures), and equity securities; e.g., common stocks. The company or other entity issuing the _____ is called the issuer.
a. Security
b. BMC Software, Inc.
c. 3M Company
d. Tracking stock

12. Established in 1941, The _____ is internationally recognized as a trustworthy guidance-setting body. Serving members in 165 countries, The IIA is the internal audit profession's global voice, chief advocate, recognized authority, acknowledged leader, and principal educator, with global headquarters in Altamonte Springs, Fla., United States.

The stated mission of The _____ is to provide dynamic leadership for the global profession of internal auditing.

a. Auditor independence
b. Event data
c. Audit regime
d. Institute of Internal Auditors

13. An _____ is a term used in behavioral economics to describe those types of behaviors that impose costs on a person in the long-run that are not taken into account when making decisions in the present. Classical Economics discourages government from creating legislation that targets internalities, because it is assumed that the consumer takes these personal costs into account when paying for the good that causes the _____. For example, cigarettes should be taxed because of the negative consumption externalities that they impose, such as second-hand smoke, not because the smoker harms him or herself by smoking.
a. Operating budget
b. Authorised capital
c. Internality
d. Inventory turnover ratio

14. Internal auditing is a profession and activity involved in helping organisations achieve their stated objectives. It does this by utilizing a systematic methodology for analyzing business processes, procedures and activities with the goal of highlighting organizational problems and recommending solutions. Professionals called _____ are employed by organizations to perform the internal auditing activity.

Chapter 20. Information Systems Auditing

a. Auditing Standards Board
c. Internal Auditing
b. Auditor independence
d. Internal auditors

15. _____ is a concept that denotes the precise probability of specific eventualities. Technically, the notion of _____ is independent from the notion of value and, as such, eventualities may have both beneficial and adverse consequences. However, in general usage the convention is to focus only on potential negative impact to some characteristic of value that may arise from a future event.
   a. Risk
   b. Risk adjusted return on capital
   c. Discounting
   d. Discount factor

16. _____, in auditing, is the risk that a company's internal controls are insufficient to mitigate or detect errors or fraud.
   a. BNSF Railway
   b. 3M Company
   c. Control risk
   d. BMC Software, Inc.

17. In accounting and organizational theory, _____ is defined as a process effected by an organization's structure, work and authority flows, people and management information systems, designed to help the organization accomplish specific goals or objectives. It is a means by which an organization's resources are directed, monitored, and measured. It plays an important role in preventing and detecting fraud and protecting the organization's resources, both physical (e.g., machinery and property) and intangible (e.g., reputation or intellectual property such as trademarks.)
   a. Audit risk
   b. Audit committee
   c. Auditor independence
   d. Internal control

18. An _____ is the buying of one company by another. An _____ may be friendly or hostile. In the former case, the companies cooperate in negotiations; in the latter case, the takeover target is unwilling to be bought or the target's board has no prior knowledge of the offer. _____ usually refers to a purchase of a smaller firm by a larger one. Sometimes, however, a smaller firm will acquire management control of a larger or longer established company and keep its name for the combined entity. This is known as a reverse takeover.
   a. ABC Television Network
   b. AIG
   c. AMEX
   d. Acquisition

19. _____ is a step in a risk management process. _____ is the determination of quantitative or qualitative value of risk related to a concrete situation and a recognized threat (also called hazard.) Quantitative _____ requires calculations of two components of risk: R, the magnitude of the potential loss L, and the probability p that the loss will occur.
   a. BMC Software, Inc.
   b. BNSF Railway
   c. Risk assessment
   d. 3M Company

20. _____ or audit log is a chronological sequence of audit records, each of which contains evidence directly pertaining to and resulting from the execution of a business process or system function.

Audit records typically result from activities such as transactions or communications by individual people, systems, accounts or other entities.

Webopedia defines an _____ as 'a record showing who has accessed a computer system and what operations he or she has performed during a given period of time.' ()

In telecommunication, the term means a record of both completed and attempted accesses and service, or data forming a logical path linking a sequence of events, used to trace the transactions that have affected the contents of a record.

a. ABC Television Network
b. AMEX
c. AIG
d. Audit trail

21. In a company, _____ is the sum of all financial records of salaries, wages, bonuses and deductions.

A paycheck, is traditionally a paper document issued by an employer to pay an employee for services rendered. While most commonly used in the United States, recently the physical paycheck has been increasingly replaced by electronic direct deposit to bank accounts.

a. Tax expense
b. Payroll
c. 3M Company
d. Total Expense Ratio

22. Established in 1988 the _____ is the professional organization that governs professional fraud examiners. Its activities include producing fraud information, tools and training. It also governs the professional designation of Certified Fraud Examiner.

a. Association of Certified Fraud Examiners
b. AIG
c. AMEX
d. ABC Television Network

23. _____ is a designation awarded by the Association of _____s (ACertified Fraud Examiner.) The ACertified Fraud Examiner is a 41,000 member-based global association dedicated to providing anti-fraud education and training.

In order to become a _____ one must meet the following requirements:

- Be an Associate Member of the ACertified Fraud Examiner in good standing
- Meet minimum academic and professional requirements
- Be of high moral character
- Agree to abide by the Bylaws and Code of Professional Ethics of the Association of _____s

Generally, applicants for _____ certification have a minimum of a bachelor's degree or equivalent from an institution of higher education. Two years of professional experience related to fraud can be substituted for each year of college.

a. Certified Fraud Examiner
b. Certified public accountant
c. Chartered Certified Accountant
d. Chartered Accountant

Chapter 20. Information Systems Auditing

24. _____ Corporation of America was a Los Angeles-based U.S. financial conglomerate that marketed a package of mutual funds and life insurance to private individuals in the 1960s and 70s. It collapsed in scandal in 1973 after ex-employee Ronald Secrist and securities analyst Ray Dirks blew the whistle on massive accounting fraud, including a computer system dedicated exclusively to creating and maintaining fictitious insurance policies. Investigation found that from 1964 onward, as many as 100 company employees had engaged in organized deception of investors, auditors, reinsurers and regulatory authorities.

   a. AMEX
   b. AIG
   c. ABC Television Network
   d. Equity Funding

25. A _____ has several related meanings:

   - a daily record of events or business; a private _____ is usually referred to as a diary.
   - a newspaper or other periodical, in the literal sense of one published each day;
   - many publications issued at stated intervals, such as magazines, or scholarly academic _____s, or the record of the transactions of a society, are often called _____s. Although _____ is sometimes used, erroneously, as a synonym for 'magazine,' in academic use, a _____ refers to a serious, scholarly publication, most often peer-reviewed. A non-scholarly magazine written for an educated audience about an industry or an area of professional activity is usually called a professional magazine.

The word 'journalist' for one whose business is writing for the public press has been in use since the end of the 17th century.

Open access _____s are scholarly _____s that are available to the reader without financial or other barrier other than access to the internet itself. Some are subsidized, and some require payment on behalf of the author. Subsidized _____s are financed by an academic institution or a government information center.

   a. 3M Company
   b. BNSF Railway
   c. Journal
   d. BMC Software, Inc.

26. The term _____ usually refers to a company that is permitted to offer its registered securities (stock, bonds, etc.) for sale to the general public, typically through a stock exchange, or occasionally a company whose stock is traded over the counter (OTC) via market makers who use non-exchange quotation services.

The term '_____' may also refer to a company owned by the government.

   a. Governmental Accounting Standards Board
   b. MicroStrategy
   c. Professional association
   d. Public Company

27. _____ consists of the sale of goods or merchandise from a fixed location, such as a department store, boutique or kiosk in small or individual lots for direct consumption by the purchaser. _____ may include subordinated services, such as delivery. Purchasers may be individuals or businesses.

   a. BMC Software, Inc.
   b. Retailing
   c. 3M Company
   d. BNSF Railway

28. _____ LLP, based in Chicago, was once one of the 'Big Five' accounting firms among PricewaterhouseCoopers, Deloitte Touche Tohmatsu, Ernst ' Young and KPMG, providing auditing, tax, and consulting services to large corporations. In 2002, the firm voluntarily surrendered its licenses to practice as Certified Public Accountants in the United States after being found guilty of criminal charges relating to the firm's handling of the auditing of Enron, the energy corporation, resulting in the loss of 85,000 jobs. Although the verdict was subsequently overturned by the Supreme Court of the United States, it has not returned as a viable business.

a. ABC Television Network
b. AMEX
c. AIG
d. Arthur Andersen

ANSWER KEY

Chapter 1

1. d	2. d	3. b	4. a	5. d	6. d	7. d	8. d	9. c	10. d
11. b	12. d	13. d	14. d	15. d	16. d	17. d	18. b	19. d	20. d
21. a	22. d	23. d	24. a	25. d	26. d	27. a	28. a	29. d	30. b
31. d	32. d	33. c	34. d	35. a	36. d	37. d	38. b	39. a	40. d
41. a	42. d	43. d	44. b	45. d	46. d	47. b	48. d	49. a	50. b
51. a	52. d	53. c	54. d	55. c	56. b	57. b	58. d	59. c	60. d
61. c	62. b	63. b	64. b	65. a	66. a	67. a	68. a	69. b	

Chapter 2

1. a	2. d	3. d	4. b	5. a	6. b	7. d	8. d	9. c	10. d
11. d	12. d	13. a	14. d	15. b	16. d	17. d	18. d	19. a	20. a
21. d	22. c	23. d	24. b	25. c	26. d	27. a	28. b	29. d	30. d
31. b	32. d	33. d	34. a	35. d	36. d	37. d			

Chapter 3

1. b	2. d	3. d	4. d	5. d	6. d	7. b	8. a	9. a	10. c
11. c	12. d	13. d	14. d	15. b	16. d	17. d	18. d	19. b	20. b
21. b	22. a	23. d	24. a	25. a	26. d	27. b	28. d	29. d	30. b
31. c	32. a	33. d	34. c	35. d	36. a	37. d	38. d	39. a	40. a
41. a	42. b								

Chapter 4

1. d	2. d	3. b	4. d	5. a	6. d	7. d	8. b	9. d	10. c
11. b	12. d	13. d	14. a	15. d	16. d	17. b	18. a	19. b	20. a
21. b	22. d	23. b	24. b	25. a	26. b	27. b	28. c	29. d	30. d
31. c	32. d	33. a	34. a	35. b	36. d	37. c	38. d	39. c	40. a
41. b	42. a	43. d	44. a	45. a	46. c	47. d	48. d		

Chapter 5

1. d	2. b	3. c	4. d	5. b	6. a	7. b	8. d	9. a	10. d
11. d	12. a	13. d	14. c	15. d	16. d	17. c	18. d	19. b	20. b
21. a	22. d	23. a	24. d	25. d	26. d	27. d	28. d	29. a	30. b
31. d	32. c	33. c	34. d	35. d	36. a	37. c	38. d	39. d	40. a
41. a	42. d	43. d	44. d	45. a	46. d	47. d	48. b	49. c	50. d

Chapter 6

1. b	2. d	3. c	4. d	5. d	6. a	7. b	8. d	9. a	10. d
11. d	12. b	13. c	14. b	15. d	16. d	17. a	18. a	19. c	20. d
21. d	22. d	23. b	24. b	25. d					

Chapter 7

1. d	2. d	3. c	4. c	5. d	6. c	7. c	8. d	9. d	10. c
11. b	12. d	13. d	14. b	15. d	16. d	17. c	18. d	19. c	20. d
21. a	22. d	23. d	24. d	25. d	26. a	27. d	28. a	29. b	30. d
31. d	32. c	33. d	34. a	35. d					

Chapter 8
1. c	2. d	3. b	4. d	5. b	6. b	7. a	8. d	9. b	10. a
11. b	12. d	13. d	14. d	15. b	16. a	17. b	18. d	19. c	20. c
21. a	22. d	23. d	24. d	25. d	26. c	27. c	28. d	29. b	30. d
31. d	32. c	33. d	34. b	35. b	36. b	37. d	38. d	39. c	40. b
41. d	42. b	43. d	44. d	45. b	46. d	47. b	48. d	49. d	50. d
51. d	52. d								

Chapter 9
1. b	2. d	3. d	4. d	5. b	6. d	7. d	8. d	9. b	10. c
11. c	12. d	13. b	14. a	15. d	16. a	17. b	18. a	19. d	20. a
21. c	22. c	23. b	24. d	25. d	26. a	27. c	28. b	29. d	30. d
31. a	32. a	33. c	34. d	35. b	36. d	37. d	38. d		

Chapter 10
1. b	2. a	3. a	4. a	5. d	6. a	7. b	8. d	9. a	10. c
11. d	12. d	13. d	14. d	15. d	16. d	17. b	18. b	19. b	20. a
21. d	22. b	23. a	24. c	25. c	26. d	27. d	28. d	29. d	30. c
31. d	32. c	33. c	34. d	35. c	36. c	37. b	38. d	39. a	40. a
41. c	42. d								

Chapter 11
1. d	2. d	3. d	4. a	5. a	6. d	7. b	8. c	9. d	10. d
11. b	12. d	13. d	14. d	15. d	16. c	17. d	18. d	19. d	20. d
21. c	22. c	23. c	24. a	25. d	26. b	27. d	28. d		

Chapter 12
1. d	2. d	3. d	4. b	5. d	6. c	7. d	8. d	9. d	10. d
11. d	12. b	13. b	14. d	15. d	16. d	17. d	18. d	19. d	20. d
21. d	22. d	23. b	24. d	25. b	26. d				

Chapter 13
1. d	2. d	3. d	4. a	5. d	6. b	7. c	8. c	9. c	10. d
11. d	12. d	13. d	14. b	15. d	16. d	17. d	18. d	19. c	20. d
21. d	22. d	23. d	24. c	25. a	26. b	27. d	28. d	29. a	30. d
31. d									

Chapter 14
1. c	2. d	3. b	4. b	5. c	6. d	7. d	8. c	9. c	10. b
11. d	12. b	13. b	14. d	15. d	16. b	17. d	18. a	19. d	20. d
21. a	22. b	23. d	24. d	25. d	26. a	27. b	28. c	29. d	30. d
31. b	32. d	33. d	34. d	35. a	36. b	37. a	38. d	39. d	40. d
41. c	42. a	43. d	44. d	45. d	46. c	47. b	48. d		

ANSWER KEY

Chapter 15
1. b	2. a	3. b	4. d	5. d	6. c	7. a	8. d	9. d	10. c
11. b	12. d	13. d	14. d	15. d	16. d	17. c	18. c	19. a	20. c
21. c	22. a	23. d	24. d	25. d	26. d	27. d	28. d	29. a	30. d
31. d	32. d	33. a	34. a	35. d	36. a	37. a	38. d	39. d	40. b
41. d	42. c	43. d	44. b						

Chapter 16
1. d	2. a	3. d	4. c	5. b	6. c	7. b	8. d	9. d	10. c
11. d	12. b	13. d	14. d	15. b	16. c	17. b	18. b	19. a	20. d
21. b	22. a	23. b	24. d						

Chapter 17
1. d	2. d	3. d	4. a	5. a	6. a	7. d	8. d	9. b	10. b
11. d	12. b	13. d	14. b	15. a					

Chapter 18
1. c	2. d	3. d	4. b	5. b	6. b	7. a	8. c	9. d	10. b
11. d	12. a								

Chapter 19
1. b	2. b	3. b	4. c	5. d	6. d	7. a	8. b	9. d	10. c
11. a	12. d	13. d	14. d	15. d	16. c	17. a	18. a	19. c	

Chapter 20
1. a	2. b	3. d	4. a	5. b	6. b	7. a	8. d	9. d	10. d
11. a	12. d	13. c	14. d	15. a	16. c	17. d	18. d	19. c	20. d
21. b	22. a	23. a	24. d	25. c	26. d	27. b	28. d		

www.ingramcontent.com/pod-product-compliance
Lightning Source LLC
Chambersburg PA
CBHW082203230426
43672CB00015B/2883